RUNNING WILD

MIKE TOMKIES

Whittles Publishing

Published by
Whittles Publishing Ltd.,
Dunbeath,
Caithness, KW6 6EG,
Scotland, UK

www.whittlespublishing.com

ISBN 978-184995-123-4

Printed by Bell & Bain Ltd, Glasgow

Also by Mike Tomkies

Books	**Novels**
Alone in the Wilderness	*Let Ape and Tiger Die*
Between Earth and Paradise	*Today the Wolf is Dead (unpublished)*
A Last Wild Place	
My Wilderness Wildcats	**Autobiography**
Liane - A Cat from the Wild	*My Wicked First Life*
Out of the Wild	*Backwoods Mates to Hollywood's Greats*
Golden Eagle Years	
On Wing and Wild Water	**Videos and DVDs**
Moobli	*Eagle Mountain Year*
Last Wild Years	*At Home with Eagles*
In Spain's Secret Wilderness	*Forest Phantoms*
Wildcat Haven (new & revised edition)	*My Barn Owl Family*
Wildcats	*River Dancing Year*
Rare, Wild and Free	*Wildest Spain*
	Wildest Spain Revisited
	Last Eagle Years
	My Bird Table Theatres
Biography	*My Wild 75th Summer*
The Big Man (The John Wayne Story)	*My Wild 80th Year*
It Sure Beats Working (The Robert Mitchum Story)	*My Sussex Wilderness*

Contents

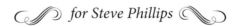 *for Steve Phillips*

1

FROM SPAIN TO FALCONS

When I drove off the ferry at Plymouth after living for five years in Spain, where I had filmed wild brown bears, lynx, wolves and other rare species, I really didn't know which way to go next. I had no home in the UK to go to. I certainly did not dream that within a few days I would be filming nesting peregrine falcons on a dramatic sea cliff in Cornwall. This is how it came about.

Once clear of Plymouth town I pulled up Mi Caballo (Spanish for My Horse and the name I'd given my faithful old VW camper van) into a lay-by and tossed a coin – north or south? It came down south. I then remembered that one of my most loyal readers lived near Truro, Cornwall – not far away – and always exhorting me to visit if ever I was in the south of the country. Well, I met her and it so happened that a lady friend of hers had a large garden hut with primitive utilities laid on, which she would make available to anyone who took care of her garden – weeding, mowing and the like. I was pretty good at mowing, I even liked mowing, so I moved in. And it was this lady who told me about the peregrines on the cliff at St Anthony.

I unloaded and sorted my belongings into the hut and next day went to meet National Trust warden Julian who was in charge of the area. He told me that, the year before, a pair of falcons had arrived out of the blue and had succeeded in raising three chicks. Now, in mid-May, they were back and the female was again on eggs. The nest was extremely vulnerable, low down on an easily-climbed cliff in a small cove. It could be seen from a public footpath and was only 250 yards from a car park. After much discussion with Julian, we agreed that these rare birds, our most magnificent falcons, needed to be monitored – watched as closely as possible in order to protect them from egg- or chick-stealing gangs.

Peregrine falcons in Britain had come close to the point of extinction by 1963, when there were only 63 pairs left. They were heavily shot in World War Two for killing carrier pigeons bearing vital messages, and in the late 1950s and early 1960s were decimated by organochlorine pesticides in agriculture. The poisons accumulated in the bodies of their prey, causing sterility or eggs that were added or so thin-shelled that they broke in the nest. After the most lethal pesticides were banned, peregrine numbers slowly built up again until today there are an estimated 1,450 pairs. Even so, an average of more than 50 nests a year are still robbed of eggs or chicks. A maximum fine of £2,000 is apparently not enough to deter some diehards, perhaps not surprisingly when the young, or eyasses, can fetch up to £3,000 each in illegal falconry markets in Germany and some rich Arab countries.

An enthusiastic group of amateur bird watchers who already knew about the falcons was mobilised, to be led by local naturalist George Jackson, who had first discovered the birds. One or several of this band would mount guard as often as they could from amid the blackthorn bushes that lined the top of the cliff, along which ran a footpath popular with many hikers. While this protection may sound haphazard, the very public nature of the site would probably deter any nest thief except during the early hours. Anything suspicious would be instantly reported to the police and, as warden, Julian would keep a close eye on the kind of people visiting the car park.

There was now a way I could do my part in this work, putting to good use my half-century of studying rare animals and birds at close quarters in the wild. We decided to erect a screen across the end of a narrow gulch, halfway down the cliff on the opposite side of the cove, and that I should spend as much time in that hide as possible.

To reach the gulch I had to climb down a 25-foot rockface which, although sheer, had plenty of ivy growing over it, giving me thick, knotty stems to cling onto. The narrow trench was over 120 yards long and filled with spiky blackthorn bushes, yet more ivy and festoons of thick, barbed bramble runners. Without gloves or a machete it was a terrible battle to get through, a foot or so at a time. I cut my ankles, knees, hands and face, and it was more than an hour before I emerged into a superb open spot near the lip of the gulch. Stalking carefully, I slid on my stomach through the bluebells and red campion until I could see over the edge, above a 250-foot drop.

The falcon had not seen me and stayed on her eggs in the usual makeshift scrape of a nest, right up against the cliff wall which formed the backdrop of a long ledge. Through the binoculars I could see her white eyelids moving up and down as she dozed. It was a wonderful spot, allowing me to look right down into the nest and, even though people would be passing on the public footpath above, the narrow end of the gulch would be easy to screen from view with a hide.

Unfortunately, I could not start the real work there and then as I had to go to London and Scotland on urgent work for two of my wildlife books. I did scramble up the ivy-covered rockface again and set up my movie camera in a hidden spot not far from the clifftop footpath. I was twice as far from the nest ledge as I would be at the hide site but I was still able to film the female sitting tight, probably by now on very small chicks, while the male, or tiercel, flew in and landed with some small prey to feed her. I returned to the garden hut and quickly mowed my new benefactor's lawn to keep her happy before I went away for a few weeks.

The work in London and Scotland took longer than I'd expected and I could not return to Cornwall and the falcons' cliff until late June. Phone calls to Julian had elicited the delightful news that three chicks had hatched and that so far they remained unmolested. The watching team had done their work. Now it was time to do mine.

26 June: Skeins of fairly thick mist boded ill for peregrine work but Julian met me on time, and after I had climbed down the sheer rockface, he roped down to me two packs, a heavy tripod and the hide netting. It took three thorny journeys to struggle with everything through to the edge of the cliff. I put up the screen well out of sight of the falcons, cutting and weaving in to it many forms of vegetation, including young ivy. It took two hours and my hands were soon cut all over. Actually installing the screen along the edge of the cleft took only minutes. The mist helped as it obscured my activity from human gaze above, and the falcons were away hunting. After I had tied a on a small roof section over the curve nearest the hikers' path, it was an even more effective screen than I had envisaged.

I first heard the chicks calling at 9.32 a.m. but I could only see two. Had some chick-stealing criminal taken one, after all? At 10.25 the mist cleared a little and I filmed both chicks, one lying down on its belly, the other reaching back with its beak to preen its tail. Through the telephoto lens I could see that they were a good seven weeks old. Forty minutes later the chicks intensified their whiny squeaking and in swept the mother falcon with prey, a small brown bird that I could not identify in the wefts of mist. She ignored the two youngsters, flap-dragged the prey across the middle of the ledge – and fed Chick Three, the youngest, which had all this time been lying down at the very back of the ledge, under the cliff face itself. It was hard to locate the chicks when they did not move as their plumage was much browner than the dark slate-grey of the adults' backs, blending perfectly with the earth and debris on the nesting ledge. No wonder most of the hikers never even knew they were there. For a time the first two just stood on the far right of the shelf, near a tall tuffet of grasses, just watching the other being fed, but the sight of the falcon tearing up the prey proved too much and they soon waddled over, to be fed in turn. The mist thickened and cleared, so filming was difficult, but I took some useful first footage.

At 11.25 a.m. the falcon left, running over the ledge with wings beating, launching herself over the sea. The two older chicks began leaping about, exercising their wings and grabbing onto tufts of vegetation with their yellow feet and dark talons so as not to go over the edge too early. The youngest chick was definitely smaller than the other two, younger by about three days, I thought. Now they had been fed, all three dispersed to separate parts of the ledge, which was unusually long and broad for peregrines, as if putting two or three feet of territorial space between each other. The oldest then began flapping its wings with a curious, circular, almost winding motion, afterwards leaving them hanging open, rather like a cormorant drying out its wings after diving for fish. It then grabbed a silvery-white sliver of wood and started to leap about the ledge with it, clutching it hard with one set of talons, constantly tugging and looking down on it. When the middle, or second, chick saw the oldest had something in its talons it flapped-ran over to take a closer look but did not try to wrest it from the other.

Already there had been plenty of action at this eyrie, which offered me such a perfect (but for the mist) view down onto it. While this pair were tolerant of humans, it was clear that they could not see me at all, so I was causing them no disturbance whatsoever. Any birdwatcher or photographer, whether amateur or professional, must establish this early on, and if there is any sign of distress they must strike the hide quickly and abandon the project. The birds' welfare must always come first. I noticed that when the falcon was actually in with prey, the chicks' normal 'raich raich raich' squeaks changed to a much deeper, harsh, even hoarse, chittering call, which I felt I ought to record. If I dared to risk leaving some gear behind, hidden in the thorny cleft, I decided I would also carry in a tape recorder on subsequent visits.

At 11.50 a.m. the chicks began calling again, staring intently out to sea. I pushed the button fast and filmed the falcon zooming in, one chick run-flapping up to her, and her briefly feeding it a sliver or two. Then she half-dragged, half-lifted the prey, a young blackbird, right across the nest ledge and began to feed the youngest chick in the top right-hand corner. One of the lower chicks squirted faeces which almost landed on the other's feet. The falcon turned to face me – ideal – as she fed the youngster before the second ran up to her and she fed that one too. Then, though, the sea mist returned and in ten minutes the nest ledge was totally obliterated from sight. When it cleared again lines of hikers, dressed in absurd blue, red and yellow anoraks, went by on the clifftop path, talking loudly, but clearly unable to see me through the hide netting's vegetation. Neither, then, could any potential chick stealer!

Just after midday the chicks began calling again and as I looked to see if an adult was coming in, I suddenly noticed a fulmar on its nest in a dark crevice, partially covered by vegetation, only three yards above the peregrines' nesting ledge! I had already discovered five other fulmars incubating eggs on ledges some 40 yards to the left of the falcons. Fulmars are certainly taken as prey and, out of more than 40 recorded species, rank below only puffins, rock doves, petrels, waders, gulls and terns, and pigeons in the coastal areas of the Scottish Highlands. It seemed these nesting fulmars, especially the pair just above the eyrie, were living dangerously. It would be interesting to note if any were taken as prey.

After another quarter-hour spell of enveloping mist, I saw that all three chicks were lying down close to each other, facing in towards the cliff face, all calling loudly as if competing to make the most noise. Peregrines have always been the loudest of birds of prey, the adults often screeching protests and flying over the heads of human intruders, so giving away the location of their nests sites even to non-expert observers. This is, though, the only 'foolish' act that can be ascribed to a bird that is otherwise, perhaps, the most perfect and co-ordinated killing machine in avian nature.

By half past one the chicks had stopped calling and all were resting, squatting down on the warm humid debris and broken-down rock of the ledge. Occasionally, they stalked about on crayon-yellow feet, holding on, flapping wings, looking like giant moths which had hit a light, burnt their antennae, and were running about, wings fluttering, out of control. A quarter-hour later, they called again, the light was better and luckily I pressed the button just as the falcon came in with a large light-coloured bird. I tried hard to see if it was a gull or even a fulmar, but the varying blue-greys of the feathers showed it to be a rock dove or, and more likely, a feral hybrid.

Each of the three chicks raced over to her and she plucked out feathers very quickly, holding the prey down with both set of talons and feeding snippets to all the chicks. They were definitely all feeding. There did not seem to be any sibling rivalry here, none of the chicks trying to beat up another with vicious beak stabs, as often happens with young eagles or buzzards. The mother did not systematically offer morsels to each one but let each snippet go to the one that was first to reach out with its beak and take it. I also noticed that the youngsters watched how the falcon pulled off the bits she fed to them, learning how to do it, for they also reached between her feet and plucked bits off the carcass for themselves. After a few minutes of this, the first chick walked off, stood still, looked back, watched, then waddled up again for another helping! At 1.58 p.m. the eldest chick walked away, then the second, leaving the youngest continuing to be fed until 2.09 p.m. Then into the nest flew the tiercel, the smaller male. One chick turned to him, instinctively, as if for food but he just turned his back. When he left again, the female followed him out, as if he had come in just to ask her to fly with him. The pair flickered away down the cove, twisting, turning, and touching talons in pair-bonding play.

Then the eldest chick grabbed a heavy stick with its left foot and began flapping, so hard that it went round and round in circles, anchored by the stick, as if on a merry-go-round. By 3.20 p.m. the mist was back. It was obvious that it would not clear completely that day so I packed up, hiding the tripod and some of the gear in undergrowth. After struggling up the cliff face, clutching onto thick ivy roots with just the valuable camera and lenses in the pack, I left.

2

IN THE FALCONS' LAIR

I spent next day still looking for my own 'nest'. I met the owner of an old forge near Porthtowan, who was prepared to sell a fully-fitted caravan inside a wind- and watertight building for £7,000. This extraordinary bargain was nipped in the bud by the planning department of Carrick Council who told me that if I slept just one night in the place I would be in breach of planning regulations. The place was only permitted to be a storage building. If caught trying to live there, even for a few days at a time, I would be taken to court and fined heavily. I was glad to turn my back on the absurdities of modern bureaucracy and return to the real world of the wild falcons, where I could do what I loved and knew best.

28 June: Up at dawn, I caught the first ferry, climbed down the rockface and was all set up by 8.42 a.m. Once again, there seemed to be only two chicks on the nest ledge, Twenty minutes later, both adult falcons began circling in the sky above and when I heard the chicks calling, I realised that this time it really had happened: Chick One had flown! Its voice was coming from the cliff below me and away to the right, completely out of my sight. At least it had not been stolen. Now the adults had vanished but soon I heard Chick One giving the harsher screams, loudly, as if it were being fed. Chick Two started walking about the nest, flapped its wings hard for over a minute then went to join Chick Three, whereupon both started to preen their wings and tails, flirting out the feathers like a fan.

By 10.23 a.m. both chicks were sleeping, Chick Two with its head back under the left wing, so they did not call out when the tiercel suddenly swept in with a dead feral pigeon in his talons. The older chick jumped, grabbed it and hauled it clumsily away from the other into a crevice at the back of the ledge. Chick Three climbed up to the tiercel, giving thin 'raich' squeaks, but he just turned and flew off. The younger then flap-walked up to its nest mate as if hoping for a few pecks at the pigeon, but stopped two feet away as Chick Two gave no ground, eating its fill with its back turned.

Twelve minutes later, once Chick Two had had its fill, I was filming the third chick walking over to the pigeon remains when in swept the falcon and dropped what looked like a vole. Chick Two, who was now full up, ran-flapped towards her. Chick Three kept eating, the falcon just looked about, and Chick Two went on calling without trying to eat the vole. With bated breath I waited until the falcon looked like leaving (glaring out over the sea with up and down head movements) and filmed a fine pan sequence of her flying off the ledge. By 11a.m. the smallest chick was still eating but Chick Two was showing signs of wanting to leave too, looking out intently and making sudden little crouches, as if about to spring into the air and fly. Minutes later it climbed clumsily down to a lower dusty shelf, preened its neck and wings, then dozed. Chick Three finished eating at 11.10 a.m. and stalked back up to the top tufted corner for a snooze.

All the time I kept an eye on the nesting fulmars, which hardly ever moved. I had seen no changeovers of egg incubation duties. Sometimes other fulmars, no doubt their mates, went flying up to the birds on the nest ledges, half-hovering nearby with shivering, shimmering wings, to be greeted with deep grunting noises before plunging downward again. It was as if they were just zooming up to say 'Hold on, mate. You're not forgotten!' With their thick, white torpedo bodies and exceptionally straight blunt wings, the fulmars breasted through the air like miniature galleons. The peregrines did not harry them, not even the one just above the nest, nor did the fulmars show any fear of the killers in their midst. Cormorants, returning from early morning fishing, now slept on many little crags and projections in the horseshoe of cliffs, but I could see only one nest ledge, which held two well-fledged young.

At 11.40 a.m. Chick One began calling again, this time from further round the cliff below me. It must have flown from one crag to another and was now more than two bulging cliff faces away. It was making so much noise, in fact, that the parents would easily be able to locate it. At 11.59 a.m. the tiercel came soaring into the bay and made two circles, which showed me that it had either a linnet or a sparrow in its left talons. It cried out harshly as it came towards the screen for the second time, then sailed down into the cliffs below me. Within seconds I heard the racket of Chick One being fed!

For the next hour and a half the other two were entertaining. Chick Two stood up, scratched its head with the centre talon on its right foot, amazing me with the sensitive accuracy of so deadly a weapon, for it could easily have pierced its own eye. Then the chick pushed one wing right over the ledge slowly, extending one foot to full length below it in a ballet-like movement, showing incredible balance. It finished off this performance with both wings arched high above its head and back in a double bow, in what I call the 'Hottentot' stretch.

At nearly one o'clock, Chick Three walked out to rest in the sunlight which now fell on the centre of the ledge, while the other climbed further up the lower shelf and lay on its stomach. Although its wings were folded back they were held out slightly to the side, so it looked like one of those wooden decoy woodpigeons used by hunters. Twenty minutes later, up got Chick Three and peered over the ledge's edge, crouched as if to fly, but simply hopping a few inches higher onto a rock and whirring its wings. After a further quarter hour it climbed down to the lower chick, waddled past it, made a Hottentot stretch, then stumbled into a dark grassy crevice so that one was in the dark and the other out in the blazing sun. They were impossible to film.

Both chicks climbed back up to the top ledge just before 2 p.m. Chick Three lay down with beak open, panting as dogs do to keep cool in the heat, while the bigger one scrambled back down again. As it went it flapped its wings and, in pure inherited instinct, struck out with its right talons in fast, comical strikes at bits of vegetation, as if practising how to kill.

The mist prevented me from realising that it wasn't until 2.15 p.m. that the sun would ever shine fully on the whole ledge. I was wasting my time paying such early visits, when the light was too poor for filming on this west-facing cliff. I had no need now to watch the nest to protect it from chick stealers: to our great relief, they were now beyond capture, as Chick One was flying and anyone climbing near the ledge now would 'explode' the rest of the brood too.

With the whole far cliff now fully lit by sunshine, I searched it more thoroughly with binoculars. I was amazed to find that a herring gull, which I had noticed perched on a projection just four yards north of the falcon's ledge, had a grey downy youngster with it. The chick stood on a tiny shelf of grass and would for some weeks have been easy prey for the peregrines, yet they had left it alone. Perhaps young herring gulls don't taste too good? From time to time I could hear Chick One calling out, and now it sounded even further away.

At 3.30 p.m. Chick Two was lying down again, drowsily watching Chick Three having a few brief tugs at the pigeon carcass. Fully up again, the younger one walked back up to the lying chick, flopped down right beside it and began to preen its sibling's back feathers with its beak. Chick Two really enjoyed this, showing no alarm whatever, and even rolled over onto its back like a dog, so that the other could riffle through its chest feathers. They also fenced briefly, almost fondly, with their beaks. I heard Chick One calling, then so did the others as one parent flew past but did not go into the eyrie. At 3.58 p.m. both rose at the same moment and began a long session of preening wings, tail and chest.

I noted that they followed the flights of many other birds - gulls, fulmars, cormorants and jackdaws - with their eyes and heads turned upwards but never calling out. They obviously knew their parents' outline, the silhouette of the falcon.

Chick Two went over to the prey, which I now saw was not a vole but half a young rabbit, tore a few pieces off and had soon eaten enough.

Changing my hunched position at 4.24 p.m., easing the pain in hips, thighs and knees, I glanced out to sea. I was just in time to see the falcon soaring over the cliffs of the far headland, just a dot in the distance. Suddenly she baulked, turned and dived fast, headlong, with both wings almost fully pulled in. Just then I saw a pigeon or dove flying eastwards, just above the line of the cliffs. Down, down, down she went at tremendous speed, then out came the feet and talons, and while I could hear nothing at that distance I saw the explosive puff of feathers as she hit her luckless prey. It was breathtaking, marvellous, but the force of the strike carried both pigeon and falcon below the distant cliffs and though I kept breathless watch for a minute or so, I saw no more. I had no time to film it as the lens was trained through the mesh of the hide onto the nest and had limited leeway. I intended to specialise in flight sequences later, but I knew well enough that any hopes of seeing another hunting strike like that were slim.

At 4.45 p.m. Chick Three began flapping exercises while clinging hard to a spur of rock, really jerking its body up and down with powerful, fast wing beats. Then Chick Two came up to it and started some comical mock-fencing, darting its beak forward as if to give a vicious jab or bite but never going closer than about four inches, all the time making jerky lifts of its wing 'shoulders', as if saying to the other 'Garn, get out of it'!

Ten minutes later the tiercel flew right past the herring gull chick, now unguarded by any parent, taking no notice of it, and equally ignored the two falcon chicks which gave their 'raich' calls. At 5.09 p.m. a falcon landed on a slanting rock five yards left of the eyrie. I thought it was Chick One returning. It kept craning its neck towards the others as if wanting to get back with them, then it scrambled onto a rock that was higher and nearer. In the bright sunlight I saw its back plumage was much darker than theirs and its chest much lighter. It was the tiercel. I ended a film on him scratching his head, then holding one foot out straight and high so he could nibble between his talons.

He moved exaggeratedly, floppily, then at 5.43 p.m. he set off, flying towards the eyrie. He seemed about to land but he either muffed it or decided that the excited, screaming chicks would be too much trouble when he had no prey for them, for he just briefly checked his flight above the ledge, then flew on downwards, out of my sight. Moments later Chick One appeared in the air below my cliff, sailed over the cove and landed in the crevice the tiercel had used, to the left of and below the nest ledge. The reason for the tiercel's odd behaviour now seemed clear: he had been trying to entice Chick One back to the eyrie before darkness fell. I wanted a good feeding sequence in bright sunlight but the parents simply would not oblige, so I started a new film on the two younger chicks flapping and leaping about, as if wishing they had the courage of Chick One. At 6.40 p.m., aching in every limb and having heard that the last ferry went in less than an hour, I took a big chance. Leaving all the film and photographic gear in place, covered with my camouflage jacket, I scrambled up the rockface to my van. The chicks could all be flying any day now so I would be back on the morrow, after my usual morning search for a new home.

29 June: I was in place by 2.30 p.m., all my gear untouched, and all three chicks back together on the ledge! I filmed Chick One flapping and leaping down to the broad lower shelf, then being followed by Chick Two. Both birds began pulling at green vegetation with their beaks but did not appear to swallow any. The smallest chick was very hungry and kept calling out, then it jumped and flapped to the top of a small rocky pinnacle flanking the far top side of the ledge. Right above the other two, it screamed again, flapped more and kept staring out to sea. The other two wandered right off their lower shelf and into the cliffside vegetation of grasses and small bushes, re-emerging a few minutes later. Chick Three watched them, its head on one side, then flapped down to join them. By 3.08 p.m. all three chicks were among the vegetation, as if playing hide and seek, wandering on foot like mammals through the lovely new green jungle until they all disappeared from view.

Moments later it began to drizzle. Had the chicks known it was going to rain and were seeking shelter? The eyrie ledge was now completely empty and even a knowledgeable hiker along the clifftop path would think that they had been stolen or had flown. I dismantled the movie gear, afraid that I would get no good still photos before the chicks dispersed. No sooner had I mounted onto the tripod my stills camera and its 2ft 6ins Novoflex lens than I heard loud screams. In came the female, with prey, and the chicks came out of the foliage like bullets. They rushed up to the nest ledge, having no trouble at all in flying. Chick Three, the one that had done most of the screaming, got there first. The mother fed it, between bouts of furiously plucking out the feathers of a young gull-type bird, of which one whitish, soft-looking non-adult foot could be seen. The other two chicks were also fed amid their clamour of squeaky screams and, as the feeding session lasted over twelve minutes, I was able to bag off 21 good shots before switching back to the movie gear for the good feeding footage I wanted.

After the falcon left, the chicks stood around for a while before Chick One, which definitely had darker back plumage than the others, headed over to the carcass for a few more pulls at the meat. Luckily, I had the cine camera going as it turned away and Chick Two came sidling up and started preening the other's back feathers. The two then fenced with their beaks, but gently, peacefully, almost like humans kissing. It was endearing to see. I was again surprised at just how busy a peregrine eyrie with three chicks can be, each one often doing something quite different from the others, and all moving. It was a photographer's delight.

By 5.20 p.m. it was pouring and the weather had clearly broken. I was almost soaked through to the skin. I left the heavy tripod and one cine battery hidden in a thicket but packed all the rest along the thorny trench to the rockface. I tied both packs to ropes, carried the rope ends up the face, and one by one hauled the packs up. As I drove to the ferry, I resolved to return as soon as possible. Those chicks would be away any day now.

3

Flying to Wild Heritage

Wind and rain the next day made work at the hide impossible so I busied myself with letters, mostly about properties, and did my best to dry out my clothes and photographic equipment in my hut lodgings.

1 July: It was still windy but there were bright periods with scudding clouds, and I was all set up on the cliff edge by 1.30 p.m. Chick One had gone again, this time probably for good. The other two were on the lower shelf but there was a young, headless, semi-plucked rock or stock dove in the top shadowed corner. All the fulmars were still on their eggs, even the one just above the eyrie, and the gull chick was still there, all alone on its tiny grass platform. It seemed clearer now that none of these birds would be molested by the falcons. Perhaps peregrines are a bit likes foxes, who do not like to kill prey too close to their own breeding dens. Just before 2 p.m. Chick Two ran-flapped back to the top, preened for a minute, then when Chick Three came up too, the action stimulated it to go to the prey and rend morsels. At 2.18 p.m. Chick Two tug-carried the prey across the nest and plucked it. By the time I had changed a film, Chick Three was pulling at the prey with its nest mate watching amicably from two yards off.

I switched back to the movie gear, still wanting that good sunlit feeding sequence, and spent the next two hours filming various antics. The chicks preened, did more wing-whirring exercises, performed lovely ballet stretches of wing and foot together, but it was difficult to film. The scudding clouds kept the sun coming in and out, so I had to keep adjusting the aperture in seconds from f16 up to f5.6 and back (or to any stage in between) and it was hard to get the exposures right.

When the falcon flew overhead I tried to tape record the chicks' screams but awful wind noise over the mic made it impossible. At 4.09 p.m. the falcon came winging back over the far headland and flew into the cliff below me, from where came the hoarse chittering calls of Chick One, which was undoubtedly being fed there. On the far side the other two youngsters watched this feeding and kept yelling their heads off, but the mother did not go over to them. They were surely full up and she must have known that.

At 4.31 p.m. Chick Two began leaping about the ledge, batting out at the vegetation with its talons, instinctively practising kill clutches. I was filming this just as Chick Three came out of the top corner, made a perfect Hottentot stretch, then ran towards Chick Two. They then had a wonderful mock fight, hitting each other with their wings. They bounced about, mock-fencing by darting their heads at each other, then pulling back without actually making any contact with their beaks. They ended up 'kissing' one another, twisting their bills sideways and upwards. It was terrific, better, in fact, than stock feeding sequences. After a few minutes' pause, Chick Three went down to the lower ledge. Chick Two followed it, tugging with its beak at vegetation tufts on the way, then they bounced about again like fighting cocks, but without actually hurting each other. They then bounce-flapped across the shelf like small versions of black vultures, awkward on landing, and Chick Two ended up back in the far corner of the upper ledge.

Both dozed for about an hour, then at 4.45 p.m. the younger chick flap-walked back up to where Chick Two had laid down, put its beak under the other's and lifted up its head, very gently. They fenced tenderly with each other's beaks, then Chick Three sat down in front of Chick Two and they leaned their heads together, looking straight into each other's eyes. They then went to sleep like that, resting their heads together. It was as if they felt suddenly lonely after a whole hour far apart. After three more minutes Chick Three again preened the other's chest feathers, a wonderful sight. They were certainly not at all like golden eagle chicks. At 5.06 p.m. the falcon flew close to me, screamed and again dived down to Chick One which, as it gave more high rasping calls, I assumed was being fed. Why would she not go into the main ledge across the cove when I had all my movie gear waiting? Damn her!

At almost a quarter to six I heard more high calls and saw Chick One winging round the bay to the left below me, coming to land right back on the nest ledge. The way the other two were calling naturally made me think that it was the falcon or tiercel, but the browner plumage and awkward landing soon set me right on that question. I ended another movie film on Chick One bouncing about the nest with the dove carcass remains, being pursued for food by Chick Two, and trying to tug morsels off. The big youngster appeared very hungry so maybe the mother had not fed it on her last visit but simply checked that it was alright, being so far from the nest. I switched back to the stills camera, fitted on an X2 extender, giving me a massive 1280mm lens as the sun was now very bright, and took a lot of shots. I varied shutter speed from 125th to 500th and the apertures too, down to f11 at times to improve the depth of field. I thought that I must have got some good shots, the last of which was of Chick Two having a playful tug at Chick One's tail feathers.

The chicks were all asleep in the sinking sun at 6.40 p.m. and I was sure the parents would not be in until near dusk, when I could not photograph anyway, so I packed up and left. The great weight of both full packs made me stumble, my legs and hand were torn again, and I gave the inside of my right knee an awful crack when I slipped while climbing up the rockface. After such a wonderful day, none of this mattered. Only the peregrines were making up for the nightmare of insecurity my life had become.

2 July: One of the amateurs who watched the falcons from the clifftop path had guessed what I was up to, and as I heaved the heavy camera pack from my van told me that all the chicks had flown, for the ledge was now empty! Knowing that they would not be far away, I climbed down the face and was all set up again by 2.20 p.m. I soon located Chick Three, high on a slanting beige rock at 1 o'clock of the nest ledge, and just above it was Chick Two. The falcon came winging over and dived into the cliff below me where I again heard the eldest chick calling out. After an hour, warden Julian scrambled along the thorny cleft to join me for a watch, and was both delighted and amazed, as most folk were, at the close and intimate view of the birds the great lens gave him.

It was soon obvious that all the chicks could now fly quite well, for they changed positions most of the afternoon. Chick Two flapped up to the left and spent half an hour perched amid tangles of creepers which, in the sunlight, threw black bands of shadow across its body. At 3.30 p.m. it shot out, wheeled round with rapidly beating wings, and landed right back on the eyrie. Then the upper youngster also flew down just past the nest ledge and landed amid the lower green vegetation tunnels, as if to escape the sun's blistering heat. A quarter of an hour later, Chick Two flew over to my side of the cove, landing somewhere near Chick One, and Chick Three emerged from the grasses to perch on a low rock. A few minutes after that, it looked nervously intent, launched itself, flew right round the cove and possibly funked landing on my side for it went back into the eyrie where it performed a few Hottentot stretches. At 4.15 I took more photos of it with wings wide open, looking intent, then it also flew into the cliffs below me. All three chicks were now on my side but out of my sight. Patience was called for! I thought that the bird watcher above kept putting his binoculars onto me, or where the screen was, but realised he must have located the chicks too. Julian, with urgent work to do, then had to leave.

At 4.30 the tiercel flickered over, calling out, followed by the bigger falcon, and both apparently landed near their young for again I heard the rasping calls. A few minutes later the falcon came circling upwards, went right round the bay, pausing above the eyrie with shimmering wings, glinting steely- blue in the golden sunlight, before going back to the chicks again. A minute later she repeated this manoeuvre precisely while the chicks maintained a constant, raucous chorus. There was no doubt that she was performing flying displays for them and telling them in falcon-talk: 'Go back to the eyrie. Go back home!'

By the time I had put my last movie film into the cine camera and mounted everything, the falcon had returned to the ledge, this time with a pigeon in her talons, and I fancied I caught a glimpse of something red on one leg. I thought it was probably just blood. She made no attempt to feed herself but kept tugging and dragging the pigeon round the broad ledge, pecking occasionally at it and even holding it up with one powerful leg against the dark plumage streaks on her white chest. The chicks were screaming at her from this side all the time and there was no doubt that she was trying to tease the chicks from across the cove, to tempt them back to the eyrie. She also clearly did not want them to roost on the more insecure cliffs on my side for the night.

Finally, Chick One was brave enough to fly over the bay, grabbed the prey from its mother and tug-hopped it across the ledge and into the crevice by the cliff wall. Then the falcon left, her job done. As the prey had not been plucked at all, the chick turned it over twice, prising little flesh off and getting feathers stuck all over its beak, which it did not much like as it tried to shake them off with violent flicks of its head. It gave up for a while, 'attacked' vegetation with its claws, returned to the prey, dragged it round the ledge while looking down, and smashed its talons into it until it opened up a little. It fed briefly then flew right across the cove back to my side at 5.10 p.m. Fourteen minutes later Chick Three flew over to the pigeon, plucked and ate some, then also flew back.

At 6.31 p.m., the falcon landed impatiently back on the eyrie ledge and picked up the now half-eaten pigeon. This time I was able to confirm my original suspicion that it had a red band round its right leg. It was, or had been, a racing pigeon. She fed herself a few snippets, then again dragged it around the ledge, holding it up, and in swept Chick Two, who snatched it from her and took it into the crevice to feed. The falcon watched the youngster feeding for a few seconds, her black 'moustaches' giving her a solemn look, then left the ledge.

A little later, I was surprised when the tiercel flew in and took the remains away from the eyrie, probably to leave the errant chicks to do what they were intended to do – exploring their new territory, keeping to rocks and ledges up high, and getting to know the terrain. At 7.30 p.m., with no more action, I packed up to catch the last ferry and drove home for a late supper. Over the next two blustery, rainy days, I continued my abortive search for a new remote home, including a 100-mile drive to Dartmoor to see a cottage which I could caretake free for a year. When the owners admitted they had suffered trouble with sets of squatters, though, some of whom still lived in the district, I realised my gear would not be safe whenever I left the place, and I returned still homeless.

5 July. Another sunny day with small passing clouds. I was in place by 3.23 p.m. but the ledge was empty and I could hear the chicks calling from below me to the right. Twice the falcon, with rasping cries, came flickering round the bay from the east,

finally landing on the creepers above the nest ledge. I took a few photos but soon realised there would now be little or no action at the actual eyrie and that there was certainly no need to keep a watch on it any more. I cleared the hide of vegetation, rolled it up and packed the lot out and up the rockface, leaving the site pristine apart from a few flattened grasses.

I then carried the movie gear over to the public path at the top of the cliff. The only amateur ornithologist there that day was the one to whom I had spoken on my last visit. John Mason, from Solihull, turned out to be an enthusiastic, knowledgeable fellow who had taken early retirement to wander Britain in search of his favourite birds. He said he would be glad to be part of any future team mounting watch on the nest as soon as eggs were laid, an idea Julian and I had already discussed.

We soon located Chicks Two and Three, lurking together in the shadows of the creeper tangles, and before long Chick Two flew across the bay and landed on one of three little rocky pinnacles to the left of the thorny cleft where my hide had been. It was a nice and shady place, which would have appealed to the youngsters, and was clearly the spot from which I had heard all the cries. At 4.34 p.m. Chick Three also flew off, circled the bay twice on slightly quavery wings then, to our astonishment, landed only seven yards away from us on the top of the cliff. I cursed myself for not bringing the still camera too but the young peregrine just stayed there, showing no fear. I actually had time to change the lens and swivel round. Even then, I couldn't quite get it all in frame so I filmed its head and chest, and even completed an up and down panning sequence before it flew away again.

At 5.06 p.m. Chick One appeared in the air before us, circled the cove at eye level and tried to perform some short-lived soarings before flapping with short glides to the east and over the far headland. An hour later I saw the tiercel returning and was lucky to get the 400mm movie lens onto him at first go. What a terrible job it was trying to stay on him as he twice circled above the bay at great speed, meteoring round invisible corners like some daredevil rider before diving down to land below Chick Three, which had returned to the creeper tangles. He struggled up to join his youngster and when he began to preen his wings, the chick copied his actions.

8 July: Again the chicks flew well all afternoon, from the creepers to the ledge, across the cove to the shady side and back. The mother peregrine again fed them on the ledge, using the same teasing tactics as before, and at much the same time – 4.30 p.m. Despite the pressure of my search for a home, my gardening and work commitments, I could not resist one more visit to the falcons.

9 July: I was in place on the clifftop by 4 p.m. and how glad I was that I had come, for I was treated to the most wonderful displays of all. I immediately located Chick One on the right-hand cliff, on one of the rocky pinnacles below the vegetation line, and Chick Three was in the creeper tangles on the left cliff. Then Chick Two came zooming over from round the far headland to my left, crossed the path of Chick Three which had leaped into the air, and they chased each other to the far headland again. Then back they came at breakneck speed, diving on and calling to each other, occasionally grappling briefly with their talons. Their wings seemed soft like those of giant moths, the pinions extended like the fingers of a spread hand with each swishing turn. They were right in front of me when Chick One joined in, launching off like a rocket, and all three winged over to the headland. Then back they came again, banking, dipping, wheeling and turning, into gorges and back out, before they landed, one by one, back amid the shadows of the creeper tangles. I noticed there was a cormorant perched nearby but it seemed not one whit put out by the proximity of the young falcons. Then another cormorant arrived, followed by a third, so in the end I got photos of the three chicks and the three cormorants together, which was most unusual.

A quarter hour passed, then Chick Three flew round the far headland to the right. Suddenly I saw the falcon heading along, way out, going towards where it had clearly landed, for as she vanished behind that cliff I could hear the chick calling out. The sight of their mother galvanised the other two for they also left their perch and vanished round the same headland. I thought that would be that but at 4.55 p.m., the tiercel came flapping along from the left headland with some prey in his right talons. This slowed him down so much that a herring gull pursued him, diving low upon him, as he obviously posed no threat. He took the food right to the eyrie and Chicks One and Two, who had clearly seen their father, flew in to join him. Chick Two grabbed the prey, a brown bird, and took it up to the high tussocky corner.

After it had fed, the three chicks again gave me tremendous displays in the air, each lasting about twelve minutes. They zoomed about, chasing each other, banking and turning wildly, and they chased passing gulls and cormorants, dive-bombing them but never making an actual strike.

There was no doubt now that all three chicks were safe and flying well. No thief could get at them, and any mortality now could only be the natural first-winter death, which can be up to 70% of all flown young birds of prey. It was magnificent to witness them feeling at last the power of their wings, their skills in the sky, and the wild British heritage their species had fought so hard to reconquer.

4

RUNNING WILD – TO OTTERS, SEA EAGLES AND OSPREYS

After filming the peregrines, there followed the most hectic, and often horrendous, period of my whole life. I began charging all over England and Scotland looking for that ever-elusive small, isolated new home. Sometimes I stayed with friends near Truro, or in Chertsey and Blackheath writing my book Last Wild Years, making visits to my publisher Jonathan Cape and many more to London studios to finish the film and videos of my first main wildlife production Eagle Mountain, which took over a year to complete. My belongings were scattered all over; some at my three friends' homes, some in storage, some in a frequently-overloaded Mi Caballo, my faithful old VW camper, and some still in Spain.

This period lasted nearly two years. I drove thousands of miles, spent thousands of pounds on petrol but never stayed in a hotel or a bed and breakfast – my old 'horse' Mi Caballo was my main home and at times we shared some very dodgy wild camping. The one glue that held me together during this long and frenetic period was that, almost everywhere we went, I had fascinating wildlife experiences.

On the way up to Scotland I camped in a small secluded forest clearing on Dartmoor. As my supper hissed away in its little pressure cooker I began to wonder if it might not be better for me to live the true gypsy life – just wandering at will, filming at will. Not paying council tax, not paying income tax, with no noisy neighbours and just burning wood in a small stove whenever I got to woods. True, I was getting older and could be found dead in the van, but wouldn't that be better than dying in some hospital ward or old folks' home? I could locate places where I could camp for a few days at a time to get my writing done. Maybe I was not meant to own property...

I was woken before 6 a.m. by old Caballo being shifted about, this way and that, quite violently. I shot to a window to see Dartmoor ponies, with foals at foot, rubbing their backsides on his fenders, two dear little youngsters the main culprits. I didn't have the heart to drive them off so dressed quietly, then went out to take photos. They were all very friendly, nudging each other out of the way to be stroked. I liked most of all the sweet little foals which had such thick furry legs, socking big hooves and huge, long-lashed eyes.

I was sitting in the sun, loth to leave that superb spot, when I saw three buzzards up in the sky. I kept watch in the hope that they would lead me to a nest. Two displayed like eagles, making roller coaster 'golden ball' dives, but not flapping upwards after each dive, as do eagles. One did five dives with trussed wings - terrific. If only the film gear had not been packed away. They did not show me a nest but they were revelling in the strong winds, rising higher and higher, some even vanishing into the clouds. I had never seen buzzards do that before. I drove off, loving the beautiful wooded and valleyed country I was in, but when I went in to estate agents in Bovey Tracey they just laughed at my limit of £45,000. 'Houses on the moor cost more!' they told me.

A few days later, after walking round the Worthing-Ferring area, I became fairly sure that Sussex, where my love of nature had begun, was beyond my purse. Even so, I decided to take a last look at the huge (for Sussex) Friston Forest near Eastbourne, which had appeared both wild and interesting when I had visited it on a Monday morning the year before. On that visit I had met and made friends with the working forester there, Cyril Fuller. I now drove to his home in West Dean and took him for drinks and dinner at his favourite pub, the Sussex Ox. What he told me was rather off-putting, to say the least.

'I've only been here for three years but the Forestry Commission car park is now full every weekend, and cars that can't get in park on the grass verges,' he said. He added that visiting populations had doubled each year, as they had at the nearby Seven Sisters Country Park, now charging £10 per car. The Commission's selling of many woods into private hands meant they were more protected by gamekeepers and owners, so putting more pressure by the public on the remaining FC woodlands, out of which they could not fence people. The wooden bath and lavatory complex had been burnt down last year and replaced with portable loos, which he sometimes had to empty once a day! He could not shoot any more, certainly not to kill rabbits and squirrels with a small bore rifle, because he never knew when or if folks were in the woods. He said that so many people drove up the private roads and tracks, even camping at night, that he could no longer do anything about it unless they had guns. He had even seen dim lights at night up the log roads three miles away, and found motor cyclists – with tents! I will never forget the look on Cyril's face as he said it. 'People have far more free time now than they used to. We all have to change with the times – me and you too!'

These were some of the biggest woodlands in Sussex and they were infested with humans. On the other hand, why shouldn't folk enjoy the remaining woods that are free? Even so, I now realised it would be totally useless for me to try to do wildlife studies of these woods or camp in them for peace and quiet while doing so.

Three days later I was camped in a sheep field by Haweswater in the Lake District, the nesting area of the only pair of eagles in England, when I saw some lapwings with chicks. I got out and stalked the nearest chick and it tried to hide in a tiny peat hag below a rock. As I got nearer it just crouched lower as I took a photo, so I reached out slowly and managed to pick it up. Its eyes were blinking rapidly with fear and I saw the familiar lapwing, or peewit, crest was already sprouting on its head. When I put it down again it ran off but only in very short sprints, stopping to look back at me. Once it even ran a few steps back, towards me, which I could hardly believe, before thinking better of it and carrying on its way.

I was parked in that spot to meet a reader called Julie who was holidaying in the Lake District. She had written that she had never seen an eagle and would like to, and also that she had an isolated steading for sale up in Banffshire, where I was ultimately heading. I had already made a trek to the Haweswater eagles on my 62nd birthday in May, even though I'd been told by an RSPB worker who watched it that the nest had failed. The single egg had, apparently naturally, rolled out of the side. I had been lucky enough on that occasion to film a long sequence of the male eagle flying the entire length of the glen, landing in trees twice, and being followed by the larger female who joined her mate in a tree at the end.

When Julie arrived we drove to the end car park then trekked round, up the steep hill to the top of the ridge, then left along the top official path used by all the many hikers. At intervals we could see the RSPB hut way down on the valley floor, halfway along the glen. Julie was as amazed as I had been when I pointed out the main eyrie, now unused, and realised that it was within 100 yards of the path. She wondered why the RSPB didn't put a hide nearer to the nest crag. I told her I had made exactly that point to the RSPB the previous year. The terrain was such that one could make one of my 'invisible' hides and set it to film, photo or just keep watch from 100 yards from the nest, and much the same distance from the path. It would be, in other words, an undetectable hide in an undetected place. I felt it wasn't much use having RSPB staff in a hut keeping folk back over half a mile away in the valley bottom if walkers could pass within 100 yards of the eyrie without challenge. I only recall that they said that they didn't want to put any kind of hide that close. At least Julie got her reward that day, for we had two sightings of the male eagle, albeit at a fair distance, flying above the ridges on the far side of the glen.

After Julie left I headed up to the island of Mull as a fellow eagle enthusiast had told me there were over thirty golden eagle eyries there, as well as the two pairs of re-introduced sea eagles. I reached the ferry point at Lochaline, only to find caravans with their legs down and other cars and campers parked by the side of the road. It was Sunday and the ferry was shut. All were camping there until the next day. I asked myself whether I really wanted to come back to Scotland. I had lived for three years on a Scottish island and, even if I found the right home on Mull, did I want all that ferry and boating trouble again? I drove up the minor road towards Drimnin but after a few miles couldn't find a camp spot so I pulled into a passing spot, ready to turn back. Almost immediately three cars pulled in around me, although I hadn't seen a single car in almost an hour. I waited until they were gone again, then looked out, down towards the shore. There was something in the sea, moving westwards: one dot, then another, then a third. Up with the binoculars.

Three otters! They were playing around, diving with their poker tails following last, grappling with each other, biting muzzles, and swiping round heads with their paws. I took a few distant photos from Caballo then stalked down to the shore, dashing when the otters dived, freezing when they re-appeared, dash and freeze, dash and freeze. I crept behind some rocks on the shore and took better photos of them leaping out of the water, descending on each other with paws out wide, like fox cubs.

I followed them to the west but couldn't see a den, or holt, and then they vanished round a bend. I dashed back up to Caballo and drove to the headland but they were travelling back east! I drove back, located them again, made another big stalk down to the shore, but they'd gone. I thought perhaps the otters had come out of the water and there, sure enough, were two glistening lumps on the seaweedy rocks, the same browny-green colour as the rocks and the sea wrack. They had a large crab between them and were chewing it from opposite ends, tugging the claws off. Two big cubs, I guessed. I put the lens on them until one moved its head into sideways profile and I got two shots. I tried to stalk closer but when I raised my head around a boulder they had slipped back into the sea.

Just past them, I now noticed, was a superb small wood, about four or five acres, where the trees went right down to the sea. Just the wood I had always dreamt of! I drove to a better view of it behind some willow trees, then investigated. There were small cliffs and rockfaces and many deciduous trees among the Scots pines – beech, sycamore, larch, ash, silver fir, hazel, oak, rowan – making the most beautiful woods and sea combinations I had ever seen. If I could buy it I would be quite happy just to camp there, especially as my little 12-volt TV worked perfectly, whereas it seldom did anywhere else. That night it treated me to an interesting programme on the rise and downfall of Diana Dors, whom I had known quite well. I later made efforts to obtain the 'great wood' but there were complicated ownership disputes and in the end I failed.

Next morning, after the ferry trip from Lochaline, I was driving along by Ardachoil when I saw a huge bird flapping along and into a tree on the far side of Loch Spelve. Up with the bins and there seemed to be two nests in the trees, found within an hour of arriving on Mull! I had lunch in a layby then hiked up a peninsula to the north of and opposite the nests, noting fish tanks right below them, but after a long wait saw no more sea eagles and nothing moving on the nests. I drove all the way to Fionnphort but found it as touristy as Mallaig and the beaches along Loch Scridain rather bleak, as was the Ross of Mull. I'd been told the eagles there had little to eat but fulmars, but I did pick some fine big cockles at low tide to make a paella. I also gathered a few large mussels but they were full of gritty white 'pearls' which needed to be picked out if they were not to break my teeth. I drove back to camp opposite the sea eagles' spot, and the midges were so bad I didn't even dare open Cab's door to throw the dish water out. I'd forgotten about the midges.

Next morning, as soon as I stepped out of Caballo, I saw a sea eagle flapping along towards the nest trees, followed by two hooded crows trying to mob it. It looked vulturine, wings floppier than a golden eagle's and broader too. I went into the van to get my binoculars but by the time they were up and focussed, it had gone. I drove round Loch Spelve to Croggan to get a better view but a sea mist came in and obliterated everything.

When I stopped for petrol I was very surprised when the garage man who served me said that I was right about the sea eagles' nest, and that a month before there had been a chick in it, which had probably flown by now.

As an exercise to keep the legs and eyes 'in', I decided to look for a golden eagle eyrie which my friend had told me about, up the gorge of the River Scarisdale. If it did have a late chick in it I would try and work it, if the terrain was right. After five minutes, having crossed a marshy patch and battled through thick bracken, I had just started climbing the steep ground when I realised I had made a mistake. After so long a gap I had got it all wrong. I was looking for a nest on the left-hand side of the gorge so should have gone up the right side, so I could keep glancing over. But here I was, on the left. Oh well, I wasn't going to go all the way down to try again so I just kept going. Halfway up Beinn a Ghraig, the mist I had started out in began to clear and roll away from me, so I was lured into carrying on.

I crossed above a super waterfall between two rocky towers, took a photo of the view between them, and saw that I was by then above the whole main gorge. It was extremely deep and I could see no eyrie on the right or left sides. I saw only shallow faces up to the top of the hill and was sure no eagle would nest in them. I began to go down the right-hand side of the gorge and, sure enough, I found the eyrie! It was some 100 yards below the waterfall, on a recessed ledge. It had a small oak growing out in front of it which, in terms of photography, would cut any bird in half if one didn't work out the best angle. It was empty, with no sign of this year's use, but it was not a wasted trip as it gave me the rare opportunity to see down into it. It would be a very good place to work when it was next occupied. On the way back down I had to negotiate a sheer chimney out of a side gorge which had my heart in my mouth as I climbed out of it, but I managed it safely and felt quite proud of myself as I tramped on down to Caballo. I dashed to the ferry as I only had a two-day excursion ticket and, arriving just in time to see it coming in, I was lucky enough to be the last vehicle on it. As we steamed back to Lochaline I reflected that Mull was a wonderful island with rare species and infinitely varied scenery but realised that I didn't really want to live on an island again. I could, however, come back and film the sea eagles one season once I had the necessary permissions.

I drove up to northeast Scotland but reader Julie's steading turned out to be an almost derelict barn with no doors or wings, a leaky roof and right by the side of a road. It was filled with hay bales and cowpats from which oozed puddles of something browny-red which looked like blood. Even at £16,000 I didn't think it a good buy, and it wasn't a good wildlife area. I went to look at a cottage near Drummuir which Julie's husband Graham had recommended and having heard that Lord Seafield's estate sold cottages, I rang his agent's office on the way. Mr Fitzjohn just said 'Come back to Cullen now and get our 'what's on offer' list!' I groaned as it mean backtracking twelve miles but when I found that the Seafield office was in York Place, it seemed a good omen, as York Place was the address of my friend with whom I often stayed in Chertsey. I wasn't sure I really wanted to live all the way up there, the landscape so rolling and bleak, but decided to give it a go now that I was there.

Fitzjohn was a really nice man, with a spaniel that took a real liking to me and in a vast office which gave it enough room for exercise. He said 'Up here we have space and time. It's the last land in all the UK that time forgot!' He gave me a sheaf of property particulars and suggested I take a look at an isolated farmhouse near Deskford which was screened by its own belt of trees. I did just that, drove down there, and took an immediate liking to the place. It was a huge farm, with E-shaped steadings, roof in fair nick, dry inside although missing two skylight windows, and its front garden was screened from the minor road by a five-yard-thick belt of trees, mainly sycamore. There were five rooms downstairs, two big bedrooms upstairs, with a wonderful landing like a minstrel's gallery, on which jackdaws had been nesting. With very little work, one could just move in! I went to see the cottage which Julie's husband had suggested, and another near Huntly, but the Deskford farmhouse seemed the best prospect so I drove back there to camp for the night, even more delighted to find my little 12-volt TV worked perfectly on all stations.

I woke up after a long dreamless sleep to see something large and brown at the end of the farm track. It was a hare! It lifted itself up into an arched-back bow, raised one forefoot and licked between spread toes. It grabbed one drooping long ear at the root with both paws and drew the ear through them, grooming and drying it from a rain shower. Then it did the same with the other ear. It stood on tiptoe on back feet only, arched its back, flapped its ears, and boxed its forefeet out to the front, pawing the air madly to dry them of droplets. All the time its great brown bulging eyes flashed in the sun. What a performance! So much more complicated than a rabbit's, and in an animal twice the size too. I took a few good pictures. Deciding now to make an offer for the farmhouse, I went all round it measuring the broken windows, of which there were, in fact, only five.

I drove away and after a few miles spied an oystercatcher's red beak by the side of the road. It was sitting on a nest scrape on a gravelly strip between the road and grass verge, with traffic thundering by a mere two yards from her. I tried to pull up to get a closer look or a photo, but there was nowhere. Maybe she knew that! As I drove along I was somewhat mortified to hear on BBC radio precisely the kind of eagle trek which I had proposed, with a detailed script, back in 1983. The same producer had told me their schedules were full but that he would bear it in mind for the following year. I hadn't heard from him again but now, seven years later, they were doing it with someone else! I listened to the species mentioned on the trek and felt a sense of frustration: even back then I could have shown them nesting eagles, buzzards, black-throated divers, peregrines and otters, all in one trek. Oh well, their loss, I thought.

I drove on to Stirling to meet fellow nature writer and friend, Jim Crumley. At the time Jim was chief feature writer for the Edinburgh Evening News and had written some fine pieces praising my books, especially the three on golden eagles, and we had met and become pals. I must say I soon began to feel Jim was a better writer than myself and I confess to encouraging him to leave his newspaper job and write books himself, even introducing him to my publisher Jonathan Cape, who went on to produce three of his books. I still consider Jim Crumley to be the finest wildlife writer in Scotland today.

In the morning Jim took me to an osprey nest near the Lake of Menteith, atop a 150-foot Scots pine, which could be seen from the road but only by an expert eye. I took a few photos, including two of an osprey flying in with a stick trailing from its talons. It dropped the stick onto the nest and landed with winnowing wings on the topmost green sprays above it before dropping down on the right side of the nest. As it did so, we saw the white heads of two chicks rear up, as if expecting food.

After I cooked us lunch in Caballo, we set up the movie gear, Jim carrying the hefty tripod and I the camera and its batteries. We didn't need a hide but set up below a small birch which I saw had branches spreading enough to make a fair screen. Within minutes I filmed the male coming in with a fish, and he gave high-pitched ringing kite-like calls before he landed. The female put one set of talons on the fish then wrenched bits off to feed the chicks who were sprouting their first browny adult feathers. During the afternoon we noticed the female occasionally give what seemed to be greeting calls when the male arrived, and sometimes they flew round in circles together before one broke off to feed and, usually, bring back a fish.

The ospreys normally come back from their African winter in early April and Jim told me that one year a young female came back first, just after the male, who impregnated her. She and he then built a nest. The older female then returned and the male courted and impregnated her too and fed her on the nest. He then ignored the young female on the nest so she had to feed herself. Jim said every time she had to eat she left the eggs, but was back with a fish inside three minutes, as if she knew that the eggs should not get cold. This showed how efficient an osprey can be when it needs to be.

As we were talking, the female came off the nest when the male had returned and headed our way, allowing me to take two super sequences of her flying, once turning on her side so the sunlight lit up her wings.

On the way back, Jim showed me an oystercatcher on its nest on the top of a wall and I began to think that these birds are rather weird. She had found a suitable depression in a mossy-ferny section of the wall and to see that bright crimson beak suddenly jutting from atop a wall right by the road was quite a shock. She clearly felt safe from predators up there but I would have thought that a stoat could easily enough have got her eggs.

Next day we worked the ospreys again, then hiked round a wood where Jim had seen rare capercaillie but we didn't find any. We were passing through the trees below undulating mossy rockfaces when Jim heard the sound of young chicks calling. The calls were coming from our right so we looked up and saw a woodpecker hole in a broken-off spar. I put up the binoculars. It was a new hole, with many golden bits of fresh wood showing. Then the great spotted woodpecker turned up, 'kik-kik-ing' like mad when she saw us. She stopped in the branches to scold us but it must have been kind of difficult with a beak full of caterpillars and insects, and the urge to feed her young was just too great. She flew to the hole and thrust the lot into the unseen beaks of her bairns, then flew off fast.

As we were leaving, I suggested we return the next day but put up a hide now. Jim said we didn't have any hide materials but I said there was plenty! We tore up bracken and, after dragging in small branches to bridge a tangle of uprooted tree root clusters, we covered it all in to make a nice, hidden tunnel. We returned to the hide the next day and I took some excellent photos and film of the woodpeckers coming in. I waited each time for a full side view of its body, head, beak and prey and of it bracing its tail against the trunk in order to bend its body right into the hole to get its beak far below and into the youngsters' mouths.

5

WILDLIFE ON THE RUN

Back in the garden hut near Truro, which a reader friend was letting me use, I struggled fitfully with my book *Last Wild Years*. I also met the National Trust head warden who was very keen on my suggestion that I do a wildlife survey of their Predannack area, an idea I put forward in the hope of ingratiating myself with the Trust which might let me buy or rent a run-down holiday cottage. He told me that their current survey was mainly of a botanical nature, so it would be a great help if I categorised the mammals and birds. He even gave me an Honorary Warden's badge so I could go anywhere I liked. He said that otters had dwindled in recent years, partly due to mink, of which some 500 had recently been trapped in a single year. I was asked to do a badger census and a raptor survey, if I could manage it, and he told me that there were 400 golden plovers nesting on Predannack airfield, which was used by helicopters only.

While doing the survey I found, in a steep wood, a buzzards' nest which had been used that year, so I could have filmed them as well as the peregrines. I sat for a while and then saw three buzzards come sailing over my head. I gave my usual buzzard whistles and – blow me – the smallest swung round, half hovered, circled twice, getting lower and lower, and called back! Later I was by Caballo, parked on the edge of the wood, when the three buzzards came back, the small one, probably a male, calling loudly. I called back. Again he swung out from the other two as they went north, and hovered, coming lower and lower. There was no doubt about it now: he was curious about me. I held out my arm, bent like a falconer's, in unlikely hope, but he didn't land on it.

I spent a week tramping everywhere on the Predannack survey, located five badger setts, one with 22 holes which could have been two or three combined, three fox earths with blackberries in the scats, and two stoat holes, one freshly dug. I also located two more buzzard nests. I wrote my report, made a detailed map of all my findings and sent the lot off, hinting again that I would like to buy or rent any sub-standard holiday cottage which they might want off their books.

Some weeks later I received the reply. I recall that it said, in summary:

Dear Volunteer,

We thank you for your survey and work with the volunteer section. We would be pleased if you would carry on the good work next year. A list of properties for sale or rent can be obtained from the Land Agent.

Yours faithfully…

I should have remembered the advice I was given in the army: Never complain. Never explain. And never volunteer!

In November I visited BBC Bristol where a top producer bought some of my peregrine film. I went on to my lady friend's home in Blackheath and finished a lot of work in film and video studios in London. By now I had heard from my Spanish lawyer friend that the isolated Red Villa, in which I had lived in Spain, had been burgled but he had locked up what remained of my belongings there.

Partly to retrieve them, partly because my friends in Chertsey and Blackheath were having family problems, and partly because I needed somewhere quiet to write, I drove back to Spain in December. I was lucky and managed to rent a large seaside villa on a cheap winter let, emptied everything from Mi Caballo into it and next day drove up to the Red Villa in the mountains above Totana to retrieve what the burglars had left. The burglary had happened six months before so as I approached I was sure it would have been taken over by squatters, who might lynch me, or that I would find it boarded up. But no, as I reached it the windows were open, the small side door was wide open and so were the back gate and door. I had obviously lost everything. Only the huge main door was locked. I used the heavy key I still had and undid the lock.

Amazingly, while they had taken my 16mm Projectior (which had been a free gift anyway) and my pup tent, Canadian bucksaw and fishing rods, they had left my small bed, my book-writing swivel chair, the wood stove and smoke pipe, a big woolly rug, 40-metre hosepipe, Spanish wildlife notes and my treasured hazel-honeysuckle spiralled walking stick. The house had been open to the world for six months yet all this gear was still there. They had left most of the cutlery and crockery too. I lost no time in bundling it all into Cab. On my way down from the Santander ferry I'd stopped off at Candelada so that a Spanish pal could show me two fincas for sale. One was a circular hectare with a wall right round it, a big chicken shed which wouldn't cost much to convert to a cabin and its own water well. When I took my Red Villa key back to my lawyer pal, Gregorio Parra, who lived in Totana and in fact owned the villa, he looked at the particulars and said I should have nothing to do with the place. The wall, the well and the chicken house were not on the excritura, and three families had the right to take water from where the well was situated. For the rest of that winter, apart from occasional noggins and meaningless jocular conversations in local bars, I did nothing but finish my book.

Back in England in mid-March, I had to leave the garden hut near Truro as my friend there still had family problems. I had to put most of my belongings hastily into storage there. My friends in Chertsey and Blackheath put their homes up for sale but I rented a room in the latter until mid-June, by which time, after many visits to London studios, I had 500 videos made for £1,560 and finished revisions and photos for my book. I didn't work eagles on my 63rd birthday but did make a seven-mile trek round the top of Leith Hill near Dorking, the highest point in southeast England, after visiting the gothic tower at its summit. I found a roebuck skull, a fox den and a badgers' sett but now saw only a few common garden birds and no birds of prey at all. I got lost on the second far hill, had to ask my way and then had to hike all the way back round the horseshoe to the car park, all while carrying a hefty camera pack. That would make a good story – the 'great trekker' of rugged high mountains in Canada, the Scottish Highlands and Spain, getting lost in a Surrey wood! My left hip was very painful towards the end, too. Well, I thought, my eagle days are probably over but it had been a very wet late May and June and I probably wouldn't have got much anyway.

On the day I had to leave Blackheath I really didn't know which way to go. I was 'running wild' again. To go back to Cornwall, or to head north? A woman editor of Pan Books who lived in Hereford had just bought the paperback rights to Moobli, my book about my great Alsatian tracker dog, and had invited me to visit. And my eagle worker pal Dave was running an RSPB reserve near Penrith and had found a peregrine's nest you could look down on without doing any climbing at all. I drove off and camped for the night in what I felt was a secluded glade in the New Forest.

I was woken just before 6 a.m. by a ranger with a pogo stick picking up litter, but he didn't come over, so I dozed with my clothes on until 9 a.m. I had just got up when a Forestry Commission van arrived. The ranger said they had seen me eating in Caballo last night but didn't want to disturb me, for which I liked him. He informed me that there were twelve official camp sites in the Forest but that wild camping was not allowed. I promised not to be a naughty boy again and showed him some of my books. He seemed impressed and asked for my autograph. Even so, I drove off feeling rather a lost soul, reliving the nightmares of years of wild camping and of being turned away. I took the lady editor out for supper, perked up by her cheerful company, but disaster struck on the way to meet Dave at the Geltsdale reserve above Penrith.

Just before Shap there was a loud bang and a flapping sound and Cab slowed down as I pulled to the side. A socking great screw had gashed through the rear off tyre. I tried to change the wheel but one nut refused to come off, and my violent efforts with the wrench only rounded its edges. Police came by and tried to help with a handsaw, to no avail. Eventually, an AA mechanic came at their request and had to hammer and chisel it off. I camped near Swindale and next day drove to Penrith, where a most helpful firm, Tyre Services, on the Carlisle road, not only made repairs to the hub, fitted a new tyre, sold me a new battery as my old one had gone flat overnight, but gave Cab an oil change to boot. I had been away from Blackheath for only three days but the cost of all that, including petrol, came to a total of £159.49. I tell you, wild camping can cost more than renting a flat!

Dave took me on a seven-mile return trek but it was easy, in fact rather boring moorland terrain – boring, that is, until we reached the peregrine's nest. It was quite extraordinary. It was on a long, dark ledge in a small ravine with a stream running through it. It was only about fifteen feet above the ground and on it were three well-grown peregrine chicks, still in the white downy stage but sprouting the first dark grey wing and tail feathers. We were standing on the opposite bank, not more than twenty yards away, and while one chick crept to hide behind a dangling sprig of heather, the other two stood their ground, just glaring at us, making me feel like the intruder I was. Once, one of the parents flew over to their side but did not kick up the harsh calls which are usual when humans appear close to the nest, maybe because it felt that the chicks were safe enough on the far side of the ravine, small though it was. I took a few photos of the chicks, of course. The chicks were surrounded by many pigeons' pinions, some of which had numbers painted on them, clearly from racing birds. Dave told me there were five pairs of the falcons in the 36,000 acres of the reserve but that no others nested as low as this pair.

Next day Dave and I hiked up into the great Riggindale valley at Haweswater in the Lake District, where the only pair of golden eagles in England nested. We only went as far as the official RSPB hide in the valley bottom but through our binos we saw both eagles were in eyrie 4, one of the five I had located on a memorable October day seven years before. It was the highest eyrie, a really good deep nest with a small rowan tree supporting the front of it. We could see only half of the large female as she was standing behind one well-grown eaglet. The male stood proudly on the right side of the nest, his rich chestnut breast towards us, golden nape and silvery streaks just discernible on his powerful 'shoulders'. I took two photos but they were too far away for top class images and, after the long trek yesterday my hips told me that we need go no further that day.

Dave left me in a lay-by and I didn't know whether to head north or south. I had no home and was, again, alone. I'd heard of Keilder Water so headed for the beautiful lake. I found nothing for sale but did find that it was a tourist trap, clearly a haven for pleasure seekers. Onto Morpeth I went, but agents there said it was a very expensive area, being a dormitory for Newcastle. Before Alnwick I saw some magnificent cliffs and crags but when I got to them they were covered with climbers, ropes and pitons, and I heard the yells of humans. In the town of Hawick I found nothing under £40,000 but poky town flats and flats in rundown terraces. I headed for the sea, came to a sea lagoon I could live by but found, further on, a big sign: Lindisfarne Nature Reserve. Heading away from the No Parking signs, I camped up in the Lammermuir Hills, grouse moorland but seemingly well-managed, the burnt areas small. I'd seldom felt so far outside society, lonesome and depressed. I needed a tonic and knew just where to go.

I drove to Jim Crumley in Stirling and we did a long trek round the crags of Glen Fathan, part of the Balquidder estate. From about three-quarters of a mile I spotted some white splashes on a cliff ledge, evidence perhaps of a peregrines' nest. Up with the binos – and we saw three young kestrels flying about a crag some twenty yards away. It was likely that the droppings had been made by the parents roosting nearby when the chicks had grown too big to leave much room in the nest. Such white splashes on cliffs can always be indicators of the nesting sites of golden eagles or any bird of prey, as well, of course, as nearly all sea birds.

Next day we went to watch ospreys fishing in the Lake of Menteith and for once I did get photos of one diving, catching a fish, flapping hard to pull it to the surface then flying off with it, turning it into a more streamlined torpedo position as it flew. It is most amusing to see salmon and trout fishermen in their boats, patiently waiting, sometimes for hours, for a bite. Along comes an osprey, dips its foot into the water right by a boat, takes a 2 lb trout, shakes its feathers as if to say 'Thank you, gentlemen!' and away it goes to its nest. Some men get angry; I saw one shake his fist at a retreating bird.

Next day Jim and I had an enjoyable book signing in the main bookshop in Callender, then I drove on to nearby Doune to visit an old friend, Phil Corcoran, whose phone call to the owners of Eilean Shona had led to me living in an old croft there for three years. He now told me that the prestige magazine *Scotland on Sunday* were trying to trace me to do a big interview, with photos, preferably in my old area of Moidart-Sunart-Ardnamurchan, from where I had written most of my wildlife books. I hadn't intended to go back but realised that this might be a chance to get over my homeless state. Maybe some landowner would say 'I like Mike's books and we've got this little old run-down croft…' I could also do a recce of the property situation there. I rang the magazine's assistant editor and arranged to meet the team at Strontian.

My first shock on arriving in my old area was to find that a seafront bungalow at Camus Inas near Glenborrodale, on the market for £20,000 before I went to Spain, was now up for sale at £95,000! And this steep rise was reflected over the whole area. I simply couldn't afford to come back! I duly met the team and did a full interview and photo-shoot along the shores of Loch Shiel, opposite my old home. The article was excellent, occupied a full page in the magazine, and not a single landowner responded! After the interview I went to camp at Dorlin where I used to launch my boat on the sea, and rang the new owners of Shona. I was told they had nothing for sale on the island but that my old croft was now a holiday home for a

Welsh school teacher. Not far from the phone box were some wooded cliffs and I heard a buzzard calling loudly from somewhere on them.

In the morning I started climbing, trying to find the easiest route but coming again and again to bulging, heathery, granite faces which I could neither get round nor over. I struck off further north, up a gully filled with big rocks when – wush wush wush - off went the buzzard, from a nest actually on the rocky cliff. My eyes had met its eyes just before it left and I was just thinking that I would shrink back and leave it be when off it flew. I had never before found a cliff-nesting buzzard. Still calling, it went round my head twice, quite close, so that I felt the draught from its wings. I was sure no-one knew this nest so I climbed about, found two ideal sites where I could get good shots, especially of flying in and out. The bird, clearly this year's chick, was flying strongly so it must have flown from the nest several times before. I doubted it would come back after my intrusion but it was a place to bear in mind for next season.

Two more good things happened that day. The lady who ran the outdoors shop in my old home village said that the three eagle videos she had bought from me on my way through had gone in one day. She thought it 'so dense and fabulous' that I was under-pricing them and she bought ten more from me, handing me £155 cash. Feeling that property in my old area was now just too pricey, I headed north but stopped off at Lochailort to fill Caballo with petrol. I was astonished to see four magnificent red deer stags which had, apparently, elected to graze around the garage/pub complex. They were tame and all bigger and better than the stags on what was in reality poor grazing in the mountains around my old home, Wildernesse, which I had studied and photographed for years. All were still in velvet and one which showed interest in me, raising its head and taking a few steps forward, was a Royal, with twelve tines on his antlers. I got some tremendous shots – all without any effort at all – making sure that nothing of the pub or garage showed in the important, useable ones.

I headed on north, looking at likely properties. I found an ideal little cottage below a huge crag but it was at the start of a drive to a Residential Home for Alcoholics. I spent an afternoon finding and looking around a school and ruined church I'd been told about. Both fitted the bill as they were not too close together, and I saw a buzzard fly into a tree with a big nest, dippers in the burns and ptarmigan on the tops of Ben Rinnes. When I rang the Dufftown agent, both had been sold the very day I found them. And so it went on. I saw seven more cottages in the next week but there were always problems. Hope began to fade and I felt that this was the worst period of my life, endless driving, often in heavy rain… I'd probably end up in a ditch like Ira Hayes in the Johnny Cash song. It's all going to end in heartbreak. No, it can't, I have no heart left.

On 18 July I had to dash to Insh station to make a programme for Grampian TV, arranged by my publisher to coincide with the release of my book *Last Wild Years*. I was a few minutes late to meet reporter Ann McKenzie, her soundman and cameraman, but I took them to a secluded wooded site and did most of the interview standing up and sitting in Caballo. To make a dramatic point at one stage I dropped copies of my books, one after the other, on top of each other while explaining that after writing so many, I was still homeless and, in comparison with most folk, virtually penniless. I hoped, as before, that some landowner might offer a wee bothy…

My spirits lifted when I spent a long weekend with my old newspaper editor Arthur Redford and his wife at Culbo House on the Black Isle. We exchanged many hilarious memories and anecdotes from the stories we had worked on in the past and both said they hadn't spent such an enjoyable weekend for years. Arthur said they were selling up and moving to Dorset where it wasn't 'so cold for so long'. Why didn't I buy their home? I could maybe buy a *room*, I replied. I was with them when I found out that North Tonight, the program for which I'd been filmed, was on Grampian TV the next night, when I was due to be in Fort William to meet the Forestry Commission land agent there.

Next afternoon, the agent revealed he had nothing for sale that would suit me but he put me onto an isolated house that was being offered at a very reasonable price in Glenhurich, which was right back in my old eagle area. It also contained two of my best ledge eyries and I said I would drive over to see it on the morrow. When I told him my TV programme was on that night, I got a shock. He said that Grampian TV did not extend as far as Fort William and that I would have to get to the Fort Augustus area! Cripes! I shot to old Caballo, drove him there and had to try several spots before, in a tiny lay-by by a small loch, I got the last part of North Tonight on my little 12-volt telly. Luckily, my bit was on it. Well, they did me proud, really. I was 'the angry environmentalist who can't find a home… Despite all his critical acclaim and popularity, he has come back from five years' exile in Spain, and finds himself homeless and disillusioned …' and so forth. Then I came on, bunging down my books and moaning about my plight. A bit sad, really, but good professional material. This time I did eventually hear from one landowner, a lady up in Dornoch Firth offered me a room in her flat at a cheap rent, provided I did her heavy chores and gardening!

I caught the ferry to Ardgour next day and eventually found the Glenhurich house. It was isolated, bigger than Wildernesse, its roof fine, with just a few busted windows. I could move into it but I'd forgotten how gloomy and misty this glen was, surrounded on all sides by the high crests of the mountains. Today it was mistier than ever but, despite the conditions and the fact that I was wearing heavy new boots bought in Fort William, I made a six-mile return trek. Towards the end of it I binned the two ledge eyries but neither had been used that season, and a new forestry logging road had been made, running directly under the cliff.

As I put the binos down I saw something moving down the track towards me, near the grasses at the side of a bend. A pine marten? No, it was too big and too grey. A badger? But as it trotted nearer I saw it was too small. I had moved slowly to the side of the track and put up the glasses, keeping dead still. Suddenly it paused and lifted its head. It was a wildcat! On and on it came, putting one foot in front of the other, each time a paw obscuring the one behind, a sort of pigeon-toed walk, like an unathletic girl running. It got nearer and nearer and I could see the golden eyes.

Suddenly, it stopped, saw me, not quite sure if I was a human or not. It stretched its head up fast, and I could see the twin black bands on the tops of its forelegs and its long white whiskers and salmon pink nose. It was now quite close and I couldn't think of what to do so I gave out a loud 'meeeow'! It jumped up, turned, shot away from me, showing its thick black-banded tail, and dived into the undergrowth by a forestry deer fence. A superb sighting and I cursed that because of the gloom and mist I had not taken the camera.

I was even more angry with myself later when I was hiking back to Caballo. A roe deer fawn came out of the heather and bracken ahead of me to the right and stumbled brokenly across the track. I reckoned it was about three weeks old, quite wobbly on its feet. I took in the Bambi face, twitching velvety black nostrils and lustrous big eyes with long lashes, a darling creature, as ever. Then I saw the red-brown form of its mother, further back in the heather. She was plucking off hawkbit flowers along with grasses and the tenderest shoots of heather, while her bairn was nuzzling and licking grasses and sniffing strands of herbiage.

Slowly I slid onto my knees then belly-crawled to between two baby pines. I kept quiet and still and the fawn moved slowly right up to me, saw me, though I hadn't moved, did two double-takes, then tottered back to its mum, grazing by the trackside. They went a few yards up the track then turned, came back my way, grazing here and there, then began trotting right up to me. Suddenly the mother noticed my still form, stopped, stared – and bolted, quickly followed by her fawn who that time round was not at all tottery! It was as close as I'd ever been to wild deer.

It began to rain heavily so I ran the last few hundred yards to Caballo and camped for the night right by the deserted house, enduring yet again the forgotten hellish biting of the midges. In the morning I kept an appointment arranged by my publisher to meet Andrew Eames, a top freelance feature writer, who wanted to go with me on a trek in my old eagle area and write a piece for The Independent newspaper. Again I agreed, as it would help the book and I might hear from a landowner who…

First, I took Andrew on an easy drive along the forestry track on the south side of my old home loch and glassed eyries 27, 28, 33, and 41. We saw no eagles but I was delighted to see a full-grown eaglet in 28, too far away to photograph as it was across the far side of the loch. Then I took him on a trek along Glenhurich but a shorter and higher one than the previous day's, and showed him the two ledge nests. Being higher and closer, I could see them better, and was fairly sure neither had been used for two or three years. I answered his questions, he took all the photos he wanted, and we parted, he with the intention of driving as far south as he could get and camping in his car, which I thought was rather brave.

The Fort William agent had said I would probably get the house for £20,000 but when I rang the owner I felt that to be a bit too optimistic and cheap and offered him £30,000. To my surprise he said he wanted over £45,000! For that gloomy, rainy, misty glen? No way. As I drove away, I felt it was just not meant for me to return to the western Highlands. As if to emphasise the point, I reached the last ferry just as they were lifting the drawbridge and setting off to Corran. I had to drive right round the long way, through Coal and Fort William to get to the main road south at Corran, an extra forty miles out of my way.

6

A WILD PARADISE FOUND

The second half of the summer was spent in more futile chasings around Scotland, looking for my new ideal home, and by the end of it I had decided to return to Spain. Then, though, something strange happened. I was driving through Perth after visiting a loyal reader in the town when I spied a big colourful notice in the window of Bidwells, the estate agents: Hideaways In Scotland. The street was clogged with cars, with nowhere to park, and I was about to carry on when a big car in front of me signalled to leave. I stopped, flashed my lights to let it out, then pulled into the gap and marched in for the brochure. I camped near Douglas Water and saw that the brochure had several promising properties.

Next day I checked a sawmill on the River Nith but it was too near other buildings, and a small cottage near Selkirk which could have suited me if it had not already been sold. I motored on eastwards to look at a weirdly- named Ropelaw Farmhouse in the middle of the 10,000-acre Craik Forest near Hawick, which was described as the 'ultimate hideaway'. It looked to be so from the photo and, at offers over £35,000, seemed to be a very good buy in an idyllic spot. I finally reached the remote Forestry Commission gate. The instructions said that one had to drive 5.6 miles down the forestry track to find the farmhouse but the gate was padlocked! It was now pouring with rain so I was damned if I was going to walk it and back.

However, I well knew the habits of FC rangers. Sure enough, there was a key under a rock by the side of the gate. I used it, put the key back where I'd found it and began driving down a seemingly endless gravelly track. To my surprise, I saw a Rolls Royce driving towards me! I pulled into a hardcore layby and waved frantically, hoping to stop the driver and tell him to leave the key for me. But he just waved back airily, barely glancing at me, and went on. Oh hell, he's probably bought the place already, I thought, but decided that I may as well take a look at it anyway and drove the 5.6 miles. I found no left turnings as stated on the route, so went on, still found no turnings so went back, counted the two miles I'd overshot and looked more carefully. I then found, rather than a turning, a tiny weed-covered two-wheel track forking to the left. It was muddy and soaking wet and old Caballo could easily get stuck so I backed down it a few yards. The farmhouse was said to be two hundred yards down the track. I marched on and on and after some five hundred yards felt like I must be on the wrong track. I was about to turn back when I spotted a chimney through the trees. I hiked on down.

What a fantastic place! It was huge, three-bedroomed farmhouse, in excellent order, with mains electricity and septic tank drainage laid on, and with its own water supply. There was a huge byre to the side and a separate garage/workshop, both in good condition. To the front of the 3 1/2 acres ran a burn with salmon and sea trout spawning pools, 160 yards of which belonged to the property, and the whole view beyond was of supernal hen harrier-type unplanted pastureland stretching to the next section of forest on the horizon. Again, quite fabulous. I looked through the windows and saw stacks of nice furniture, good quality carpets and curtains, and even a Rayburn. In the kitchen I could see racks of crockery, cutlery laid out, an ironing board and an iron. Crikey, I could just move in! Without thinking, I put my hand on the front door and made the Wildernesse prayer: 'If you want me here, help me. I will love and look after you if you will love and look after me.'

I felt that living here would be a totally new experience, new terrain, new wildlife. No eagles but surely I'd trekked enough on them? Maybe I'd give up my bondage to the king of birds and get down to serious writing, maybe some memoirs. I very much wanted to camp by the place but in the continuing downpour was afraid the track might wash out and Caballo would get stuck, six miles from the nearest road. I drove back to the gate but the key had gone - the Roller driver must have taken it! In vain I searched, scratched, scrabbled the ground under and around the rock but it was gone. I was stuck behind the barrier all night. I couldn't lift the gate off its hinges as the hangers were reversed. I could have axed through a side gate but destroying government property could mean big trouble and would ensure that I didn't get the farmhouse. Oh well, camp here for the night, then, I thought. Soaked almost to the skin, I laid out my clothes to dry a little, had a few drams, made a meal and went to sleep, hoping some forester would come through tomorrow.

Not until ten o'clock next morning did a battered jalopy turn up and a man got out to walk his greyhound. He didn't have a key either but told me I could just drive out of the forest by going back to the open end at Craik village. I was getting short of petrol so I asked how far it was. He said it was fifteen miles but that it was a complicated route and that many folk had got lost in Craik Forest. In the end he postponed walking his dog, apart from giving it a brief run, seized his own 4-gallon can of petrol and guided me all the way to Craik. I then had to drive him back to his van, from where he guided me to Hawick and a petrol station. He would take no reward but when he said he had won many shooting competitions and wanted to be a deer stalker, I said I'd write and recommend him to Louis Stewart MBE, head of the Red Deer Commission whom I knew, which I later did.

That very day I rang Bidwells to say that I definitely wanted to buy the farmhouse. They told me that there had already been two closing dates but that no-one had come up with the money. I dashed south to complete some business with my publisher, make more videos, get Caballo through his MOT, sort out tax affairs with my accountant and conduct negotiations by telephone, which took almost three weeks.

When I first entered the farmhouse with the estate factor I was delighted to find that the electricity and water systems were working perfectly and that there was far more useful gear in the house than I had seen through the windows. The biggest surprise came when he told me that everything in the house was owned by the previous tenant, the world-famous yachtsman Chay Blyth. The good news continued when I went to the Scottish Power office in Galashiels and, on asking how much it would cost me to help maintain the five miles of private line that went to the house, was told that it would cost nothing at all. It was their responsibility to keep the line in good repair, and if a pole fell down they would be out in 24 hours to put up a new one. My only responsibilities were the meter and wiring inside the house. What was more, Chay Blyth had paid up to date, and they even gave me his phone number, in Petersfield, Hampshire, where he was working for British Steel. At the Forestry Commission office in Hawick I was told there would be no tree extractions around me for at least five years and at the postal sorting office in the same town, from where I'd hoped to collect my mail, I was told that there was a daily delivery right to the house, which would clearly be the most isolated place I had ever lived. Everything was looking better and better.

I will never forget the day of the handover at the farmhouse when I met Chay Blyth. I had already spoken to him by phone and he said he'd received a letter from the Estate stating that once he and I had agreed what gear he was taking and what he was leaving, I could move in, as 'the missives would be concluded'. I expressed the hope that he would bring a big van as I was a writer and didn't want removal men coming in again and again over a long period. He said he understood. We met – he was shorter than I expected and had white hair – and shook hands at the top of the 600-yard track. It was not what I'd call a handshake at all and I thought 'This is the hand that rowed the Atlantic!' He wanted to drive me down to the house in his car but I needed to see if Caballo could make it, which he did, easily. After Chay had showed me around – more fine furniture than ever, wardrobes, chests of drawers, cocktail cabinet, folding desk, the lot – I said 'Well, what do you want to take and what leave? I thought you'd come with a big van?'

'Oh, I don't really want to take anything!' he replied. He reached out and picked up two small framed photos of himself in some winning water polo team and added, 'I'll just have these'. And that really was all he wanted.

Now came the tricky bit. There must have been £2,000 worth of gear in the house. We went out into the garden and I asked how much he wanted for what he was leaving. He muttered something about the storage heaters being worth the most. I was ready to go up to £800 but found myself saying 'How about £400?' He said, without a pause, 'Make it £500 and we have a deal'. I have never written a cheque so fast. I needed to buy nothing at all. I could just move in, into total luxury.

After Chay left, I sank to my knees inside the house, hardly able to believe the long search was over, and thanked the Great Spirit. I knew it was mine now. I'd never owned a brick before so this was the first home I had ever owned, and I was coming up to be an old age pensioner. I went to Caballo, where my most needed belongings still were, wrote the biggest cheque of my life, for £35,350, drove to Hawick and posted it to my lawyer in Edinburgh fast, before I changed my mind and did a bunk to the Yukon! I moved in on 20 October, the very day, twenty two years before, on which my Scottish odyssey began, when I landed in Scotland from Canada to find a new wild home and hiked into Camusfearna, Gavin Maxwell's home.

I had a lot of fast work ahead to prepare for winter. The track in was bow-shaped and clumps of thick rushes threatened to knock off Caballo's sump, so I hired a strimmer to cut them and spaded off the worst rocky bits. I gathered sacks of shale and rubble from the shores of the forest lochs, spread them over the marshy bits and used Caballo's wheels like a steamroller to make his own 'road'. To ensure my water supply I drove to Clovenfords to buy a huge black 320-gallon tank which had been used to ferry orange juice in bulk from Israel. It dwarfed Caballo but somehow the store manager and I got it strapped to his roof. As we drove back through Selkirk and Hawick, pedestrians stared, pointed and laughed at the weird apparition. To get the ballon off the roof into position by the house, I made a wooden plank 'bridge' but it fell off halfway down and nearly flattened me. I got out of the way just in time but it actually bounced and rolled right to where I wanted it. I had a Hawick blacksmith make me an 11 ft metal barrier but had a hard job lifting and fitting it onto a stout post I'd driven in at the top of my track.

In these first few days I realised I had seen no wildlife at all, not a single bird of any kind, but I did once look up to see a flock of redwings winging over to the west. Suddenly a far larger shape with long wings zoomed over between them, passing over my head and the house with tremendous verve and speed. A peregrine? It was twisting and turning, its long wings held half back. What a sight! It glared down at me before vanishing over the roof. I ran round to the side but there was no sign of it. It had been travelling twice as fast as the redwings and probably snatched one when out of my sight. The flock broke into two groups, one swinging back over the house before joining the main flock. I went in to check my books: surely I had seen the much rarer goshawk, bigger than the peregrine? I came out of the house and heard some barking but higher up. I looked into the sky – a V-shaped skein of whooper swans, also heading west, great long necks extended, bugling as they went. That, too, was a fine sight but I was still not seeing any birds near the house.

I was standing to attention outside during the two-minute silence on 11 November, remembering old friends in the army, when the feeling came upon me that, as much as I loved this house, the place could never truly be a 'home' to me. It seemed dead. Not one bird had come to the scraps I set out from the very first day. The forest was said to be full of roe deer but I hadn't seen a single one. It was beautiful but like an idyllic postcard, blown up and shoved outside the window. Well, I'd give it a year...

I began to feel this wild place had somehow teased me with that sighting of goshawk, redwings and whooper swans because for almost three months I saw no wild creatures at all. When the first snow fell, covering the undulating ground with a two-foot thick white shroud, my world became a deadly blue-tinged hush. I was marooned, for old Caballo could not get up the steep, slippery track, and neither could any four-wheel drive vehicle, according to the foresters. When that first snowfall melted I dashed to Hawick 18 miles away and spent £100 on tinned foods, flour and pulses, not to mention sacks of tatties and onions. There now seemed only one thing to be done – do up the place and sell it.

Every fine day I assaulted the property, wearing out three wire brushes to scrape lichens and mosses from each square inch of wall, slapping on paint until my wrists rebelled. I scraped, painted and re-puttied all the windows. I dug under long swathes of winter-dead white grasses looking for old fencing nails and stobs, finding just enough to fence the 70 yard gap on my northern boundary. Having no sledgehammer, I hefted up a big flat rock in both hands and whacked it down on the stobs to drive them in. The sheep netting I spotted, second hand, in the yard of an engineering works 30 miles away.

The roof I feared the most of all. Gales had clattered some slates to the ground and there was a leak in the attic. The chimney brickwork had broken away in places, sprouting ugly cushions of moss. One stormy night I was woken by odd clanks on the roof and two thumps on the ground. The tin chimney pot covers had blown off. Now I had to get up there. On the fine morning I chose to start, I went out to find five chaffinches on the roof's apex. Birds, at last! I was as thrilled to see those cheeky pink-breasted cocks in this bereft place as I had been to see my first golden eagle in the Highlands. So to hell with the roof today.

I had always believed that most wildlife spends most of its time foraging or hunting for food. So if you want to see any, put out the grub! My scraps hitherto had clearly not been enough. I chainsawed an 8ft slab off a fallen tree then nailed it, bark side up, across three stout posts I dug in, so that it ranged the entire length of my study window, complete with perching twigs, partial covering moss and a nut bag. I bought large bags of mixed grains, peanuts and fat balls, spreading them liberally over the bark crevices and moss of the table. It made a perfect natural-looking scene I could photograph from the warm inside of my study which by now was an improved replica of the wildlife museum I had first established at Wildernesse.

It was three days before the chaffinches dared approach, and they were followed by a cock blackbird whose 'kip kip' calls alerted me to his presence. Then one day I saw a canary on the nut bag. A closer look showed it to be a cock siskin, with blazing yellow on his chest and rump and in patches on his constantly flirting tail. Within ten days I could hardly see the table for squabbly chaffinches, counting 37 at one point. Four pairs of siskins moved in, duffing each other up with vicious beak stabs, the females often bettering the males. My old theory of putting out a lot of food was at last proving right. Then came a coal tit, a great tit and even a pair of dunnocks which crept about like mice, fast dodging the darting attacks from the finches. A flock of fieldfares moved onto my front field for a few days and as spring began the wistful songs of the willow warblers vied with the calls of the chiffchaffs, and a charm of goldfinches landed on my electricity wires, raiding the last of the dock seeds that had survived the winter. Occasionally a goshawk wheeled slowly overhead. Thrushes and blackbirds appeared from nowhere, making the morning woods ring with song. Then the tree pipits invaded my meadow, fluttering up to a height and parachuting down in courtship display, fluting a crescendo of 'see-er, see-er' notes.

Once the bird table tribes were used to my presence, I launched my attack on the roof. I was about to start cementing the chipped bricks when I heard a loud fluttering and felt a sharp pain in my left ear lobe. I turned, in time to see a cock siskin making off to the woods. It had taken umbrage at my being on the roof, so keeping it away from the nut bag. Fancy that – assaulted by a siskin! In the end these wee birds became so tame I could occasionally stroke them with a finger when they were on the nut bag.

It took many days of hard ascents (and muttered prayers each time) to replace the chimney tops, clean up, cement and paint the stacks, and replace damaged slates. After four months of work the house looked like new. Now I could surely sell at a profit and move back to the west Highlands. But when I went out to order from the blacksmith six burglar-proof metal grilles for my downstairs windows, I also rang Mr Fitzjohn, the factor at Seafield Estate who had written that the Deskford farmhouse was still for sale. I told him I had bought Ropelaw, fearing he might be peeved. Far from it! He knew Ropelaw well, had stayed in it when working as a stalker on the next door Buccleuch Estate. 'It's a super place,' he said. 'The finest wild home in Scotland!' I began to think again.

It was the eagle that changed my mind.

I had made a firm friend of Tony, the new young Forest Ranger who had knocked on my door in the first week of taking over and whose main job it was, among all his other ranger duties, to control and keep in balance the roe deer populations in the huge forest. When he had said that to him the whole essence of being out in the wild was the skill of getting close to an animal or bird so that it does not know you are there, I knew we would get along. When he added that he didn't like the methods used by one wildlife quango body, I said 'Put it there, pal!' We shook hands heartily. Over the next three years we did a lot of work together, cruising the forest's three lochs for signs of otter and pine marten, analysing the invertebrate life in the burns (using my study as a lab), experimenting with hides for owls, buzzards and goshawks, putting up nest boxes. Once we even built an osprey nest, in a tree on the biggest loch. Currently I was helping him to find occupied goshawk nests, not only for the long-term study of the bird and its needs but also so that he could inform his chief Ian, who would ban any felling or forestry work within 400 metres of the nest in the breeding season. The other purpose was to officially close-ring the chicks, so that illegal falconers could not steal them and pass them off as captive-bred birds. After long treks, necks aching from constantly squinting upwards at hundreds of trees, we located one occupied nest.

Tony felt sure that another pair inhabited a huge stand of larch three miles away and he had driven us up a long track to a high clear spot from which we could overlook the area. We were sitting in his van talking about eagles, our binoculars up on a buzzard that was wheeling in hunting circles over grassland by the larches. She gave up and glided away to our right as Tony said he had not seen any eagles since he had started. Following the buzzard, my binocular vision ended up on Tony's out-of-focus ear! I put them down, turned to the front, and could hardly believe my eyes. There, away to my left, flying with ponderous flaps alternated with long glides and nearing the van every second, came the largest female golden eagle I had ever seen.

'No eagles here, eh?'

'Aye, that's right.'

'What's that, then?'

Tony turned and gasped his surprise. The massive bird was now only some 40 yards above and in front of the van. We could see the eagle had big oval whiteish patches under her wings, proving that she was not fully mature. She made a wide circle and then began to sail to the west, ahead of us. Within a minute she was a mile away. We drove to the end of the track, just in time to see her disappear over a long humped ridge. We waited. A minute ticked by, then suddenly, from behind the ridge, came a big bird (but not as large as the eagle), followed by another. At first we thought they were goshawks or buzzards but they began, with hardly a wingbeat, to soar around each other. Then, like a shot from a cannon, the giant female appeared. She zoomed right up between them and as they all wheeled and turned, wings flashing in a burst of sunlight, we realised that the other two were both immature male eagles. Sighting eagles in the Borders is a rare enough event but to see three together like this was unforgettable.

We both knew of the one pair that nested in the Kielder Water area and that while they had raised a chick in the previous year, they had failed in two before that. Indeed, on first taking over the farmhouse, I had trekked into their eyrie with a friend but had lost interest on finding that the nest was on an ugly metal contraption put up by humans, watched by the local Rangers and a fair army of volunteers from quango wildlife bodies and a raptor study group. But could any of the eagles we had just seen be the past progeny of that pair? Or could any of them be old enough to be breeding birds? The Kielder pair were nesting over the border in England that year, guarded by an SAS team, so it couldn't have been either of them we had seen.

By the end of that week we had located a second goshawk pair with eggs. At last I had worthwhile projects; trying to find any eyries of the new eagles and, especially at weekends when the foresters were away, keeping an eye on and photographing the goshawks from my 'invisible' hides. When the eagles had been seen twice more in the same area, I located the nest crags on my map, parked Caballo in a deserted quarry and, with camera pack on my back, set off. Down a steep slope to a burn I marched, a lapwing spiralling madly with 'peeoowit' calls over her running chick, the triple liquid alarm calls of curlews mixing with the shrill 'kleep' cries of a pair of gaudy oystercatchers as I crossed some natural stepping stones. A slog through heather and bracken to the top of the a hill, half a mile of tussocks, another hard descent to a burn and then I was plodding my way up to the crags at nearly 1,500 feet. I stumbled on and up. There was only one ledge that could have held a nest – and it didn't.

Looking into a fold in the mountains I could see a small, dark gorge near the top, about a mile away. I knew an eagle could use such a site, so with a groan I set off again. It was hard going now, the last stretch covering steep short-heathered ground. At the head of the gorge I saw a big wall of etiolated rockface with ledges that had mossy or wood-rush covered tops. As I neared it I paused to catch my breath before the approach to the lip of the gorge.

Suddenly I heard the magic 'keeyew' call of an eaglet, only here it seemed a weaker 'keeyi'. Twice more I heard it and knowing it was a bird of prey, if not an eaglet, I started forward. A big bird hurtled towards me, zoomed over my head and gave the familiar harsh 'raich raich' calls of the peregrine falcon. She flew about above me, hollering loudly. I soon found the nest, on a tiny ledge behind a small rowan, and I could see two white downy chicks. I took a few photos then turned to leave, but not before taking advantage of the mother's wrath. I got several pictures of her flying over me, her beak open with raptor cuss-words. My hips were giving me hell by now but I left feeling triumphant. While I had not found an eagle eyrie, a peregrine's was no mean discovery.

7

INTO OLD AGE WITH EAGLES

For about five years I had sworn to myself that I would mark my 65th birthday by working with eagles from a hide, and that I would do it back on Eagle Mountain in the west Highlands, which had been the focus of my eagles video and where I had enjoyed many golden eagles adventures years before. And, having done that, I would hike down the mountain, triumphant, head for the Post Office and claim my first old age pension. This dream seemed doomed when the government refused me any eagle licences that year, the licensing officer, who I understood had recently left university, saying that the 'quota' for my old area was full (whatever that meant) and adding that surely I had done more than enough photographing over the years and that it was time to give younger men a chance.

Up early on 23 May, I drove to Stirling to pick up a pal who had sworn to be with me on the project. After lunch at his house, we drove our own vehicles to the boat pool on the river near the shores of my old home loch. There were five boats there and we were just wondering if we should 'borrow' one when along came the man who ran two of the boats for a hotel twenty miles to the south, who was with his wife walking their dogs. For a tenner he let me have the hotel's old heavy wooden clinker-built sea boat, and the three of us man-handled it into the river. I put in the oars, strapped on the engine and pulled the starter cord. It would not work. Try and pull as I did I could not get it to fire. By then the light was fading so we had to forget all ideas of looking for eyries on Eagle Mountain this day. Luckily my old key still fitted the forestry gate so we were able to drive along the track that ran along the southern shore of my old home loch. There, we chose a clearing to camp overnight then set up to glass four of my old eyries across the loch, but although we kept checking until dusk, they all seemed dead. There was no sign of eagles anywhere.

While we were doing this, Tony Millard, the man who took over Wildernesse from me, drove by from a shopping trip and gave me some deadly information. He was now leaving himself; the estate would not let him sell on the remaining ten years of the lease and he had agreed to accept £1,000 to surrender it and was buying a little semi-derelict place on the south side of the loch. More than that, he told me that the estate next door was doing up the old croft ruin just across the burn at Wildernesse as a deer feed store, but he reckoned it would become a holiday chalet in the future. That ended any thought of going back there myself. When I asked if we could borrow my old small boat from him tomorrow, he said it had been smashed up completely by the previous winter's storms. He did have some good news though: Moobli's grave was fine and he had taken my advice to let it grow over, as some of my readers were boating or hiking in to see it.

I had not seen my pal for a long time so we had really good crack and didn't get to our beds until 11 p.m., having consumed rather too much whisky. In the morning he confessed he would be useless for the day as he was being ill all over the place, and it was clear that whisky did not suit his innards as it suited mine. I suggested he try and get more sleep and, if he didn't feel better, to go on home. I drove back to the boat pool and kicked the heavy old boat off from the bank down the river. The motor still would not start and I spent a frenzied twenty minutes fending off with an oar from one bank or the other until the river deposited us on the loch itself.

It was only a mile to the shore below Eagle Mountain so I decided to forget the engine and began to row. I was only a quarter of the way over when the left rowlock burst out of the decayed wood of the gunwale and could not be wedged back. The only way I could use the oar was to make a sling 'rowlock' for it from the anchor rope and tie it to the empty seat in front of me. I never had a more awkward now. Halfway across a fisherman I knew came puttering from the other direction and yelled 'Hello Mike. What ya up to?'

'Just practising for the Atlantic!'

It took nearly an hour to reach the shore and I felt just about knackered already. If I had known I was to tackle all this alone I would not have attempted it but now it seemed I had to. I bundled all the film gear and netting hide into some bog myrtle bushes and slogged over the mountain without a pack. I struggled over the first tussocky steeps until the hard climbing, then sweated up to eyrie 34. Dead. Neither was there anything in Eyrie 11 on the big rockface. I was about to give up, my birthday project doomed, but in spite of a feeling of despondency I forced myself to go round one more bluff and at last located the eagle called Juno. I had reached a heathery ridge about two hundred yards from a small but sheer cliff across a shallow valley, when she came sailing along and flapped leisurely into a nest on one of the ledges. Through the glasses I could see she had landed beside a downy white chick, almost a month old. What a relief! I now knew exactly where to pitch my hide for my birthday vigil next day. Stiffly, I clambered back down to retrieve my gear and get back to the boat. I worked harder on the engine and it was lucky that I got it going for the return trip, or I would never have got it back up the flowing river.

I was up at 4 a.m. next day, telling myself that this really was to be the last time. I would not trust the boat again so had to park Mi Caballo in a sandpit quarry over the river bridge a mile back from the boat pool and on the very slopes of Eagle Mountain itself. I checked the movie gear and hiked up with it and the netting hide, on a far longer trek than yesterday's. Over the tussocks, below low trees, over a forestry fence and a wide burn, into which I almost fell, I struggled on up to the north and then northwest, luckily finding forest rides zig-zagging roughly in the direction I needed to go. Hellish hard climbing now, sweating profusely, stopping often, shoulders aching with the pack weight, arms aching from carrying the hide. I slogged on and on, the long rockfaces up to my left passing only very slowly. I had a hard task re-locating the right face for Juno's eyrie but when I reached the previous day's spot on the heathery ridge, I got onto it at last.

Juno was on the left of the small ledge, beside a small rowan, and now and again I caught glimpses of the chick's white head. I backed out of sight and camouflaged the hide's front with grasses and heather, though it was not strictly necessary, as I was over two hundred yards away – a bit far for first-class filming but the terrain was such that I dared not go closer. I spent nearly five hours in the hide watching Juno feeding her chick, grooming it gently with her huge beak and just squatting beside it while looking about her in a leisurely manner. I could see her looking down towards me now and then, felt sure she knew I was there but she was not alarmed and in all that time did not once leave the nest. The distance and a heat haze made it foolish to waste film unless I could get better material than ever before so, apart from a first few feet of general view and one zoom in, I resisted the temptation. As I had seen years before, she really 'loved' her chick and was spending all her spare time by it. I felt a surge of pride that I had pulled it off at last. 'I'm an old age pensioner now!' I told myself, '… but I ain't done yet!'

I ate an egg and tomato sandwich, sat for a quarter hour, then struck the hide and carried the lot back down, at a fair speed too as, oddly enough, my legs felt good, even after the previous day's trekking. I'd promised to visit Tony Millard at the semi-derelict cottage he was now doing up on the south side of the loch. I found he had done some good work, after battles with the planning authorities, but the more he told me about his last months at Wildernesse, the clearer it became that I could never go back. For some moments I had wanted to boat over and sit by Moobli's grave but, as I mentioned earlier, he had taken my advice to let it grow over so that it would not become a shrine to readers. A fair gale had blown up on the loch and Tony's big engine was in bits on a rack, undergoing repairs, so we didn't go over. I could see, though, where Moobli's grave was and the 18-inch spruce I'd planted there was now about 20 feet high. Only his mortal remains were there. I made a short prayer to the Great Spirit to look after Moobli in the Happy Hunting Ground, saluted the old dog, looked at Wildernesse for the last time and drove away from the loch for ever.

8

REARING YOUNG EAGLES AND GOSHAWKS

Back at the sandpit quarry I swabbed myself all over, went to bed early, slept like a log and next day drove to meet a young man who described himself as a freelance photographer. He had been writing to me often with queries about eagles, claiming that he had found many of my eyries and that he was interested in all my movie gear. Now, I thought, I can sell it and retire! I drove to his home in Kilchoan, knocked on the door and out he came – Steve Phillipps.

I took a great liking to him immediately, a handsome, fit lad of 23 who was not only mad keen on wildlife but who soon turned out to be the most talented young man I had ever met in the field. He was certain that what we came to call the 'windy glen' eagle pair were nesting in my old Eyrie 10 and so were the pair in the high sheer sea cliff to the south. 'Right,' I said 'Let's go – now!' 'Fine!' he said, and off we went, Steve carrying more than his share of everything including my netting hide. I was looking forward to working with these eagles as they were the first pair I had ever photographed from a hide, exactly seventeen years before.

It was an easy two-mile hike in, but harder towards the end of the glen as we approached the rocky eyrie buttress, where we paused and optimistically camouflaged much of the hide with heather. We carried it up to a site between two large rocks which Steve had found - higher and better than the one I had used, which had been on the ground - and glassed the eyrie ledge. We were shocked to see that the two eggs had gone. Steve's face fell: he looked utterly woebegone. He had seen the eagles exchanging incubation duties on four separate days, the last time only the week before, so the eggs had been stolen since then.

Steve had also found this pair's second nest, in an easily-overlooked rocky crevice a mile to the east. We dropped the hide where we could pick it up on the trek out and hiked over but, of course, it too was empty. Steven commented on the fact that we had seen no eagles all day. I told him that when eagles lose their eggs or chicks like this, they invariably desert the immediate nesting area, as if it would be a constant reminder of their bereavement, and spend their time hunting in a distant part of their territory. Sadly, we climbed down and walked out, my hips and knees telling me they had done just too much trekking in the last three days. I camped overnight in a small quarry beyond Kilchoan while Steve went back to his parents' house.

He arrived, keen as mustard, at 8 a.m. but I told him I wanted the morning off. We set the hide up beside a stream near Loch Mudle and filmed dippers landing on rocks, swimming, diving and flying into a nest box some kind soul had erected under a concrete bridge. I skived a bit more time off, buying groceries and having lunch in the village, but then we set off to try and film the nesting eagles on the huge sheer sea cliff face to the south. Steve happened to know that the new owner of the estate was away in London, so we took a chance and drove Caballo up a private track, so taking almost a mile off the two-and-a-half mile trek down to the base of the cliffs. My hips began to hurt again but I got there safely. Almost immediately, as we trekked between big rocks on the shore line below the great cliffs, we saw an eagle flying over. I quickly set up on a high grassy knoll on the east end of the bay and filmed superb sequences of both eagles being mobbed by ravens, flying about, twisting and turning, the male once trying to grab a raven.

When that show was over we hiked over to the west side and set up again, behind a much higher flat rock, as the eagles were still flying about, sometimes landing on top of the cliffs. I then shot three fabulous sequences of both the female and the male flying into the eyrie, which held a large white chick, the female on one occasion coming in with a gull in her talons. Twice she came down dramatically from on high, wings folded half up, so forming, as Steve described it, an 'M' shape. She rocketed down as if through an invisible chute, then flattened out and shot into the eyrie with a few wide backward wing flaps for a steady landing. This had to be the best material I have ever taken of a bird flying in and landing on a nest ledge.

We started to climb higher, hoping to get a clearer view of the nest ledge, but by now my legs felt weak and I was scared my knees could suddenly give way at any time, sending me falling to my death. Steve, who said he only weighed 9 ½ stone, was far more agile than I was on the rocky terrain. I also found out that, although he looked like an angelic choirboy, he was in fact a judo brown belt and had practised the martial arts for years. The more we worked together, the more I liked and respected him.

Next day I drove us right across Scotland to Strathconon, where readers had written, with photographs, to tell me that a pair of eagles had three eyries just above a road. We reached what we thought was the right spot. I handed Steve the photos, then went to park Caballo in a layby two hundred yards away. When I got back he had already located two of the three, and we soon found the third, which had a chick in it . We noticed that someone was occasionally raising binoculars on this nest. I felt sure it was a warden or volunteer on guard, keeping watch, so we hiked back two hundred yards, cut down through a fence to near a burn, then sneaked back, hidden by a heathery ridge, to just past where his car was, above us, and quickly set up. As I did so, Steven located the male eagle through his binos and said it was tugging at twigs on a small rowan tree with his beak. I tried to get onto him but it was difficult on the dark rockface so I switched to the eyrie as Steve hissed 'He's flying!' I was just in time to get the full sequence: the male flying to and into the eyrie with a twig in his beak, landing, then walking to beside the chick which obligingly stood up at just the right moment. It was super stuff. We filmed the female coming in with prey which we couldn't identify, the male leaving and her feeding the chick, and after an hour we packed up, hoping to catch the last ferry back to Ardgour.

After stashing all our gear in Caballo we casually walked past the car with the man in it. He was a volunteer warden with the RSPB and told us he had seen one eagle taking twigs to the eyrie and the other feeding the chick. Although we had been much closer than he had, we had not been so close as to disturb the birds and thus break the law, but I managed to resist the temptation to spoil his afternoon and say 'Yes, we just filmed it all!'

I was most gratified on my return to Ropelaw to find two licences among my mail, allowing me to examine and photograph rare goshawks at the nest. I had not applied after the refusal for eagles but the Forestry Commission bosses wanted me to work with their ranger, Tony , and had got them for me. Tony had also left a dead buck rabbit hanging on my front door handle which he felt would help me with the eagles, but he had come with it just minutes after I had left. I quickly bunged it into the freezer – it could still come in useful, as I'd promised Steve to go back for the sea cliff eagles again in a few weeks' time. Tony had also left a scribbled note, washed out by rain, and all I could read was 'male gos perished'. By now we had found three occupied goshawk nests, and as goshawks were Britain's rarest breeding raptor, it seemed we had a major loss on our hands. When I next saw him, Tony explained: he had found the male of the Meadshaw pair dead on top of an electricity box. It had got its pinion feathers stuck in some wires and, when flapping about trying to get free, had made contact with the top wire and electrocuted itself. He had made a rough feed table and put two rabbits on it, cut open, so the female wouldn't starve, but she had not come to it and eventually had deserted the eggs.

The good news was that two pairs – one near a hairpin bend and the other near an old tin shed - had hatched chicks,. I had also found a buzzards' nest with a healthy chick in it. We would soon have hides up on the hairpin nest and the buzzards' nest and began keeping a close watch on the tin shed goshawks. The first time we went there, the male stayed on the nest when Tony's van stopped and I got two shots of him glaring at us, head cocked to one side, while the heads of two white downy chicks sprouted comically from his sides. When we put up the big buzzard hide I said it was best if we could have it facing north (and the nest, of course), explaining that the sun would fall mainly on the nest and behind the camera, and not into the lens.

On 6 June I was up at 5 a.m. and in the buzzard hide less than an hour later. The chick was on its feet, flapping its wings and often toppling over. I twice heard a distant 'keeyoo' call from an adult but none came in. About 8 a.m. the chick stood up from a long lie down and entertained me well, flapping wings and trampolining about the nest sticks. Once it shook its head with beak open, tried to close its beak but something from inside forced it open again. It shook its head again, and again, then lowered it towards the nest bottom – and out came a pellet. The chick looked down at it as if thinking 'What's that? Where the hell did that come from?' It then picked up the pellet and dropped it, several times, trying to break it up to see what was inside, before giving up. My feet were getting cold now.

Half an hour later I heard a faint flap. The mother was on the nest and I took shots as she looked first at her chick, then my way, then sort of tumbled off the nest again. The chick took about five minutes to rend a mole she had brought in and to swallow bit by bit, black fur and skin stretching its neck far from its pinning-down feet to beak tip. This darn chick didn't call out when a parent came in so I had to keep my wits sharp. My feet were so cold by 9.30 a.m. that I hiked to Caballo for a cuppa and to warm myself and my boots on his gas stove. Back in the hide, the chick was up from a slumber at 10.21 a.m. and rending the last of the mole. Half an hour later an adult shot in behind me at great speed, dropped a vole and left fast. Knowing their chick could feed itself, the parents were spending no time in the nest. I should have started earlier. I figured the chick would fly inside two weeks.

I went back home for lunch, packed up a lot of videos as I was now getting plenty of orders, then did another stint in the hide. Two days later I went back, this time with all the movie gear, and shot similar material but also a nice sequence of the mother circling around the tree with a small bird in her talons, then landing, holding it up before the chick for a few seconds (it looked like a tree pipit) before dropping it, looking fondly at her youngster, towards me, then flying off. The chick seemed sated, almost backed up by the amount of food its parents were bringing in, and made no attempt to eat. It finally flew on 20 June, when I found the nest empty and located the chick perched on an old small flat-topped pine fifty yards down the hill, where I filmed it for a last scene.

The real goshawk work began on 9 June when Dave A., the official bird ringer for the region, Craik forester Ian, Kielder forest ranger Gordon, Tony and I trekked in to the hairpin bend pair. I filmed Dave climbing the tree, banging in the leg irons as I had once done years ago in Canada but couldn't attempt now, and lowered the three downy chicks to the ground in a linen bag so that he could ring them more easily. Tony and I quickly made an improvised 'nest' to allow us to take photos and film them. I was surprised by how calm the chicks were; they didn't cry out or struggle but lay, blinking rapidly, more in bewilderment than fear. Job done, Dave carried them back up and put them in the nest. We then went to the Meadshaw nest – Tony had been right, the female had deserted after her mate had been electrocuted. Dave climbed up and took three eggs for analysis. We then went to the buzzard nest where Dave ringed that chick too. I stayed in the hide to see how the chick reacted to its traumatic experience – it lay down and had a long sleep. Dave knew goshawks well and revealed females weigh between 1,500 and 2,000 grams with males only 900 grams and not a lot bigger than female sparrowhawks. I also learnt that the way to sex fledged chicks is to check the tarsi: in females they are longer and far thicker.

I then had to spend a week in London to have all my films and photos developed, buy new stock, have 200 videos made and have meetings with my publisher, among other business. Back at Ropelaw, I found over £1,000-worth of video orders awaiting me so I was kept busy packing and posting them and didn't get round to making and setting up a hide on the hairpin bend nest until 27 June. After half an hour I heard a goshawk calling away to the right, with another – doubtless the female - answering with far deeper, harsher calls from just left of the nest. Then the calls mingled to the right and, after about two minutes, in swept the female and dumped a half-plucked woodpigeon on the nest. The male may have had the pigeon on the usual plucking post and been calling her to 'Come and get it!' which she did. I was disappointed she didn't stay longer but I managed two shots of her before she left. At this stage, almost fledged, chicks are well able to feed themselves.

I noticed they didn't seem to compete for food like many birds of prey. Indeed, the biggest chick just did a wing flap-leap up to a higher branch and began preening. It seemed the hungriest chick feeds itself while the others stand about. When one wants to take over there is only a slight confrontation, 'kik kik kik' calls, raised hackles, wing flapping, and the newcomer gets his way! I took about twenty shots of the chicks, which I now named BC (Big Chick), MC (Medium Chick) and LC (Little Chick).

Two days later I hid the photographic gear in bracken at the start of the two hundred yard walk-in, parked Caballo a quarter mile back on the forest track, so that he could not attract attention to our operation, and walked back. I was in the hide by 10 a.m. With the movie camera I filmed the chicks doing just about everything! They scratched, preened neck feathers and wings and LC flirted her tail feathers into a fan-shape and reached back to tweak them with her beak. Then MC tried to preen BC's chest and belly feathers while LC turned and looked on in faint interest. BC soon got fed up with this and jumped back up to the higher branch above the nest.

Next, I heard the male goshawk's weak ringing drawn-out calls over to the right, a 'rrrringoo rrringoo'… then the female's staccato 'kik kik kik' over to my left, as before. This time, though, she did not appear to go over to the plucking post and the calls got fainter, as if the two were meeting on the far side of the tree. Then came a pause, before I saw the two lower chicks dancing about, squeaking, eyes staring, wings shuffling. It was obvious that a goshawk was coming in. I pushed the button, got them doing all that, then in swept the female from the left, landed, dumped the prey at the feet of LC and almost immediately took off to the right. I captured it all.

LC started rending the prey, which had been plucked and looked like a young duck. She pulled off bits for a quarter hour and MC, though clearly hungry, just watched her, moving as if to go forward but desisting as if knowing that was not the protocol. BC saw LC feeding and became agitated… just as I had to change films. LC pulled away at the duck, tugging it about with one foot, striking out with the other to 'kill' it. I just missed BC leaping down onto the nest from the upper branch but I got him walking towards the feeding LC, then going behind her while MC still watched from the front. No attempt was made by either bigger chick to intimidate or oust the smallest chick, or fight over food. Again it seemed that the one who got to it first was allowed to eat its fill.

I filmed more, then BC clearly felt really hungry, came out from behind LC and made several sideways, furiously fast pecks at the carcass being held by LC's foot. LC could feel the need, the determination of BC although there was no attacking movement, and slowly gave up, relinquished her grip on the body, backing away then turning and walking to the right edge of the nest. BC then fed for about twenty minutes, by which time MC was looking rather put out but did not attack BC. I just missed the changeover, for when I looked back MC was stepping onto the prey as BC was relinquishing it, moving backwards from it with two odd bows. I filmed MC tugging away then got them all doing wing flaps, Hottentot stretches, with wings up and arched above the head, and wing stretches across the nest.

By then it had gone 2 p.m. so I packed up, snatched a tuna sandwich at home, then dashed to Hawick to post a large batch of videos and – even more importantly – make a check at my bank. For weeks I'd been having protracted and worrying correspondence with the authorities over my old age pension. They had asked many awkward questions. How long was I in Canada? How long was I in Spain? In the end, though, they had written that I would get it within five working days. I paid in the video cheques, took out some cash, then checked. My first old age pension had been paid in – £126 for four weeks – and in three working days, not five. A super ending to a super day.

I put Tony into the hide twice more, he using my stills gear as he didn't yet own a powerful telephoto lens, then went back in myself on 1 July. It was much the same as before except the chicks were hopping on and off the branches round the nest. I got one hilarious sequence when MC jumped down from one and started pulling LC's tail up, hard, two or three times, as if trying to shift her, forcing poor LC to get up and shift over to the other side of the nest. Once, after the male had swerved in front of the hide and dropped a semi-plucked young rabbit, BC and MC almost undid my theory about non-fighting. They squared up all right but it was just upraised bodies, wings flapping, BC calling faint 'kik kik kik' but no real beak or talon contact. All the chicks preened and did much more jumping about, trampolining around the nest. On leaving I was about 150 yards from the nest when the female came behind me, calling loudly. I called back with my best goshawk whistles. She shut up. I wonder what I said?

The afternoon of 4 July was spent in the hide, just for still photos. Only LC was in the nest. MC was in the upper branches but there was no sign of BC. Maybe it had flown? The only prey in the nest was a partly-plucked crow, red meat showing. After overnight gales, I went back two days later and the whole right-hand side of the nest was gone! The left half still looked secure and there was a semi-plucked woodpigeon on it, with LC perched on a branch above, clearly not hungry. Of BC and MC there was no sign. As I hiked back to parked Caballo I saw the two adult goshawks flying along with BC between them. I drove behind them at a discreet distance and it was superb to see, because every time BC stopped, as if tired, they landed near it and urged it to go on. They were without doubt teaching it to fly with them and maybe even hunt with them. Of course, all the cine gear was now in the rear of Caballo, so I couldn't record any of it. Three days later, making sure none of the goshawks were still in the area, I took the hide down and covered any traces of our having been there.

I now had a big decision to make – whether or not to drive all the way back to the sea cliff eagles, as Steve Phillipps was urging me to do. After all, I had already achieved more with eagles than I had initially set out to do. I had fulfilled my dream. I recalled that I had half-promised to let Steve use my movie gear if ever we worked eagles again as he wanted to get into wildlife filming himself. In the end, the lure of that vast, wonderful and magical sea cliff proved too strong, and I knew that any eagle chick in the nest there would soon be gone. If I was to go back I'd have to go now. On 12 July I packed everything into Caballo, made good time, and when I arrived at the wee quarry past Kilchoan Steve was cycling towards me. He had just earned £20 for taking some tourists on a wildlife walk, his first 'pro' fee. We discussed our plans for next day.

9

Disaster below the Eagles' Cliff

It was a gorgeous, hot, sunny day with superb light and as I drove Steve half a mile up the steep track leading to the huge, sheer sea cliffs I was really looking forward to filming these eagles again. I had brought the dead buck rabbit in the hope of getting them down to it. We hiked the mile of rough ground then down the last half mile of steep hill and reached our previous spot between rocks above the shore. At first we couldn't find a spot for the rabbit far enough from us for the eagle to take it but close enough for us to see. In the end Steven took it to a high rock right below the nest ledge, some 300 yards off. We hid in an ideal rocky arbour with just the tops of our heads showing.

We waited – and waited. No eagles appeared. I was sure the eyrie had failed or that the eaglet had flown already, for all morning and afternoon to 4 p.m. we saw neither an eaglet excreting (they always come to the nest edge to do that) nor a single flick of a big brown wing, which we would have seen had an eaglet been in there. I felt we were now wasting our time but I did film ravens flying above the cliffs and a panning sequence of five species of rock flowers.

At 5 p.m. I decided to give up. I put the movie gear in the pack on my back, and took the heavy tripod too, as Steve went over the rocky tangles to retrieve the rabbit. We would have a go at otters the rest of the day, and wait for wildcats in the forest by Loch Mudle that night, with the slashed bloody rabbit as bait.

I started climbing down, coming onto bigger rockfalls, great jagged boulders from 2 feet to 5 feet round with caverns between them. It became harder and harder to negotiate myself and all the heavy gear down over their murderously hard surfaces, gaps obscured by bracken, and I was still fed up we had seen no eagles. I saw grass below one rounded rock, extended my right foot, put my weight on it, and found nothing there. My foot went on and on, touching nothing, my left knee bent on the rock I was standing on, the heavy pack toppled me over and down I went.

It was a helpless, hellish feeling as I fell through a void. My right side and arm hit the next rock, the pack overbalanced me so I did a complete sideways roll. I was terrified my fall would only be stopped by hitting the next rock through the bracken, which rendered me blind. I sought only to protect face, head and neck with both arms, so I let go the tripod.

I crashed into a small cavern, my head hitting my right forearm against the next big boulder, but in the sideways somersault my legs whipped over and the inside of my left knee and calf smashed into and down a piece of sharp rock, then was slammed into it again when the tripod hit the leg too. I yelled with terror twice as each void came up. When I came to a stop I felt great pain in my left knee and calf. To my horror blood was spurting out in great gushes. I could hardly move as the pack had wedged between rocks, but I forced my way out, clamped my right hand over the pouring blood and hobbled onto an open grassy patch. I was in panic. I truly thought I was going to die. There was no way to stop the blood spurting. I must have cut or severed an artery. I knew only that I had to hold the wound closed.

I yelled for Steve and he came fast, scrabbling over the rocks. He was horrified at the sight of my blood-covered legs and boots and when I saw his horror, I was sure I would die. 'No, Great Spirit, not yet!' I thought. My life seemed to pass before me … after all that, would I die here? I would soon lose consciousness and Steve couldn't help. Galvanised into action by these thoughts, I grabbed clean loo paper from my pocket, Steve pulled antiseptic ointment from the little first aid pack he always carried, spewed it over the toilet paper and I clamped it onto the wound. I told him to tear the sleeve off my under-jumper and bind it round the paper, and tie his clean hanky hard and tight round all, and from the top of my calf, so the lot couldn't slip down. Steve had some Elastoplast in his pack too and we used strips of it to clamp the bandage on more firmly.

Somehow, somehow, the blood stopped flowing as it clotted round the paper and the rest of the bandage and I managed to limp the whole two miles back to Caballo, moaning all the time. Steve carried everything, his pack, my pack and the tripod, a Trojan effort on his part. Even so, I had lost a lot blood and was terrified that I would not even reach my van. Once there, I began to feel better. We drove back to Kilchoan and district nurse Jesse, who lived only a few doors down from Steve's parents, was in. She immediately cleaned my wound, which luckily had gone between two veins, and put on special plasters to hold the ½-inch by five-inch gash more closely together. Then Steve's father, Peter Phillipps, drove the two of us in his huge American car to Salen, twenty miles away, where Dr Maris Buchanan stitched my leg up. Man, did those stitches hurt, but it was better than dying!

I knew then that my days of working with eagles, carrying over 60 lbs of movie gear over harsh terrain, were finally over. I could not ignore such a terrible sign. Steve still coveted my filming outfit so when I reached home and collected it all together, he got the lot at a knockdown price. But I'll let you into a little secret: I wrote in the Introduction to the Jonathan Cape reprint of *Golden Eagle Years* that, after this accident, 'Back at my remote outpost in the Borders, I hung up my eagle boots.' When Muhammed Ali was asked after their fight why he didn't fulfil his promise to crawl across the ring and kiss the victorious Joe Frazier's boots, Ali replied:

'Ah lied!'

And when I wrote 'I hung up my eagle boots'...

Ah lied!

I did intend to retire but after Steve put me onto it, I bought a Canon EX1 Hi 8 camcorder which, even with tripod, weighed only 8 and a half lbs, so I was back in eagle business.

I limped about my work in some pain, reluctant to take more than half the painkillers the doctor gave me, but on the third day my left leg began to itch so I knew it was getting better. I was filming a new family of jays on my bird table when ranger Tony called round to say a pal of his had found long-eared owls feeding chicks in an old crows' nest in Wauchope Forest and should we put a hide up on it? Well, should we? I'd never even photographed a long-eared owl in my life and said we ought to move fast, as so late in the season the young might have flown. From Tony's description of the terrain I decided a lie-down hide would be best and drove off to retrieve the three long hazel poles I'd left behind when removing the buzzards' hide. On the way I saw the young buzzard fly across the track. It was good to know it was OK.

There were brief drizzly showers next morning, 20 July, and we dithered about going as we made up the new lie-down hide, but when the sun peeped through the clouds, we decided to head off. We drove to the end of a forestry track near Newcastleton and hiked over half a mile along the track until we were below high steep banks that ran for fifty yards or so. The long-eared owls were nesting in an old crows' nest in a birch tree near the top of one of the banks. We climbed the opposite bank and I located a full-grown chick in another birch some twelve yards from the nest in which only the youngest of the three chicks remained.

What comical characters they looked, with black faces, whitish basal hairs at the bottom of long Roman-nose beaks, bright golden eyes, thick golden eyebrows and sticky-up ear tufts. They could have auditioned for the Black and White Minstrel Show.

Tony told me to choose my site for the hide, then pointed down to one he liked. No, I said, it was too close. Better to go further to the southwest, not the southeast, as when the sun starts to sink its golden light will be full on the nest. Tony gave me a look that said 'Smart arse!' but there was some respect in it too. I found a super declivity in the ground with a natural grassy dais at one end on which to stand the biscuit tin which would serve as a tripod in so low a hide. On it the camera would look straight into the nest on the opposite bank. Out of sight of it, over the brow of our bank, we quickly gathered meadowsweet flowers and grasses, covered the hide netting and hauled it into place. I slid inside to set the long hazel bracer wands correctly and to lay down the ritzy luxury strip of carpet Tony had thoughtfully brought along to save our bodies from the wet ground. It was like a comfy little hotel room in there!

Tony then climbed the nest tree and expertly removed some wee branches and obscuring twigs. As he did so the chick flipped out of the nest onto surrounding twigs. 'Can you put it back, for God's sake!' I cried. He reached down, caught it, put it back and luckily it settled down fast. As he was leaving the tree one of the adult owls came over towards the nest, saw him and looped up, swerving over the top of the bank. Hell!

I had a long wait. For two and a half hours nothing happened, but I filmed the chick preening its breast feathers, sleeping, standing tall, and scrabbling between its toes with its beak, holding the foot up high to do so. Most of the time its eyes were only half open so the pupils were like black half-moons as the upper eyelids covered their top hales. Now and again it gave plaintive little cheeps and these seemed, eventually, to be answered by harsh but very quiet 'schowwl' calls from a tree away to the left. Finally the chick started peering out eagerly, crouching expectantly. I looked through a side hole in the herbage over the hide and saw an adult fly past the nest. It must then have turned for it landed on the left side, just as I pushed the button. By the time my eye got back to the camera, it had gone and the chick was just cheeping. Half an hour later this happened again and I think I got footage of the adult landing and being with the chick but was not sure because, yet again, I was trying to see it flying about. If I just kept my eye on the nest through the camera, I couldn't know if the adult was coming in or not.

By now – and as ever - the slightly uneven rises and dents in the ground were causing pains in my back and hips. My attempts to film the bigger chick in the birch tree branches were unsuccessful because it kept moving about, with foliage always in the way, and no adult came to visit. I therefore set the camera on the nest. Suddenly I saw a bigger owl flying in. I pressed the button fast and got my eye back to the viewfinder just in time to see her land on the far side of the nest from me and stand facing the camera. She stayed there one, two, three... seven seconds! She was staring about, at the chick, at the camera, with mad marigold eyes.

She had dropped a vole. The chick snatched it up and tried to gulp it down whole two, three, four times, beautifully turned to the right to give me a perfect profile and a view of all the action, the huge mother in the background, watching intently to see if the vole went down. But it got stuck and the chick turned towards me as if thinking 'How in hell can I get this sodding vole down?' Then away went the mother, the chick made two more gulps, and down went the vole. Lovely stuff at last. After a quarter hour or more with no action and silence, I slid out of the hide and took some still photos, the owlet on the branches showing little alarm although I was only fifteen yards away. I fell over once, carrying all the heavy gear down the bank, but when I reached home I did a job I'd been dreading for days – removing the stitches from my gashed left leg. It was, in fact, a snip – four snips, in fact, as I barely touched them with the little scissor tool I'd been given, and they just fell out. I didn't feel a thing.

My next project was to make a large vegetable garden. I found that the half-sack of potatoes in my kitchen had sprouted roots and realised that while I could still eat some of them, the majority could become seed tatties. The ground below the farmhouse was all grown over, thick with weeds, so I went to Jackson's Tool Hire on the Hawick-Selkirk road to hire a rotavator for a week as, if I could work it, I could more easily get two large plots ready for planting. As we heaved the heavy £36-a-week machine into Mi Caballo, Mr Jackson warned me that the rotavator tended to dig itself in before setting off.

'I hope I don't end up in Australia,' I joked. 'New Zealand, yes, but not Australia!'

He was just as fast. 'Och no, you'd really have to concentrate hard on the entering trajectory to get to Australia!'

The next day was hot and sunny, so to hell with the desk. I hauled the rotavator down to the lower patch, beyond the sheep wall, where I felt the dark loam was the best. I pulled the starting cord several times. It went off like a bucking bronco once it fired and dragged me down to the burn. I tried to stop it by hauling backwards, forgetting that my finger was on the accelerator, and the more I pulled back, the harder it went. Only by a swift hard left turn did I keep the machine – splosh! – from going into the water, closely followed by 'sper-losh' – which would have been me. It was a fair while before I learnt that I had to dig its rear spike in after it had travelled two feet or so, and let it dig itself down. Then I had to lift it and push slightly, then quickly jab the handles down again to get it digging, going forward.

The weeds, creeping buttercup, great stalks of thistles and nettles and lesser ones of rosebay willowherb, made a great two-inch mat all over the surface and I constantly had to stop the machine and pull the screwed-up weeds from around the tines with my fingers. If I didn't they built up so much that they covered and blocked the tines and prevent any digging. When the machine hit rocks, it jigged and jagged and wanted to stall, but it turned most of them up and out. I then had to bung them away to the sides, which quickly made my fingers sore. By lunch I had dug about forty feet by twenty feet, then I used the rotavator's waddling tines to march it up to dig out the top plot just below the house. There, as it was drier, I measured off one link (33 ft) by half a link (16 ½ ft), marked the corners with spade, shovel, hoe and an old walking stick, then took a short break.

After lunch, I went at it again and on the top plot found it better to pull up by hand most of the weeds and cast them aside, so that they couldn't gum up the works quite so much. Before long my back was aching badly, my fingers were sore and I had muscle pains where I hadn't known I had muscles. It really was like holding onto a bucking bronco. By 6 p.m. I was knackered but forced myself to swab down and make a meal - after a few drams, of course.

By the end of the week, working for shorter shifts, I had both plots planted up with seeds and vegetable seedlings from a Hawick nursery. The week after, I rough-fenced both gardens with old rolls of sheep netting I'd found in the woods and fence posts cut from dead, fallen lodgepole pines. From mid-summer onwards I supplied all my own vegetables, except tatties, when my small plantings ran out, and mushrooms. I was especially proud in my third year to cut a cabbage that was a foot across and weighed almost four pounds.

I next decided to dig out my own lake. Not a pond – a lake. I hired a digger machine from Jackson's Tool Hire and Gordon himself delivered it on a low loader two days later. It was raining so I asked him to drive it down to the lake site for me, as I had never in my life driven a digger. He briefly explained and showed me how to operate some twenty controls, then left. Cripes! I had to fight back waves of fear as I climbed onto the seat and tentatively started work. I was just about getting the hang of it when ...whoosh... another downpour, and I was driven back to the house.

I went back during a lull in the rain and put in three hours' work, gradually getting used to all the controls, and in fact had great fun – gouging out great lumps of mud which I could never have carried myself. The bucket had a twelve-foot reach and I had to figure out a method of getting the thirty-foot width I wanted. I did this by cutting out twelve feet from both sides, leaving a six-foot wide ridge in the middle. Next I had to go to each end and dig out twelve feet of the six-foot wide ridge in the middle. I then had to go to each end and dig out twelve feet of the six-foot ridge, so that the final lake would be dumbbell-shaped. Next day, 13 August, I worked from 10.20 a.m. to 6.30 p.m. and dug out thirty yards, also deepening what I had dug the day before. I got more and more used to it and in the end, as Gordon had predicted, it was easy.

I worked only five hours next day as I had to get supplies, put a good number of wildlife video orders into the post and buy more diesel for the digger. When it drizzled all next day, I finally got angry that I was paying so much for the digger's hire and yet couldn't use it. I donned all my rain gear and with one of Chay Blyth's left-behind kiddies' raincoats over my knees I worked for four hours. I got soaked but I loved the physically-easy work and the new skills I had discovered. I could earn my living at this, I thought. Once you have dug out a big bucketful, you have to lever it round to the side, stretch it out, lower it and unclench the bucket at the correct height and in the right place. I often had to jump from the digger and dig out clay stuck in the bucket with a fork or spade.

After ten hours' work the next day I had dug out sixty yards of one side and ten yards of the other. Pouring rain overnight had filled the lake and when I began work again it was overflowing slightly into the raging burn. My plan was already working! I just had to dig a narrow outlet channel, put in a stout mesh screen to keep in the fish, and there would be a current flowing through the lake most of the time. The digger was up to its ankles in water but, luckily, the vast beds of hard-stemmed nettles and thistles formed a mat and the digger's tracks moved easily over it.

Over the next two days I dug out all the other side and used the six-foot central ridge at each end to leave two grassy islands for any nesting birds. I also dug out a small inlet channel from a natural little pond by my sheep wall boundary, which itself was fed by a tiny rivulet from a small burn in the nearby pine woods. I confess I widened this, but ever so slightly, with a spade.

These were happy days, creating my own beautiful new lake environment with two islands, and I would plant a few saplings like birch and rowan to see what would happen. When I walked down to drive the digger back to where I could clean it, I saw there were already two toads in the lake. It was a start. I had my own lake for nothing more than the cost of the digger. And now it was time for the next big project. The following morning I transferred all my movie gear up to the loft of my large byre so that I could make a film of my barn owl family.

10

My Barn Owl Family

Perhaps the single main achievement at Ropelaw was the successful raising of my barn owls. As soon as I saw the huge airy loft in the byre I realised it was the ideal place to do some captive breeding. There were high oak beams on which to nail nest boxes and two dormer windows to the south which could be propped up to allow the birds to fly in and out. Barn owl numbers had dropped sharply in recent years, due to a loss of habitat and the conversion of old barns into homes. I wrote to David Ramsden, who ran the Barn Owl Trust in Devon, asking if he could let me have a pair of disabled owls. I feared he might reply that he could not, because of the red tape surrounding Schedule One birds.

Even so, I spent a whole day making a nesting box arrangement from a small tea chest which I had cleaned out thoroughly. I sawed a plywood sheet to the right size for a front panel, cut into its bottom an entrance hole 8 ins by 9 ins and hinged it onto the chest so that, for filming purposes, it could be pulled up and open by a cord and pulley system. I broke up an old chair, the curved and lipped back of which provided a perfect landing and perching tray in front of the entrance. I carried the whole caboodle up a ladder and through a trapdoor into the byre's loft. I then ripped out two long, old fence railings, got them up to the loft, cut them to size and nailed them onto the last two high rafters to the east. I then nailed the nest box and tray onto them. I propped open the eastern dormer window but had to replace two missing panes by cutting plastic sheet to size.

Next day I rigged an old dark green hide around the trapdoor so I could come through it, step to the side onto the loft floor, close the trapdoor, and stand on it when filming. On a long flex from the house, I fixed twin studio lights to the beam above the hide so that they could be switched on to shine on the whole end of the loft and the nest box ten yards away. I got the cord and pulley system working and, as a last touch, spread a few small bark chippings over the floor of the box. Now all I wanted was owls.

David Ramsden did not turn me down flat but sent some scientific facts and a long detailed questionnaire which I filled in with as much detail as possible. He also said the Trust needed to visit a potential release site and that I should make sure there were no barn owls breeding in my area. I added that they would be welcome and that I'd even pay their petrol. I checked with a few local folk and the area's bird ringer, a Dr Taylor, made sure that there were no breeding barn owls in the area and, after more correspondence, David Ramsden wrote that he wanted me to have some owls. He did not need to visit and the best plan would be for me to stage 'a young clutch release'. This meant that I would rear young chicks to flying stage and, if I was successful, do everything I could to help them find their own territories. He would have some ready for me at the end of the summer.

On 22 June I had an amazing experience. After breakfast I went to walk and warm myself up in the hot sun before tackling a pile of correspondence, when a huge tawny bird leaped clumsily off my sheep wall only thirty yards from the house. It raised one foot and set-off talons unusually slowly. I thought at first that it must be a buzzard, but it was too darned big. After going two hundred yards to the south it circled round and round, gaining height, looking down at me. As I saw the oblong white patches in its wings I realised it was an eagle, an immature male! I dashed in for the camera pack but by the time I got both parts of the telephoto lens out and together it was almost a mile high and I could only manage a distant shot before it disappeared into a hazy white cloud. What was it doing so close to my house? It must have noticed that the chimney ladders were up and the front door open. If only I had looked carefully before going out.

I hared down to London and spent a mad ten days doing publicity for my book Last Wild Years with Woman's Hour and Midweek on Radio 4 and Country Living magazine. I was also flown to Edinburgh and back for interviews with The Scotsman, the Daily Record and a BBC Radio Scotland programme. All this, while fitting in the usual business seeing my publisher, having films developed and more videos made.

At the end of July, I made a rat-proof feed platform in the loft from a table in Caballo which I never used and which had a shiny metal tube as a stand which no rat could ever climb. I also cleaned the floor of old chicken muck and debris, filling my hair full of dust and putting my left foot through a rotten board, scraping my leg badly enough to bleed. I also located and rang Elwyn Lewis, the boss of a chicken hatchery in nearby Earlston, who said I could have as many dead day-old chicks as I wanted. They had to cull nearly all the male chicks anyway, he said, and I could have at least a hundred a month. I would not have to pay anything but just come and collect them.

I kept in touch with David Ramsden by phone and in the end he said I would have to drive down to the Barn Owl Trust HQ in Ashburton, Devon, on 28 August. I would need to take on at least five owlets as it was usual in such releases for 75% to die or get lost on their first flights. It would be no good him driving up with just two

- they wouldn't stand a chance, he said. Meanwhile, I had to send him a detailed map of my place, with all references, describing the terrain and marking the grasslands. On 25 August, I drove Caballo to Earlston where Elwyn took two huge plastic sacks containing 400 dead day-old chicks from his car boot. I was amazed how heavy they were and could hardly carry one, never mind both. Back home, it was lucky I'd bought a large fridge-freezer as it took me nearly an hour to cram them all in.

When I reached the Barn Owl Trust in Devon, David and his wife Fran produced six owlets in a big box. They swayed as we came near and hissed continually, sounding like steam escaping a locomotive, pumping air through their beaks with some internal sac while taking in another breath with their lungs, like bagpipes. David fitted on BTO rings, which clip on, then colour rings on their left legs so that I could identify them. The first two, male and female, were five weeks old. Of the other four, three were three weeks old and the fourth, the youngest, was only just over two weeks old, and much smaller than the rest. He explained that barn owls lay an egg every three days, so if there were seven eggs there could be three weeks between the biggest chick and the smallest. They didn't attack each other deliberately, unlike some birds of prey. It was OK to mix broods, even to put the two big ones with the four smaller ones. I had to put a soft surface below the nest so that if any fell out, they wouldn't be injured. There was no need to clean out the nest box often as their pellets and droppings would just get trodden under the bark chips (I decided to clean them out sometimes anyway) but I had to look out for rotting food because of flies and poisoning.

'Do you regard them as intelligent birds?' I asked. The reply was immediate 'No, they're not, they're stupid!' He laughed and added, 'Of limited intelligence' is the nicest way of putting it. As they were captive-bred, did the parents mind them being taken away at this stage? David said that he hadn't asked them, but that the truth was that no-one knew - they certainly didn't show any sign of missing their young, such as going off their food or changing their behaviour in any way. How should I sex them? He turned the big chick over, showing me that the underside of the wing on the carpel joint was rusty brown with a row of black and white circles. When the wing was fully feathered these spots would be right across the underside in the female, while the male has a pure white underside to his wing. He pointed out that the female had a green leg ring and the male a black. He felt sure they would all get along together but that night would be the first time the two broods would share one box.

David said I should not keep them in an aviary, even a large one. I must not imprison them in any way. They had to be free to go, to clear off if they wanted to. In the first ten Young Clutch Releases carried out by the Trust, all the owls left the release site. In the next two, the owls stayed and formed breeding pairs, and no-one knew why. 'It's essential we find out more, and we feel you have a better chance with your set-up and with six owls than with just two, three or even four. It's cars which often contribute to that 75% fatality rate in the first winter, and they should be less of a problem where you are, unless the birds fly several kilometres.'

David then showed me how to serve up the day-old chicks. First, cut off the lower legs and feet as they are hard to digest. Cut diagonally through one shoulder, as the wing stubs get stuck in the owlet's throat when it tries to swallow the chick whole. Once I see that the little ones are swallowing whole chicks with ease, I should stop cutting the shoulder but still remove the legs.

I gave David and Fran my eagle video and two books and they offered me a meal but I always keep Spanish time and never eat before 8.30 p.m., so I cooked up in Caballo before turning in.

Next day we loaded the six owlets into my old wildcat den box, took a few photos and, because I wanted to get them quickly into the safe, warm nest box in my loft, I drove the 436 miles home in twelve hours, good going for old Cab. Not wanting to traumatise them further that day, I set them on my desk in the study overnight. I cut up twelve day-old chicks and slivers of half a sheep's heart between them. Oddly, it was the smallest that dived in first, working hard to jerk big portions down its throat. The biggest two were the slowest. If my hand went too close when putting in the food, these two sometimes reared backwards, lying on their backs with talons out but not actually grabbing me. I had to hold each owlet once to see which one had which colour ring, and in each case they went all soft and yielding, closing their eyes as if about to sleep.

In the morning I made last minute adjustments in the loft, re-arranging the twin studio lamps so that light went in from the left and right, diffusing any shadows when filming. The old wildcat den box was too big to get up the ladder and through the trapdoor. I had to get a cardboard wine box and transfer them by hand, one by one, to that. They did hate this operation and hissed and clopped their beaks but I got them up gently and safely, then slowly held the box on its side, letting them stumble one by one into the nest box. I was amazed by their reaction to the new environment. They immediately looked all round them, carefully, slowly, with glares like wildcats, as if assessing from where a threat might come and where the escape routes might be.

I left them to it all afternoon and planted on the banks of my lake two 7 ft trees, a birch and a rowan I'd bought from a nursery on the way to collect the owls. At 6.30 p.m. I cut twelve more chicks and made slivers of 2 oz stewing steak. As I carried the food up through the trapdoor I saw through the hide that the owlets were moving about nicely, scratching on the front of the nest box. I undid the hide cords and, as I got close with the food, all except the little chick hissed and erected high. I noticed the little one had a hard, pinkish lump in its rear crop which to my inexperienced eye looked like cancer. David had said I would probably have three die on me but although I didn't want to lose a single one, I feared I might find the wee one dead next day.

In the morning, however, it was fine and chipper and again was the first to dive into the cut-up chicks. It picked up a fat one and took a long time to hack it back down, then retired to the rear. I noticed that the distended crop now looked normal. I now had to identify the owlets by name, so I could keep notes and write about them, so they became Little Chick, Small Chick, Medium Chick, Medium Chick Senior, Big Chick Male and Big Chick Female, which I'll use in abbreviated form from now on. Second to feed was MC, third was SC, fourth was MCSr, then BCml. Last to feed was BCfem who watched the others feed and turn off to the sides and rear before slowly shouldering her way forward, but with no aggression to the others. She made circular motions with her head as if focussing on the food, then took the biggest remaining chick. She tried to jerk it down her throat, had a pause for thought, then stuck it under her left foot talons. Then she began, achingly slowly and with great delicacy, hauling off tiny bits of flesh and yellow downy skin. She took about twelve minutes to finish and my knees were trembling so much with bending strain that I feared I might go through the trapdoor. Then BCfem relaxed, looked up at the roof of the nest box and went to sleep. It was now clear that they ate one big chunk, then retired for a snooze. Half the food was left so they fed again an hour or so later. This matched behaviour in the wild where they have to catch one vole or mouse at a time and cannot and do not sate themselves.

Next afternoon I looked out of the study window and saw a jaunty little roebuck at the end of my garden. I took its photo then cut some chicken wire netting to the right sizes and went to fix 6 ft cages round the new birch and rowan trees at the east edge of my lake. On the way back I saw a lovely female kestrel hover-hunting the clear fell behind my house, the sun glinting the bronzy sheen of her flashing pinions into flames. Then I saw it – a cat, a domestic one at that, because of its small size and scrawny tail, eating from the meaty scraps I set out in the hope of attracting badgers. What was it doing here, over three miles from the nearest human habitation? I scared it away then hurried to shift the ladder up to the owlets' loft in case the cat came back and could climb the ladder.

Next morning the cat was back, and on the bird table. It was eating the bits of hamburger I had left and had put out for the birds. I found a half-size tea chest in the attic room and swiftly made the kind of box-cage trap I'd used for my wildcats at Wildernesse. I set it at dusk and kept watch through the lace curtains. After only a few minutes I saw the cat start to enter the trap, head in and reaching out with a foot. I turned away in case it caught even a slight glimpse of my face when… thump! I raced out, full of confidence I'd caught the cat and could drive it to the nearest village tomorrow, but it wasn't there. My wildcats had always gone completely into a trap, to grab the bait meat with their teeth, but this cunning old cat must have reached in with one extended set of claws and raked at it instead. The hefty sliding back door must have come down only on its shoulders or back, allowing it to make a rapid backward escape. I figured that a shock like that would stop the cat from coming back, and it didn't. When I went shopping next day, I found by my far gate a fresh scat, doubtless left by the cat when leaving of its own accord. The female kestrel was again hunting the clear fell area.

When I went to feed the owlets, there were only five in the box. Had the cat somehow managed to get up there? It was the big female that had gone, I rushed for a torch, went on hands and knees and finally located a pair of owl's feet and talons showing under a floor crossbeam. It seemed she had shuffled along the strut that supported the nest box, dropped a big white scat halfway along, and had then fluttered to the floor. I reached in, took gentle hold of both legs and tweaked her out. There was no protest at all. She just lay back and looked at me as I transferred her back to the nest box.

LC was always the first to stir at feed time and came out with eyes closed, to grope about on the bark chips for food more by feel than by sight. Once LC was retreating with a big piece when MC took a grab at it too and, after a tug of war, got it off LC. Then, with glares, BCml advanced towards the food but LC grabbed his left foot as he was going, held on while he grabbed and jerked back a bit, and still held on as he retreated into the huddle-together-for-warmth cluster. BCml then hopped about with flapping wings but couldn't shake LC off. I had to sort it out as BCml's leg – or the whole of LC – could have been hurt. I reached in among their hissing forms, took gentle hold of LC and pulled him out. He still had hold of BCml's foot but soon let go. As I brought the food towards LC – bang! – down went his beak and he grabbed a big chunk while still in my hand. I let him go but he had grabbed too large a bit and couldn't jerk it back. With my fingers beside his beak I separated the bit into two with my finger nails and he then jerked back the bit he had left before retiring backwards into the cluster.

As I climbed down the ladder I saw that two of the three young of a second brood of swallows that were nesting in the byre had gone. Once the third had flown I could keep the byre door closed, and then the owlets would be fully protected. As I rounded the house corner, the female kestrel flew off one of my garden posts and landed in a dead tree to the south. Indoors, I kept close watch. She perch-hunted for a few minutes, then flew to another dead tree nearby and did the same. It was as if she preferred to land on dead branches or twigs as there was no foliage to obscure her vision. The first two perches were about 30 ft high but the third was only 7 ft from the ground. Once she flew to a fully-needled spruce and began jumping about as if scalded, maybe finding it difficult to get a footing which didn't prick! I took some fine photos, happy that she clearly liked my immediate area.

As BCfem had already gone 'walkabout', I realised I'd better get some film of the chicks while they were all still in the nest box. It was extremely complicated to get the tripod legs right around the trapdoor, and I had to make a small platform to the rear of the hide so that I could sit on a collapsible canvas chair while filming. MC came out from behind the cluster and took a bit of heart which, being harder than a dead chick, was harder to get down. MCsr tried to snatch it but missed. LC then came out for a chick, followed by MCsr and finally BCml, who got a big bit. BCfem just looked at the others feeding from time to time but preferred to snooze on, as if she knew there was plenty of food there, the ration now increased to 14 chicks a day.

A week later, the owlets started feeding themselves while I was still there, and even when I began shifting them about slightly with a long wooden spoon! I did this to replace the bark chips, now getting too damp, with shredded dry newspaper, which was also more easily replaced. That evening I was at my desk, packing more of my videos to post, when I heard a soft thump. I turned just in time to see a sparrowhawk thump into a young plump chaffinch, more unaware than the adults, on my bird table and carry it off. I just glimpsed the mad golden eye of the hawk but how can anyone set up to photograph something like that? She comes out of nowhere like lightning, with no warning possible, and – crash – is away with her prey. I hoped she would pluck it on one of my fence posts but she vanished into the thicket of tangled lodgepole pines that bordered my land.

Over the next few days I made an extra nest box, as the first one was getting crowded for the growing owlets, and another smaller one, which I carried to the old steading by my gate entrance so the owlets would have a choice once they flew. I also saw the female kestrel catch what looked like a frog on the bank of my lake and labour with it to the high seat for shooting deer that ranger Tony had erected on the far side of the clearing across my burn. Through the binos I could see her rending the frog but she was too far away to try to take photos or film her. Later she was back on the dead pine just south of my lake and, as I walked down, I gave two what I hoped were reassuring 'kee kee' buzzard/kestrel whistles. They seemed to work, for when I drew abreast of her, only thirty yards away, she stayed where she was and started preening her wings. All the swallows had now flown their nest but as they were coming back at night to roost, I couldn't shut the byre door just yet. Realising they would soon be gone for good, I took a few flash shots of them bulging out from the nest. They didn't mind at all and had, indeed, become totally trustful of my comings and goings, one even letting me stroke its head with a finger. A day later, nice and sunny, all five swallows were flying in and out of the byre, catching insects on the wing and often missing my head by inches.

11

Best Ever Barn Owl Release

In mid-September, when the owlets started moving around the loft, often hiding from me in the floor 'cubicles' between the roof beams when I came through the hide with their food, I realised they would be flying and going outside before much longer and made a special feed table a few yards in front of the bird table outside. I dug a two-foot deep hole to hold a seven-foot length of scaffold pole. On top of this I nailed a two-foot square of thick plywood as the 'table' and round the edges of that I nailed thin strips of wood so that the dead chicks would not be blown away by any strong wind. When the owls were perched under the open dormer windows they would see the grub on this table and fly down to take it. Or so I hoped.

On 13 September, MC had gone on 'walkabout' and was hiding in the same 'cubicle' as BCfem had. Afraid of my approach, she lay on her back so as to strike up with her talons. I ignored this, gently took hold of one foot, pulled her out far enough to hold her other foot, then with my other hand under her back, I lifted her onto the perch tray of the nest box. She ran in like an old lady holding up her skirts then turned to glare at me with an outraged expression as she barged into the others.

When the food started going from the 4-foot high separate feed table I'd made in the loft, I knew they had started to fly, and from outside, working from a ladder, I fixed special perch poles jutting out from the dormer windows so they could land more easily if and when they returned from outside. David Ramsden, of course, had warned me that they might do anything but!

While I was doing this, the female kestrel started hunting around the back of the house, often hovering. I dashed for my camera, got a few shots and then saw what looked like one of my barn owls hunting high on the clear fell, a light brownish bird with broad wings. Surely not this soon? It landed on a fence post and through the binos I saw it was a short-eared owl, with the small ear tufts, but too far away for photos. In the morning it was still there, on the post. I hiked up, through long drying grasses near the top where the first blue scabious flowers were blooming, and got one photo of the owl. It flew towards me, veering off through a gap in the pines, but not before I saw the gold eyes, dark eye rings and short 'ears'. I now knew what to look for and sure enough, there was a huge, disgorged pellet below the fence post. I later dissected it – one big field vole and two woodmice. I photographed the skulls, thighs, tibia and hip bones on black paper and arranged them with the fur of the pellet into a neat exhibition item for my little wildlife museum.

On 14 September I had proof that BCfem was flying as I found her on top of the nest box, perched behind a cross beam so that I could only see her legs and feet. And, once again, the two chicks on the feed table had gone and there was a white splash below the table. Over the next few days all the owlets were flying and I found them crouching under various 'cubicles' on the floor when I went in with food. I shot a lot of film at this time as I knew they would soon be going outside and may not come back. I tried also to sex them, one by one, using David Ramsden's criteria, although I didn't like doing it. To judge by their underwings, it seemed that four were females and two were males, but of course I could have been mistaken. Although at first they hissed and made mock beak stabs, they would become totally submissive once I took firm hold, although they were still afraid: you could feel their wee hearts beating like trip hammers in your palm. I would have loved to tame one, but that was definitely not allowed.

Ranger Tony turned up on 17 September so I showed him the owls for the first time, after he had promised not to say anything to anyone about them. He was entranced with the birds and with the view from the hide and fully approved of what I was doing. BCml was missing, though, and as he didn't seem to be in any of the cubicles, I felt he could have flown. Next day Tony brought me some useful cuts of deer meat and as I was now combining the day-old chicks with cut-up bits of lamb heart and liver, roe deer venison would mix in nicely. When we took the food up, BCml was back and standing next to BCfem on the main beam by the nest box. When I put some food on the loft feed table, he flew down at me, almost in contempt, as if thinking 'I'm beyond your ken now!' Two of the owls were now using the second nest box regularly. As we left, I saw that the swallows' nest was now empty. I had not seen them for 48 hours so I reckoned they had flown south with a mass of swallows and house martins that had come down from further north, filling the air around the house and byre three days before. I padlocked the byre door, giving the owls greater security.

I woke before 6 a.m. on 20 September and crept through the gloom into the study to see what birds were about. There was a barn owl on the bird table mosses, looking into the study window. It was Small Chick, not quite fully grown. She kept circling her head, looking all about her, then she jumped onto the tits' nest box and scraped the window with her beak, peering in at every part of the study. She saw my half-face and made goggle eyes at me, so I couldn't move until she looked away. Then she crouched a few times, flying towards the feeder table but landing on a notch in the pole below the table as if unable to gain enough height to land on it. I saw her wings and back were wet, her feathers bedraggled, so she had been caught in a shower. She clung to the notch, one wing dangling towards earth, then flapped awkwardly to the top rail of my garden fence. From there, the light getting brighter, she looked at everything again, finally making up her mind that the pine pole perch jutting from the east dormer window was the way back into the loft, crouched a few times as if funking it, made a big jump and flapped upwards towards it. I couldn't see if she made it so shot out and peered round my porch wall. She had gone, so she must have been back in the loft. I saw the outside feed table still had two mice and two chicks on it so no owl had reached it yet. I went back to bed.

An hour later I got up, and the two mice had gone. I was typing my diaries prior to my usual morning walk round my little estate when the shadow of a big bird came onto the bird table. An owl? It had landed behind the main window pillar. I moved my head slightly – and off went a jay. It could have been the jay that took the mice. Damn it. I'd never know, but from now on mice would only be left in the loft. On my estate patrol two snipe shot up and away from the muddy flats I'd left at my lake's entrance, twisting from side to side as they arrowed away. It was frustrating and I should have gone more slowly, but at least the lake was doing what I'd hoped it would and attracting wildlife. A flock of bullfinches were at the meadowsweet seeds, too. At the evening feed all the owls were in the loft so Small Chick had managed to make her way back in.

I was about to make lunch the next day when I went out for some fresh air. There was a big barn owl on a fence post by the burn about four hundred yards to the southeast, and she was perch-hunting, looking down into the grasses intently. Through the binos I was sure I could see a greenish tinge on her legs so it was BCfem. I took a couple of photos but didn't want to go any closer as that could scare her away. A half hour later I went out again, in time to see her swoop down onto something in the grasses. Half a minute passed, then she was up and flapping to the left and into the lodgepole forest, with probably only a beetle in her talons, at most a mouse. 'Hope you make it back, girl,' I whispered.

When I went up with the evening feed – by now it was 14 chicks and 3 oz cut-up liver – the four youngest owls were in the nest box, while BCml and BCfem were also there, the female on her favourite perch on the beam while the male jumped from the second nest box to the floor and ran into a cubicle. It was wonderful to realise that the big female had made it back safely from her hunting trip a quarter mile away. I now gave them both proper names: the male I called Blacky because of his ring colour. As I couldn't very well call the female Greeny, I re-named her Browny.

At dawn the next morning I sneaked a look and saw Blacky on the outside feed table rending a chick, so took three photos through the study window. When I went out with the evening feed, Browny was perched on a dormer window exit pole outside the loft. She saw me, did a goggling double-take then, like a parrot, edged her feet, one after the other, back into the loft. By the end of September all the owls were flying, four of them outside. When Blacky and Browny flew close over my head at dusk I was scared my presence might scare them away but they kept coming back. I set up a hide in my garden so that I could film them flying into and out of the loft and rending the day-old chicks on the feed table. I quickly learned to nail the chicks to the table so the owls had to pull, tug, and work hard to get the flesh off them. They would otherwise just pick up a chick and fly to the loft with it before I could film anything. When they began leaving the feed chicks in the loft I guessed they were hunting quite well and that I could lower their rations every few days. When I rang David Ramsden with the good news, he said it seemed I was having 'a fantastic success'. I said yes, but that they still had the winter to face.

I was pleased the owls did not seem too worried about seeing me outside. They had, after all, seen a lot of me inside the loft. Above all, I wanted them to feel I loved them, that they could co-exist with me and that I was the provider. Fat chance, maybe, if they are of limited intelligence. All this time the female kestrel continued hunting in my lake area and had three favourite rending perches, all in dead trees. The jay returned, having found a partner, and continued to raid the small birds' peanut holders, sometimes nicking a day-old chick which the owls had loosened on the feed table. Once, at dusk, I went to pull the study curtains when I saw one of the owls on my garden gate. It saw my face looking out, but instead of flying away, it flew upwards and back into the loft. It was a most reassuring sign.

On a rainy morning in early October, I went to check the freezer in the larder and saw a barn owl on the window sill outside. It was LC and he fluffed himself up when my face appeared in front of the lace curtain. All his feathers were soaked and bedraggled, though, and there was no way he could fly back to the loft. I got dressed, put on wellies, grabbed a torch, the flash camera and a clothes peg bag and went out to the rescue. I took two photos in the sousing rain, slowly gripped both his legs with gloved hand and manoeuvred him into the soft, dark bag. I unlocked the byre door, climbed the ladder, opened up the hide and let him go. He ran off with droopy tail spikes, wings half-lifted like an umbrella on two clawball legs, and into the northwest corner. Then he saw three others in the floor cubicles to the southeast and ran over the floor to join them. I took my last flash shots of them all in the loft that day.

Next afternoon, during a break in drizzly weather, I was coming back from the lake when an owl flew with weak wing flaps from the eastern perch pole. It couldn't make it even to the fence top and flopped into a huge tangle of thick stinging nettles. It was Small Chick and she clung to the wet nettles, which looked like iron bars around her, with one wing drooping earthwards. There was no way she could launch from there and fly back to the loft with soaked wings. I took two photos, caught her round the legs, set her atop the gate for two more, then put her in a sheltered hole in the sheep wall. I shot up to the hide in the loft, dismantled the movie gear and filmed her in and atop the wall. I then carried her in the peg bag back to the loft, where all the owls were perched except for Blacky, who was doubtless away on one of his hunting trips. That was the last time I actually handled any of the owls. By now they were not using the nest boxes in the loft very much, so I cleaned them out, also for the last time.

I had no qualms about removing the movie gear from the loft as the owls hardly ever flew when I was in the hide. No matter how quiet I tried to be, I was sure, with their acute hearing, that they could hear my breathing, my heartbeat, a slight wheeze or even a hand movement. I set the lot up in the outdoor hide and had much more luck filming them on the perch poles and flying in and out on their hunting trips. I once saw Blacky hunting on the upper clear fell and he was away for three days, but came back on the fourth. I also filmed the owls flying to the outdoor feed table and tugging at the nailed-down day-old chicks, often carrying them back up to the loft once they'd got them free.

I had a nice shock one dusky evening. Sitting at my desk, I looked out and saw a big bird on the outdoor table. It was tugging at a chick but I was sure it wasn't one of my barnies: it was the wrong colour, being sort of coppery. I gingerly pulled the lace curtain aside to see that it was the female kestrel. She had become tamer of late, flying over my head when I gave the right whistles, but this was quite unexpected – and quite wonderful. Before long she came almost every day, always taking a single chick and flying over to the burn to rend it atop ranger Tony's rickety deer seat. Of course, I filmed her too.

So the owl saga continued, with individual owls missing for a few days at a time but then returning to the loft, and eating far fewer chicks, so they must have been hunting well. When Blacky had been missing for a week I feared he had gone, but he had taken up residence in the steading by my gate where I had put a nest box. Two of them took up temporary residence in a broken-down old steading in the forest, half a mile to the southwest, so I left a few chicks there. But on 20 October, all six were back in the loft! Once, on a now-rare visit to the loft hide, I saw LC standing next to Browny on the beam by the old nest box. LC started very gently grooming Browny's chest feathers, then held her beak upwards with closed eyes. They entwined beaks in a sort of kissing action which lasted more than a few seconds. It was lovely to watch and I wondered if a pair bond was forming. When I phoned the Barn Owl Trust with the latest news, David Ramsden said it sounded like the best ever barn owl release.

I now often saw my owls hunting the clear fell areas above and below the house, fanning along like giant white moths, making sudden swirls if spotting something. When the first snowfalls began in mid-November, they returned to the loft more often and I had to judge their needs by how many chicks were left and how many had been eaten. At the end of November I was driving back from a quick business trip to London when I saw a barn owl on the road near Craik. It could have been in trouble so I stopped the car and got out, but it flew up and landed on a fence post. Through the binos I could see a purple ring: it was Small Chick and she had got all this way, four miles from the loft. Back home, I found no owls in the loft but they had left two uneaten chicks. I put some new ones on the loft and outdoor tables.

Within a few minutes of my being back in the house, the female kestrel landed, tested them with her beak and nicked a loose one!

In early December I had a fright. A letter from the Barn Owl Trust informed me that on 4 November the government had passed a law making it illegal to release captive-bred barn owls without a licence from the Department of the Environment. Alarmed, I rang David, who reassured me that since our release had happened long before that date we had done nothing illegal. We had, in fact, done it with some distinction. I would have to wait until spring, though, to know if any of my owls would actually breed.

During the long winter, four owls left the barn, either to perish or to establish new territories, and had left Blacky and Browny in sole charge. LC's cosyings up to Browny had clearly gone unrewarded! In time, I was sure I could find out what happened to the missing four, although now and again, especially in snow, one or other would come for the chicks I still put out on the garden table.

By late February, I noticed that Blacky and Browny were using their old nest box, frequently going in and out, before and after hunting trips. Blacky would always fly to the highest beam when I put food on the loft table but Browny often stayed beside the nest box, just watching me. She sometimes stretched one wing and foot down as far as they would go, have a yawn, then would do the same on the other side. In early March I spent freezing hours in the outdoors hide as LC and MC were coming back to take chicks after dark. They were occasionally joined by a tawny owl – as if the kestrel and two jays were not competition enough – but LC and MC did not go to the loft.

By mid-March, Browny was sitting tight in the nest box but I decided not to check on her as I had to spend a week in London having new videos made from new master and sound tapes. This would give her time to settle down without any intrusions from me. All I did was lay down a lot more chicks than usual. When I returned on 30 March, both owls were in the loft, with three uneaten chicks on the floor. I saw the kestrel, the jays screeched and the tawny owl hooted before dusk, so all my 'pals' were still here. My hopes that she had been on eggs were soon dashed, as she began perching near Blacky on her favourite beam. The two used the loft as their home for more than another year, and I was grateful that Elwyn was still letting me have the day-old chicks I needed for free. I did find a way to repay him a little, though. Early in the year he had given me a dead barn owl killed by traffic near his hatchery. I had it stuffed in Edinburgh by Scotland's leading taxidermist, George Jamieson, and he had made a magnificent job of it. When I took it to Elwyn's showroom office he thought I was just showing it to him. When I asked where he was going to put the owl, because now it was his, he could hardly believe it and his face was a study. The owl now has pride of place in his showroom, has been admired by hundreds of people and is doing a far better public relations job than if it had stayed in my study, seen by no one but little old me.

To cut a long story short – or maybe to lengthen a short story – I found Browny incubating eggs in the old nest box in the loft when I returned from my 66th birthday filming of Highland eagles with Steve Phillipps. Her wings and tail were well in view and she was lying low and very still. Two days later she was noisily scrapping around the bottom of the box with her beak, probably scraping debris round the eggs or turning them. I continued to put food in every night, of course, but by mid-June had twice encountered Blacky flying from the dormer windows to hunt the front clear fell while Browny sat tight. I hoped he was bringing her more natural prey than my chicks. Then came the best ever day with my barn owls.

On 20 June, Browny was brooding one unhatched egg – and at least two very small chicks. The day began with a visit from ranger Tony and Dave Anderson, the licensed bird ringer for the region. It was the ideal opportunity to do everything by the book. I took Dave up to the loft and filmed him going to the nest box after I had lifted the front by the pulley, to which I had been getting Browny accustomed so that I could film her. As he got close, I was amazed to see Browny hold her ground, hissing and making a threat display with open wings but not flying off. Dave said he could see at least two very small chicks and one unhatched egg by her chest. Would I like to lift her? I said no: it wasn't important how many she had at this stage and I thought we should leave her. We agreed that Dave could come back in two or three weeks and ring the chicks when they were bigger. Outside the byre, I could not resist a little dance of triumph. My barnies had succeeded at last! The long experiment had been worthwhile.

Tony and Dave had been checking the forest's goshawk nests and had found one pair with three healthy chicks. Another pair, though, were still sitting on three eggs which, this late in the season, were obviously addled. They had found one goshawk chick on the ground, thin and half-starved, and they had it in a bag. Did I have any meat we could feed it? I suggested that we feed it well, take it to the nest with the addled eggs, remove them for analysis and put the chick in. I said I had worked on a similar project on black vultures and imperial eagles in Spain. The two men looked sceptical.

I got two unfrozen day-old chicks from Blacky and Browny's nightly ration and took them to the goshawk chick, which they had put on a brown cushion on my desk. Dave proffered it bits of cut-up chick with his fingers but it would not eat. 'It's best with scissors,' I said. They looked mystified. I fetched my scissors and held little chunks on their tip to the goshawk chick. Immediately, it reached out and pecked and swallowed them. The two men looked amazed and Dave said 'By God, you do know your kit, Mike!' It was my proudest moment in years. I explained how I'd learnt the trick from Suso Garzón, and then had to explain who Suso was . We let the chick have a sleep while we had a bite to eat, then we gave it more food and took it, well-fed, back to the nest with the addled eggs. I filmed Dave climbing up, using his leg irons, removing the eggs and putting in the chick. Five days later we checked the nest – not only had the mother goshawk accepted the chick but was now brooding it, and we could see its head peeping out from under a wing.

With the twin studio lamps re-set, I was now filming Browny in her nest box every few nights, and she was accepting the raising of the front panel because she associated it with the arrival of food. On 4 July she obligingly moved right off the chicks and I could see that there were four! It was a greater success than I had realised. I told Tony and, two days later, he turned up with a large grass-cutting machine to mow wide swathes on the clear fells above and below my house, making it better for my owls to hunt for mice and voles. They now had a near-perfect environment and Blacky responded by hunting well and taking plenty of wild prey up to the loft, still pausing now and again to snatch one of the day-old chicks I put on the outdoor table. The four owlets were finally ringed on 4 August.

All this success with the barn owls took place against the complicated backdrop of trying to sell Ropelaw. I had been there for almost three years and had completed films on the owls, three pairs of nesting goshawks, two pairs of buzzards, the wildlife of the forest and my lake. There seemed little more to achieve. There were no eagles and they, after all, had long been my speciality. The worst problem, though, for me, was the winters. The farmhouse and 3 ½ acres were at a height of 1,100 feet above sea level and often in a foot of snow, while down in Hawick town there was not a snowflake to be seen. Old Mi Caballo did his best but we were sometimes trapped for days at a time (the longest was stretch was nine days) as he couldn't get up even the first 600 yards of our track to the main forestry 'roads'. Often, when we did, the huge and heavy log-carrying trucks and loaders had gouged two-foot deep ruts in their surfaces which we sometimes found impossible to negotiate. I would then have to turn back and go out one of the other two entrances to the forest, which were much further away, one of them forcing me into a forty-mile detour to reach the town. I could, of course, have bought a four-wheel drive vehicle, but a good one would have been costly and, besides, I was unwilling to ditch Mi Caballo; we had been through a lot together, especially in Spain. Most of all, though, I felt I had done all I wanted to do in that place.

Ultimately, after many complications, I sold it to a family who had a large Range Rover and who loved the wilderness and, especially, my lake. The new owner was both intrigued and delighted with the owls. I showed him how to feed them and arranged with Elwyn to supply him with day-old chicks as he had me. Removal man Stan Purves came on 15 August to take all my belongings into storage in Galashiels. Three days later I handed the keys over to the new owner, braved the forestry tracks for the last time and drove off into the void.

The dénouement of the barn owl story came some six years later. I went back to the area and checked with all the local farms and various contacts and learned of the great success of the venture. My 'barnies' established at least three breeding pairs over that period in farms at Gamescleuch, Borthwickbrae and Craikhope, over an area of 25 square miles where barn owls had long been absent.

12

Otters and an Eagle Birthday

I was homeless again, so what to do? Head off north, film golden eagles and have a try at otters with my trekking pal Steve Phillipps, that's what to do. I rang Steve, camped overnight on the Ettrick edge of the forest, and was with him at the western end of Ardnamurchan the following evening. In the morning we hiked down a burn gorge to Otter Bay. After two hours, as usual, we had no luck, so we climbed almost to the top of the great sea cliff where the eagles had a nest in a larch tree to match their two ledge eyries on the cliff itself. We had to climb down a steep quarter-mile to reach the tree and I, not having done much hard trekking in a while, began to hate all the little sheer cliffs, strangely unsure of my footing now, while Steve cantered down like a mountain goat. The nest was huge, a spectacular sight against the backdrop of the sea. It had not been used that year but I filmed it anyway.

We hiked back and set up to take an easterly view of Otter Bay, but there were none about. Otters have always been my bête noire, a species I have never filmed well, and I told Steven despondently that as long as he was with me, we would see no otters. Ravens were skirling about the sky and I got onto them twice, but they kept going out of range. In the end we were rewarded when the sea cliff eagles were spotted by Steve and, high above us, they began their magnificent yet uncommon pair bond dives, air rolls and talon clutchings. I captured most of it on film, an ideal sequence for the second video I was making about eagles.

We set off again to Otter Bay next day on our fifth attempt overall, but with no real hope. Before we reached the shore though, we both spotted it – a big otter, swimming in the sea lagoon. We hastened down and Steve set up on top of a high mossy rock, I to the side, and took almost seven minutes of my best ever otter film. It swam to a rock to my right and ate a small fish. Then it dived, came up and swam further to the right, clambering up onto thick seaweed to begin eating a butterfish. I had to make two short stalks to get closer, then readjust the tripod legs to get it level on sloping rock, which was hard to do without the animal spying me.

Steve also had to get closer with his 300 mm lens, and I filmed him sliding sideways and lower, flattened out like a crouching panther. The otter then swam towards us, climbed out onto a seaweed-covered rock and took a good look at Steve. He didn't move. The otter slid back into the sea, swam right round the small bluff, came out on his left side and took another long look at him. It dived back into the sea as Steve clicked away, then it swam right round to the right and came out twice more, to check if Steve's still form was indeed human. It clearly decided it was, turned and paddled frantically, diving a few yards away and not emerging again in our sight. We decided not to track it to the second bay – we didn't want to scare it twice. 'That's lifted your otter curse, eh?' said Steve, as we left. I said it sure did. We spent the rest of the day looking at my recent wildlife footage, and two holiday chalets for rent, but neither was what I wanted.

Two days later I took my lawyer to lunch in Edinburgh, and she immediately handed me a cheque for nearly £58,000. I held it as if it were a gold ingot. It was more money than I'd ever had in my life. My toilings on the farmhouse and lake had not been in vain. It so happened that she owned a 13-acre wood by Cockburnspath near the east Scottish coast. It had a large wooden log hut on it, with a water supply but no electricity. If I would do a full wildlife survey of her wood, I could use the hut until I found a new home, or until she sold the property in the autumn. I thought it sounded a pretty good deal.

I did the survey over three days, surprised to find quite deep wooded gorges. I discovered goshawks, found their nest and de-feathered woodpigeon kill, red squirrels, stoats, roe deer, two badger setts, two tawny owls and two sparrowhawk nests. I also listed the trees and flowers.

Some of my gear was in storage but, of the rest, I locked the most valuable inside the hut and went south on business, to visit friends and to look at flats in the Worthing, Lancing and Ferring areas. My old girlfriend Alexandra Bastedo and her husband, theatre director Patrick Garland, let me stay at their farmhouse near Chichester during those searches. I came very close to buying a sunny seafront flat in Worthing but finally pulled out because of onerous leasehold conditions. I returned to the hut in mid-October, resigned to spending the autumn or even the winter there if my lawyer friend failed to sell it, although I did look at a few flats in Hawick itself.

The hut had been built under trees, and had a high roof, so it was gloomy and damp and hard to keep tolerably warm with no electricity and only a paraffin stove. When it rained, I often couldn't get Caballo over the wet muddy fields to the wood, never mind to the hut, and had to carry everything in on foot. I had long been discussing an autobiography with my publisher, so was spending most daylight hours assembling and writing notes for it, fingers often going white with cold. My lawyer friend had to lock her Triumph sports car in the hut as she was off on a prolonged visit to South Africa, so my desk had to be dismantled. I was relegated to working on the tiny table in Caballo and to sleeping in his bed.

After a rare bout of 'flu, my first in over thirty years, I developed long spells of pain in my hips and sides and it took ages to get out of bed, get dressed and hobble to the hut. I eventually consulted a doctor in Selkirk who had read many of my books and who treated me to a careful inspection. He said I had severe muscular pains of a lumbago type. 'Ye'd better get a dry roof over your head soon,' he added, 'or ye'll have one of green sods!' That galvanised me and I drove to Hawick. There was in the High Street a poky little attic flat which I rather liked. I had already spoken to its owner, who had turned down my initial offer. As if by some odd quirk of fate, he happened to come along as I was looking up at the flat's windows.

'If you're still interested, make me an offer.'

'I did but you turned it down,' I said. The flat was on the market at £10,000 and I'd offered him £9,000

'You can always try again,' he said.

'Well, I was thinking about… eight!' I said, sure he would turn me down again.

'I'll take it!' he said, and thrust out his hand. We went to the office of the *Hawick News*, of which he had been proprietor, got the keys and looked over the flat again. It had a large living room, with a spacious kitchen leading off it with a modern cooker and fridge. There was a small bedroom, bathroom and a hall. Nothing luxurious, but adequate as a temporary base and easy to keep warm! I immediately strode to the office of my Hawick solicitor, Charles, who said he was sure I'd got a bargain, as that was the lowest-priced flat he had ever heard of. He would get on with the conveyancing immediately. The other bonus, I discovered, was that I could park Mi Caballo in any of the town's public car parks for sixty hours at a time. On 24 November I parked him right below the flat in the High Street so as to make room for Stan Purves' removal van. He came at 9.20 p.m., having done another removal in the afternoon, and it took us about fifty carries to get all my gear up to the little flat. Cramming everything from the huge farmhouse into three rooms was difficult and I had no room to erect the bed without a great deal of further effort, so I left it all to the next day. I drove old Caballo to our favourite campsite in the forest, warmed up some leftovers, and crashed into his bed at 1.30 a.m., totally exhausted.

As can be imagined, I spent a comfy but rather boring and very noisy winter in the attic flat, although I gradually became used to the constant din of traffic below my window. I made up for this by spending two months camping round Spain in Caballo and filming rare wildlife, including brown bears feeding, swimming, rolling logs in water, mating and doing everything but write letters home! I got back, delighted that I could now make a second video about wild Spain, little knowing that ahead of me lay the greatest eagle season of my life.

When I rang Steve Phillipps in early May, he said the eagles we called the 'windy glen pair' were on eggs in their low nest, and asked if I would like to be filming them on my 67th birthday? He didn't have to ask twice, especially as I now had the lightweight super-quality Canon XL1 video camera. We agreed to meet at our usual quarry on Ardnamurchan peninsula on 23 May, by which time I had retrieved the large green netting hide that I had hidden in my old forest. It had to be totally remade.

I was saved from carrying it on the two-mile hike in, though, as when I arrived Steve said he had already set up the same kind of hide on Eyrie 10. We glassed it from afar but could see no action. It was strange to realise that these were the first eagles I ever photographed, exactly twenty years before. We trekked in and, five minutes after Steve left me in the hide, the male eagle returned to the nest, built as before in a wide cleft on a huge round rockface. About nine minutes later the larger female joined her mate and I filmed the changeover, of her taking over incubation duties, settling with little wiggles onto the eggs, and of him flying off, I even followed him soaring down the glen and vanishing over a side bluff. I filmed the female turning the eggs and when Steve came to get me out five hours later, I got her flying off too. Steve went into the hide and I had to hike back after a long four-hour lunch break to escort him out. It had been a super day but it was tough on the old legs to have to make the trek twice, even though it was one of the easiest in terms of height.

We took the next day off and I drove Steve to Fort William to buy him some posh new Barbour wellies. He had done all the work, finding the eagles viable, setting up the hide and putting me into it, without thought of reward and I felt it the least I could do to thank him. I also bought myself new trekking trews to replace the ragged pair I'd worn for years. On the way back I easily filmed a hooded crow leaving its nest, as it was by the side of the road and I didn't even have to get out of Caballo. It would make a nice little cameo in my second eagle film.

I had a fabulous 67th birthday with the eagles, as I usually hoped and planned for. I didn't get a changeover that time but the female did everything an eagle can do in the nest! She flew in within half a minute of Steve leaving. I missed her as she came in so fast. I only had time to take two swigs from an orange juice bottle and put the cap back on, and there she was, on the eggs. After a few minutes she stood up, turned the eggs with her beak and shook all her feathers so that she looked like a huge, ragged, black football. She moved twigs about, set some round herself while on the eggs, yawned, got up, walked round the nest edges, peering out to the horizon, went back on the eggs, yawned again and went to sleep. Steve came to walk me out and I filmed her leaving again. More fine material of the most tolerant eagle I had ever known: Steve and I had only gone about two hundred yards when she swept back to the nest. Steve showed me a better campsite than the little quarry, between big rocks above a lochan. I had a birthday party too, as we watched a Wild West show and the Mike Tyson–Buster Douglas fight on my little 12-volt video set-up and I didn't get to bed until after 2 a.m.

Next day, which was hot and sunny, we decided to push our luck and hiked up and down to the sea cliff eagles. I found the final rocky descent difficult. My legs were a bit trembly and at times I moved like a sloth. We set up and I immediately filmed the female looking out of the eyrie, flying over our heads, circling twice, stretching out and clenching and unclenching her talons in mid-air, and the male landing in the eyrie. About an hour later the female flew back with what looked like a white gull in her talons. She sailed in, they appeared to 'talk' and the male walked to the nest edge, seemed to drop off into the air and soared away. I had got some of the best flight material ever, and I felt happier, but took it easy on the return ascent so that Steve had to wait for me several times.

13

At Home with Eagles

What we most needed now was to find a viable nest with a month-old chick in it so that we could film the whole feeding and rearing stage up to its first flight. While we now had the fabulous flying sequences from the sea cliff nest, it had been too high and sheer to build a hide at a meaningful distance. And although the female on the nest up the windiest glen had given me a wonderful display on my 67th birthday, we were fairly sure that, with May drawing to a close, it was just too late for the eggs to hatch and that there was probably something wrong with them.

A week earlier we had checked the four old nests in a small tree-filled glen that led down to the sea, one of which had given me some wonderful still photos two years in succession, but all had been empty. We decided to check a new set of cliffs higher up, beyond a small lochan, but it was to prove our hardest day yet as the forestry gate was locked and we couldn't drive through, adding an extra mile to a two-mile uphill trek. Perspiring and puffing, we checked the new cliffs and found nothing. We almost gave up to go home, but something made me suggest a detour to the right, to check a few ridges, and then a trip back to check the four nests again. Steve had not expected this, as both he and I knew that I was not trekking so well these days, but he agreed. We set off again, climbed another steep ridge and were about to head half-right to go down to the four in the lower valley when Steve, who was glassing higher up a small new cliff, said he could see something white and moving on a high shelf. He ran back to me and, as he reached me, I saw a female eagle fly off the ledge. Then, through my binoculars, I made out the unmistakeable form of a downy white chick, about two and half weeks old.

Now we had to find a suitable spot to put a camouflaged hide. Steven started to climb and I tried to join him. It was a terrible ascent, clinging to heather tufts on high, almost sheer ground. I got stuck at one point but Steve came back down, suggesting a better route, so I slid down a little and managed to reach him. From there we climbed up and reached a likely ledge. He wanted to go even higher and set off over some nearly sheer wet and muddy rockfaces but I knew I could not trust my old legs and said I couldn't work from up there. We chose a final spot, still over a sheer drop, in that the hide would have to be on the edge of a 12-foot deep rock fissure about ten feet long and only a foot wide. Anyone who fell in would never be able to claw their way out again, as their chest and arms would be pinioned by solid rock. It would be a horrible way to die.

We decided to 'work the nest' in about two weeks' time when the small chick would be bigger and better able to fend for itself, and would be left alone by its parents more often. On the way back to Steve's home, we were just passing a small freshwater loch opposite a Forestry Commission conifer forest when we saw a large wildcat in the roadside grasses. It was almost an albino, ash white with big, dark grey rings on its tail. I knew better than to pull up suddenly but passed my camera to Steve, who tried to film it from the passenger window. The resulting film was, of course, too shaky for professional use and I binned it but later regretted doing so, as the rare wildcat could clearly be seen and it would at least have made a useful record.

I camped overnight in a small wild quarry and next day we hiked down a gorge to the beach where we had seen otters. We had no luck but on the way back through a wood I filmed a fine little sequence of a spotted flycatcher at his toilette, doing everything he could to preen and spruce himself up – tail, wings, breast and neck – before dashing up in the air to nab another fly. Back in my grotty little flat in Hawick High Street, I caught up with my mail and other business, then, knowing my legs needed to be at their old-age strongest for the eagle treks ahead, I got in some hard cycling. I once covered 21 miles in under an hour. I felt truly great and, with each downstroke and pull up of the pedals, experienced again the joy of power. If only I could experience the same when hiking on the hill! A lorry driver who could have overtaken me many times kept behind me for over a mile, then hooted loudly as finally he swept past, giving me a thumbs up. He also shouted but I couldn't make out what he said.

After filming herons and other birds on the lovely River Teviot that flows through Hawick, I took off back to the eagles on 11 June and checked Glen Etive. There were campers and hikers everywhere, though, and most of the cliffs were so tall and sheer that there was nowhere to put a hide. En route again, I met Allan Peters, the young keeper who had often helped me with eagles when I had lived at Wildernesse ten years before. He now kept watch over three eagle pairs, but two had failed this year. One, he was sure, had been robbed when the eggs vanished after two weeks. The third pair were raising a chick but there was a thick bush that would obscure any clear view from a hide. Allan reminded me that he had become 'hooked' when I had shown him eagles at the nest from my own hide in 1982 and then put him into my black-throated divers' hide on Heron Islet. He had watched both species in his terrain ever since. 'I owe you a lot,' he said. 'You set me on my road to Damascus!' Allan and a co-worker in the Forestry Commission had made a floating artificial islet opposite Wildernesse and the rare divers had produced chicks in every one of the nine years since. It was the most prolific platform site in Scotland.

After camping in the small quarry I cut some hazel pegs to help pin the hide down and watched the sea cliff eagle pair soaring over the deer calving grounds, doubtless hoping to spot a weak young calf. Steve then joined me. Our trek today was a bit shorter as the forestry gate was open but we still had a hard task getting all the gear up the last two miles, Steve carrying his big wire netting hide and I my green plastic netting gear. Away from the eyrie, out of its sight, we cut up my netting to tight-fit his hide and weaved lots of heather and grasses into its top and sides. On the way to the penultimate climb, both eagles flew towards and over us and I got the video camera out and filmed them, the female making a power dive near us then swerving away at the last moment with loudly 'woofs' of the wings. She sailed back and wafted on past the eyrie where the chick was calling. The hide was now the biggest I'd ever used, for we had really made one hide out of two, and we had a hard job lugging it up the last hill. I reflected that it would be even worse the next day, when we would have to try to get it up the last near-sheer buttress to the final hide site. I'd have just as soon camped out for the night but Steve wanted to get home as his mum had promised to have him a good meal waiting, so I drove him the twenty miles back to his home and set about making my own meal in the wee quarry.

I had told Steve that thirteen was my lucky number and, as next day was 13 June, it would be my lucky day. I was right. It proved to be my best ever first day with eagles. We met at 10 a.m. and set off for the eagles, having picked up two heavy sacks of heather which Steve had collected before breakfast. I baulked at carrying them up along with everything else, as there was plenty of heather up near the hide site anyway. No, said Steven, his was better heather! He bent down, strung both sacks together, heaved them over his pack, which was already heavier than mine, and set off upwards. I felt ashamed but said, 'That will slow you down, old son!' 'Yeah!' he replied, and kept going. He must have been carrying around 100 lbs but he outpaced me. It was quite phenomenal. I had never met any young man who could outpace him on the hill. We reached the big hide and he carried it and the heather sacks towards the steep buttress below the eyrie, while I carried his heavy pack and mine, as much weight as he now had but a much less awkward burden. I knew that day would be hell, and it was. A hundred yards from the buttress he dropped the heather sacks. I lugged both packs to its foot. He said it would be easier if he carried the big hide up on his own and asked if I would go back for the heather sacks? I felt peeved as he seemed to be trying to take over the operation so I refused and said that I would carry up my pack and the tripod. He set off up the almost sheer slope and as I saw him struggling alone, I felt amazed and suddenly grateful. He weighed 9 ½ stone, three stone less than me, yet I knew that at my age I could never have carried that huge hide up to its final place. I could have tugged it up, bit by bit, but that would have disturbed the eagles if they flew round our side of the buttress. Then I realised that we needed heather in order to finish the hide so I yelled that I would go back for the sacks. I traipsed back and they were easy enough to carry to the foot of the final climb. As I was about to start up with them, Steve came slithering down again, grabbed his hefty pack and the heather sacks and began carrying them back up too! I stumbled up with just my pack, heavier than usual, found that Steve had left the sacks thirty yards below the hide site so i dragged them up too. I felt done in but was glad to find that he had already got the hide into its correct position.

Under my instructions, we weaved his heather all over the hide, then had to pluck more from the surrounding area though not, of course, from near the hide itself. I stressed that not one single plastic netting square should show; all had to be covered with heather and mosses. I hurt my now-soft hands on the toughest heather, puncturing a vein, but luckily it quickly stopped bleeding. By 2.40 p.m. I was in the hide, having shoved all my hazel twigs into the earth and Steve having set rocks on the lowest part of the hide's frame before leaving the area.

After twenty minutes the male eagle swept in, landed awkwardly on the nest edge with what looked like the bloody skeleton of a small wader-type bird in his talons, and promptly left again. The chick, now 5 ½ weeks old and sprouting its main wing feathers, pulled off a few tiny morsels but the male had left little on the carcass. It dozed on and off for an hour and ten minutes before the male came in again, carrying nothing. I missed his landing but fortunately had the camera turning when the bigger female flew in with a small, young, headless rabbit, and the male, who had probably given her the rabbit, immediately left again.

I was now treated to the spectacle of how much care and concern a mother eagle has for her young chick. She spent more than half an hour feeding the youngster, plucking off small strips of meat and fur from the rabbit with her hooked beak and proffering them with great tenderness. It seemed to me as if she were the inferior being, kow-towing like an old courtier to a young king or queen to be, anxious to please it, to make sure it was happy and satisfied all the time. I filmed her leaving, too, taking the useless wader skeleton in her beak to dump away from the eyrie cliff.

Steve came back for his first night in an eagle hide at about 6.30 p.m. I hiked, or staggered, a bit knackered, most of the way, and reached my camper van an hour later. I found enough energy to drive to a cliff by the sea where buzzards had nested, and to make a pressure cooker meal. As I slid happily into my sleeping bag, I realised that I had taken the best-ever film of eagles on a first visit, just when I was supposed to have retired from it all.

Next morning I was filming the sunny seas and idyllic scenery of Castle Tioram and the beautiful island of Eilean Shone, where once I had lived, when Steve joined me. He too had enjoyed great success with the eagles and filmed several feedings.

I wanted a rest day before my own night-time vigil in the eagle hide so we just drove to film the main eagle cliff and I filmed a limping roe doe trying to find a way through a forestry fence. Steve then took me to a whinchat's nest he had found with 4 semi-fledged chicks, which were, unusually, all facing inwards. About six yards away we draped a sheet of canvas over some hide poles I'd bought in Spain and, to my surprise, it worked! I had been in the 'hide' for only ten minutes when the parent birds began landing on bracken stems and taking grubs and insects to their young in the ground nest. That was a nice little bonus.

I bought some food supplies for what I intended to be my last all-night stint in an eagle hide, then drove Steve to the long glen which held my old eyries 18 and 19, at the end of what I'd called the 'killer trek' from Wildernesse, as he wanted to check them. I didn't go with him as I felt I needed to conserve all my energy for the tough night ahead. I regretted that when I went to pick him up four hours later. Both eyries had roosting feathers all over them but had not been used for breeding, yet on his way back he had seen a young eagle, with the typical white immature wing patches, flying over the glen with an adult female. The mother eagle had flown low over a herd of red deer, then the youngster had flown down, picked up a deer calf in its talons, taken it up to about 250 feet and dropped it onto rocks. Both eagles had then gone down to feed on it.

'It would have made a great piece of film,' said Steve.

I agreed, knowing that if a young eagle finds that it can kill young deer fairly easily, it will try and try again, but it was too late for me to go back now. We drove to the nesting eagles and I was glad to find I felt a lot better on the long trek in than I had before. As we neared the eyrie buttress, the male eagle came flying over and began hovering right above us. I was a bit late in unzipping the camera but got some useable, if somewhat shaky, footage. The bird looked enormous in the photo lens, looming and ominous as if shaking his wings and saying 'Get out of here!'

In the nest the chick was fine but when the female shot in at 9.04 p.m. I missed her and only heard the brief double swish of her wings as she landed. The chick had been asleep and so didn't warn me with the 'keeyoo' calls it usually makes when it sees a parent coming. She tried to feed the chick but it evidently wasn't hungry for it refused to eat. She left after half an hour, taking more old remains with her. The male came in briefly, as if to assess the prey situation, and I got him coming in and leaving. The mother returned just after dusk.

I spent an agonising night. I could not sleep at all and neither could I straighten out. I got cramp in my legs and the only way I could rest them was by lying on my back and putting my feet high up on the hide's side, near the roof. It was hellish altogether!

The female stood by her chick all night, all her movements gradually slowing down, her white under eyelids often showing as she dozed, then slept with her head down her back, behind one wing. She stood to windward too, definitely guarding her chick. The view through the camera was too dark at 11.15 p.m. to film anything and it stayed like that until about 4.15 a.m. At 4.24 a.m., at what was really dawn, she slowly crept across the nest and began to pluck bits off some carcass and feed the chick. When the eaglet had eaten enough, its white crop distended like a tennis ball, my camera tape ended, although it was comical to watch the mother trying to get the youngster to swallow more when it didn't want to. I thought that I should have some great material, as I had always wanted more of the night guarding of the chick by the female, showing her obvious and tender solicitude towards it.

Satisfied that her bairn had eaten enough, she looked about, stared into space, walked to the edge of the nest and gave me a superb flying sequence, as this time she didn't come towards and past the hide as before but winged powerfully away to my right and all along the eyrie cliff, up the glen and round its far corner. I then got some interesting chick behaviour, including it stamping once, twice, three times on the remains of a dead seagull, instinctively practising killing talon strikes. I was a bit peeved when Steve came to walk me out a quarter hour early as the female had just come back around the cliff and was about to come in, but I couldn't complain as I'd got more best-ever material. 'Are you still alive?' were his first words. I was very tired, my hips, elbows, indeed all my joints hurting and stiff after the excruciating night, and on the trek out I asked Steve to go slowly. I knew, though, that I'd got the final sequences of eagles on the nest at night and never need do a night stint again. Two more daytime visits would give me the complete story of behaviour at the nest, though I still needed hunting sequences if I could get them. Steve had been a great help, for on my own I probably would not have got that big hide up there. I certainly would not have felt like doing so. I owed him a lot but he refused any payment apart from the Fort William wellies! In the afternoon we hiked down to a ruined castle on a sea beach where otters were sometimes seen but none showed up that day. Ay well, ye canna win all the time.

For two days there had been loud ominous clonking from below Mi Caballo, my old camper van, so I nursed him carefully back to Hawick and booked him into my friendly garage. I got a shock a few days later when the bill came in - £527! The offside near main spring had broken and the drive shafts had to be renewed. I had been lucky to drive on it at all, never mind so far. There had been a pile of new orders, though - and nice, juicy cheques - for my wildlife videos and books and, after all, nothing was too much for my beloved old horse.

Back in my tiny garret I copied all the new Hi8 eagle film onto VHS tape and, my goodness, I could see that I did have some truly fabulous material, now that I could view it on a big TV screen. I now wanted to film the eaglet's first flight and secure some hunting footage, which would give me a fine one-hour sequel to Eagle Mountain Year which I could call Living with Eagles. I could then pack in eagles for good! Until 2 July, when I was due to work with Steve again, I mainly repaired and decorated my noisy little flat so that I could sell it more easily. I had bought cheap, which never pays.

On the way back up I paused to film the misty islets on the lochans of Rannoch Moor and also a hunting buzzard flying forward, hovering, forward again, hovering and doing this twice more before dropping like a stone, pouncing on prey. I think it missed, for it swerved to the right then rose again to repeat the technique. Steve and I first went to check the nest in the windiest glen, which the eagles had deserted, leaving one egg with a hole in it. He wondered if the hole had been made by ravens after the pair deserted and he sent it to the Min. of Ag. laboratory at Lasswade for analysis.

On 3 July we climbed back up to the hide, Steve surprised that I was going faster than before, but the earlier treks as well as the long rest (and a few bike rides) had done my legs good. Steve started powering up the buttress with a pile of heather strapped to his pack. I picked up a single sprig of heather as Steve stopped, glared and said 'Are you sure you can manage that?' I replied 'Nope. But I'll try. If it gets too heavy I'll have to abandon it!' I picked a fair clump and joined him at the hide and while he set up my camcorder I weaved the new heather into the netting as the first lot had withered to brown clumps. The chick, which was clearly a female, now seemed huge and pecked at bits although there was almost no food in the nest. She excreted three times, squirting whirling white dollops into the void, so she must have been well fed earlier. She also trampolined a lot, flapping hard and strengthening her wing muscles. By the time Steve came for a second overnight stint at 7 p.m., the adults had not come in. I told Steve I was not worried about this. When an eaglet is about eight days old, the females often take a 'vacation' for a few days and the male dumps food once a day, or twice in twenty-four hours if he's a very good provider.

I camped by the buzzards' sea cliff again, having to be quick even about having a pee as the pestilential midges were out in force. I swatted most of them but some got me and one eye was swollen for a brief while.

Next day Steve told me he had got both eagles on the nest, the female twice, coming in finally in near darkness to guard the chick. We trekked up the long glen where he'd seen a young eagle kill a deer calf but after a three- hour wait, no eagles appeared. After lunch in the village we went to look for otters on a beautiful pine-wooded sea peninsula which I hoped to rent from the Forestry Commission. We saw no otters, but halfway along the hard trek I realised with panic that I no longer had my camera pack on my back. I recalled removing it when I took off my jacket because of the heat and tied it around my waist. But where had that happened? We hiked up an eastern gorge then re-did half the trek again, searching everywhere, but we found neither the camcorder nor pack. We drove to the nearest village, rang the police in Fort William and left all the details. We drove back and did the last half of the trek again but still, no luck. At dusk I told Steve that if we didn't find it tomorrow, then that was the absolute end for me – there'd be no more wildlife filming at all. I would go home straight away. I could not afford to replace £1,500 worth of camera gear but I would offer a £100 reward to anyone who did find it. What a disastrous day! I drove him to his mother's home then camped in the little quarry.

It rained all night and as the thick bracken and other undergrowth was soaking wet, we bought some waterproof trews at a local outdoors shop and tackled the wearisome peninsula trek again, zig-zagging wider than before. Suddenly I heard a cry: 'Here it is!' and Steve plucked my camera pack from a bracken patch! I recalled then we had rested atop a small hillock as Steve had said we could get a better view of otters on the beach from there, and I must have removed it at that point. I had offered him the £100 reward if he found it before me, so I had to pay up – and did. He deserved more than that anyway for all his help. I was so grateful to have it back I just fell on him, my arms around his embarrassed shoulders and all. I could not have sustained such a loss; it would have knocked right out of me any desire to continue filming wildlife, as I would also have lost the finest tape, one which also had on it the best of the brown bear from my recent trip to Spain. The miracle was that, despite being left out in the rain overnight, the camcorder still worked fine and all the tapes were dry.

14

A Team of Eagles and Drama at the Nest

I could not have guessed, when Steve and I tackled the high mountain behind the great sea cliff the next day, hoping to film the great raptors hunting, that I was to have the most amazing experience I had ever had with eagles. We hiked about a mile from the minor road down towards the sea, then went left and started going up, up, up until we were on top of the cliff and overlooking the island of Mull. We looked down over a 4 ft-high sheep wall, almost on the edge of the cliff, and saw far below us, heading north above the rocky beach, an eagle which was being harassed by a motley pack of five hooded crows and a few larger ravens. It did not seem flustered but kept flapping purposefully along. Then we saw a bigger eagle, the female, flying behind but slightly below the mobbing pack. She increased her speed, wings beating faster, went right underneath them and then, with what seemed the utmost ease, turned over on her left side, extended her right foot and neatly grabbed one of the ravens with her talons. She just plucked it out of the sky, like a giant sparrowhawk plucking a chaffinch.

All this time I was desperately trying to get the camera out of its pack, unroll it from its protective towel, get the battery out of its compartment and onto the camera. I fixed it onto the tripod and lifted the lot over the wall, ready to shoot - but I was too late! She had now turned south and was beating away, the sooty black form of the young raven dangling from her right foot, its tail hanging below like a fan, and pursued by the pack of hoodies and ravens. I was still trying to get onto her and push the button when I saw that the male eagle had turned and was also flying south, although slightly above his mate's flight path and, again, apparently taking little notice of the mobbing birds, none of which dared go too close anyway. They vanished round the last high bluffs as I was pushing the button and did not come back. Curses! I missed one of the greatest sequences I could ever have filmed. It was clear the eagles had been working as a team, the male going as a decoy, attracting the ravens and crows to pursue and harass him while the female stole up from behind and below, out of their sight, until near enough to pluck their dinner from the sky.

We trekked even higher and perched on the topmost part of the cliff, above a terrible drop, and located the eagle pair busily sharing the raven carcass on a grassy green slope, too far away to film. I had to be content with filming heath-spotted and marsh orchids and some fine yellow flags waving in the breeze. Next day we repeated the trek, hoping to catch some similar behaviour, but on reaching the same sheep wall, we saw both eagles high overhead and heading north at great speed. We found out why – there were many hikers about, and three shepherds came with nine dogs and began gathering the sheep. The hills were alive with the sound of humans. We left.

Next day I was back in the eagle hide for a ten-hour stint, although again I found the climb hard and felt that my old legs had done a little too much work recently. I got more good material, though. The eaglet had a full crop and spent over an hour preening its back, underwings and shoulders, the last while lying down! I got it yawning, hooking nest sticks about with its beak, tearing at prey – a red deer calf carcass - and half-lifting it twice. It jumped about, trampolining with flapping wings, standing up and fanning its tail out to preen the feathers and doing what I called the Hottentot stretches, with wings high and head down, almost touching the nest sticks. I last filmed it on the edge of the nest peering down at some red deer that had gathered below the eyrie.

Steve came in for his last night's stint and as he was running short of film I left my camcorder, saying that if he bust it I'd cancel his cheque! Next day we found he'd got much the same material as I had. As he had now landed a commission to film red deer on Rannoch Moor, we agreed to work eagles again for the last time in ten days' time, arranging to meet at the ferry on 20 July.

On the way back I had an abortive meeting at the Glencoe Outdoor Centre with whom I'd been negotiating sales of my wildlife videos; they only wanted ten on a sale-or-return basis, not actually to buy any, so I took them away. On my own again, as ever. As I drove up Hawick High Street, the local fire brigade was out in force as Woolworths was on fire, only a few doors away from my flat. I half-hoped my little garret had gone up too – when all your gear has gone, you have nowt left to worry about! The fire was put out in three hours but as I went through my door I felt it almost a miracle that I'd got 'home' alive and had not had a heart attack on one of those vicious climbs. I hoped I could do just one more stint and get the eaglet's first flight. Then eagles would be over for ever, at least for me, and wee Stevie could go on to become the ace wildlife cameraman.

On 13 July I did a 20-miler on my bike, beating a rival cyclist who'd had my measure the time before. Simple pleasures! I was also happy to find that my weight had gone back to over 12 stone; the eagle treks had done me good, my legs had thickened up with more muscle and I was in much better shape than the miserable 11 stone 6 lbs of the last two years.

It had been raining heavily all the previous day and night so when I met Steve at 11 a.m. on 20 July we felt sure it would be a wasted day. By midday, though, the skies were clearing and we decided to give it a go. We took a big chance and drove up the private forestry road, which was usually locked but which cut a useful 1 ½ miles from our trek. If we were caught, so what? This was, after all, the last hurrah! The climb up seemed easier and as we had seen through the binoculars that the eaglet was still in the eyrie, I kept the camera out, going first up the last steep stretch in case it exploded out of the nest.

Steve titivated the hide as I slid in, made sure my lens was clear and left. I filmed the eaglet over some twenty minutes, then it began to rain, so heavily that I had to turn the camera well down to keep the lens dry. Suddenly the eaglet began to call loudly. I switched the camera on and tried to get it up and focussed on the nest, but everything happened too fast. The male swept in, the chick hurried to meet him. I heard a scuffle and when I got to focus on the ledge, the eaglet was gone! Only the male was on the nest and he was looking down.

I could hear the eaglet still calling from lower down but was it on some lower rocks or ledge, or even on the ground? I could not see it through the lens, nor through the peephole in the front of the hide. Hell! I filmed the male anxiously looking around the nest and downwards again, and then leaving the eyrie.

After a long wait, almost an hour, I decided that if it was on the ground it could walk half a mile overnight and we'd never see it again. I can't end my film like this, I thought. I took a big chance, left the hide and very carefully stalked towards the 'k yow' calls. The eaglet was standing on the second ledge below the eyrie, only eight feet up, as if it had dropped straight down and not flown at all. I filmed it there, using my hand-held camera, for a minute. I wondered if I should explode it into the open myself as it had left the nest under 'natural' circumstances, but decided against it.

I sneaked backwards. The female came over, no doubt wondering what had gone wrong or to see if the male had left any prey on the nest. I don't know if she saw the eaglet on the low ledge but she came very close. Because I was now afraid that the chick might fly, I kept on it, not on the mother. It did not fly and after she had gone I got safely back into the hide, making sure that she did not see me do so. Through the lens I located the eaglet and shot what few glimpses I could, as a birch tree between me and the ledge was being blown back and forth by a strong wind.

Steve arrived on time for his stint and said that he could not see the eaglet in the eyrie. I explained how the male had come in fast and suddenly, and in its eager rush to meet him the chick had obviously fallen off the ledge. We then had to decide what to do. He took my safety rope, the one I hoped would stop me falling into the deep rock fissure if I dozed off during the night, put a lasso over the birch tree and tried to pull it down, but he was too light. I left the hide again and together we hauled it down, Steve tying it to a huge rock. I got back into the hide as Steve pulled down another tiny birch bush on a rocky pinnacle that also slightly obscured the eaglet, to make sure the view was now clear for us to film. Oddly, the eaglet showed little fear as we did all this but just watched us with curiosity, and I indulged my usual habit of talking to it in reassuring tones. While on the new ledge the eaglet had done no trampolining but did plenty of preening so was clearly not too upset by its drop. The ledge only measured about four feet by eighteen inches so there was far less room on it than on the huge eyrie ledge. After I left Steve in the hide, the chick watched my descent with curiosity, again showing no fear as it did not try to retreat or flinch as I passed by.

It was soon clear that the small size of the low ledge was giving the adults big problems. Steve saw the female come with a rabbit onto the nest ledge and she and the chick called to each other, but she could not see the youngster because of the thick overhang of vegetation. She left, came in again in near dark and the same thing happened. The eaglet was not fed all night. It rained so heavily next day that we left the eagles alone, caught up with our chores and bought a large chunk of lamb flank. It was a very good thing we did, for when we climbed back to the buttress there were no signs of prey on the nest nor on the low ledge but the eaglet was still there. It was obvious that the adults could not get into the small space between the ledge and the birch trees to feed it.

As I filmed away, Steve climbed up and round to just below and left of the ledge and threw the meat, which landed a metre beyond the eaglet. She soon found it, though, grabbing it with one set of talons and rending it for dear life. She was clearly ravenous and we might well have saved her life. At one point she held the meat up high in her beak, so it showed clearly in the lens. How obliging!

For the film's narrative, Steve filmed me getting into and out of the hide and titivating it with new foliage, then we tore out all its heather, rolled up the netting sides and carried it and all our gear out and down the steeps, Steve taking some good stills of the eaglet as we left. Again it showed no fear of us and didn't fly. We would have to check it again, and feed it again if was still there until it was ready to fly, as the adults could not even drop prey onto so small a ledge. Rains and gales next day forced us to take the day off, apart from bits on linnets and whinchats, and I was glad because my hips and elbows were again painful. I had a nagging fear that maybe the eaglet could not fly well, that it might just have bad co-ordination, as happens, though rarely, with young eagles. If it was gone tomorrow, I hoped at least we would see and film it with its parents.

On 24 July we again drove the full distance up the private forestry road. 'This time really is the last hurrah,' I told Steve. 'Even if it has not flown yet!' We climbed up and the eaglet was still on the low ledge but looking much perkier after our big meal. Steve tossed in two small slices of liver and she found them quickly and demolished them. I kept filming as he moved up higher to heave in the much heavier new chunk of lamb flank, and when she walked to the front of the ledge and started looking down, then out, then down, then out, I felt sure she would go this time.

Steve hurled up the lamb flank, I saw it land and then she took off. I captured all that but lost her for a few seconds as she dropped low behind a ridge. I then picked up on her again as she soared down the long glen. She looked fabulous, huge wings wide, gliding and tilting from side to side, this way and that, as by pure instinct she discovered what her wings could achieve. On and on she went down the glen, then banked gently to the right and vanished behind a knoll on a ridge.

We hiked on down and up the far hill onto the ridge and soon found her again, standing in the grass on a moor in the wide sheltered glen beyond the ridge. It was open there, with no trees or bushes to obscure her from her parents' sight. I filmed her there, walking and even breaking into a brief run. We turned and saw the male eagle flying right above the eyrie, and maybe he had seen her flying off. She had certainly not been abandoned and they would locate her soon enough. It had been right to feed her and get her off that low ledge. I just wished she had scoffed the second lamb flank that Steve had hurled in before she had flown, but at least I'd got what I had most wanted – the first flight of a young eagle which I had seen three times but never filmed. We kept watch from a far hill for a while but then felt we had better get out after seeing the male launch from a high crag and soar over his daughter before going off in a wide arc to the east, maybe to fetch his mate.

Back in my old camper in the wee quarry I felt done in but euphoric, for what Steve and I had shot in this last season would surely be the greatest eagle film of all time. Next day was hot and sunny and we could have tackled the great sea cliff again but I had a lot of business to attend to - apart from checking, annotating and editing all the film tapes - and as some noisy neighbours below my little garret were on holiday that week, I could get on with my work in peace. I called in at Glencoe on the way back and was delighted to hear that they would buy some of my videos up front. Even so, I felt down and dead when working in the flat the next day. I'd won. In my 68th year I had tasted victory, yet there was a sense of anti-climax. No more eagles at the eyrie. What lies ahead now? A walking stick and a retirement flat in Worthing? It seemed likely. My hips were hurting a lot and I couldn't disguise a limp as I shopped in the High Street. Little did I realise that I was by no means finished with eagles that season. Ahead lay yet more extraordinary adventures.

At this time I met a professional photographer friend who told me he had been given a licence to take still photos of sea eagles at the nest on Mull, provided he work with an Aberdeen-based BBC crew. The crew, though, had used a moveable canvas hide, putting it up and taking down every time they went in and out, causing unnecessary disturbance, and the sea eagles had failed. I told him they must have been stupid amateurs and how, two years previously, I had told the Scottish Natural Heritage official who issued the licences that I would teach such crews how to make 'invisible' hides, which would go unnoticed by eagles. He had not only spurned my offer, but had refused to grant me a licence, saying that the only one issued that year was for a Gaelic crew to bring the eagle story to schools. At any rate, he said,

I had done far more that most eagle photographers and it was time I let younger men have their chances. I laughingly told my pal that I do get angry sometimes, but never bitter.

On 3 August I was back with Steve and we hiked up to the wall above the sea cliff. It was very hot, the eagle pair did not show and all I got was a burnt face. Steve told me he had dragged a big ewe carcass up there during the previous winter and the eagles had lasted over a month feeding from it. He couldn't go back for two weeks because of constant rain but on the third week he filmed them at it and they fed from the carcass for at least another week. He reckoned that they hunted the mountain in the mornings and if they got a grouse, hare or rabbit, they would not go to the ewe that day. If not, they used the sheep as a back-up supply, a food store of sorts.

Next day we laboured up to our now-empty hide site on top of the buttress. We feared one or two large brown lumps on the eyrie ledge and the low one might be a dead eaglet, but they turned out to be mud that had been exposed by recent rains. We trekked back down to the ridge to view where the eaglet had landed and found no sign of a dead one there either, thank heaven.

What we did find, however, was that the eaglet had tried to get back to its nest – on foot! We came back to the buttress from a different angle and I found a small rocky spur on which the eaglet must have perched, as there was some white down on the heather all around it and a few white splashes. There was also a little trail of down further up, which ran out, I assumed, where she had taken off for her second flight. Where had she landed, though, as she surely could not have flown far?

We soon found out. We struck off to go left, away from the eyrie face, but after half a mile I spotted a dark dot on top of the hill, against the glowing horizon. Through the binoculars I could see it was the huge form of the eaglet! I had no time to extract the camera from its pack and set it on the tripod in case she flew. So I yelled to Steve to provide his right shoulder as a fulcrum, and I filmed her from there. Suddenly he shouted 'Look out! The female's flying towards us!'

I looked up to see that the mother eagle had launched herself from the rocky ridge above the eyrie and was heading our way. Still using Steve's shoulder as a fulcrum I got onto her, her first brief hard flapping turning into a glorious glide past us, only about thirty yards away, before she landed on a rock some three hundred yards below us. The eaglet must have seen her, for then it flew towards her but landed on the ground fifty yards away. She then hopped-flew onto another rock, clearly enticing it closer by flying, to make it fly too. We had achieved another of our targets by seeing mother and chick in close contact. It seemed they would not be needing the two lamb chops I had carried up in case we found the eaglet in dire straits, but I left them in a prominent position anyway.

As we stumbled-hiked down and out I told myself I need never 'work' eagles again. Mission accomplished. And yet… I was looking forward to giving my sweaty

Soon after returning from five years in Spain, I found myself up a cliff in Cornwall filming a peregrine falcon family. These three chicks, calling for their mother, all flew successfully.

At my first wild camp after the falcons I was woken at dawn by Dartmoor ponies rubbing their rumps against my camper van.

When making a wildlife survey for The National Trust in Cornwall, I often saw foxes, like this young vixen.

The goshawk, pound for pound, is the fiercest and most voracious of our birds of prey.

Two adult ospreys in their nest. Both hunt fish to feed their chicks.

A long-eared owl chick in the nest looks quite comical with its black face.

My barn owls soon found the dead chicks on the outside feed table.

It wasn't long before a lonely female kestrel spotted the chicks on the feed table and came for one, at most two, a day. She was so lovely, became quite tame, and I was sad when the goshawks killed her in the third winter.

At my desk, I was too slow to get film of the sparrowhawk's kill but she caught and ate a chaffinch, then came back to the table with a full gut!

I had a large byre at the farmhouse and decided to try and raise barn owls. Here, David Ramsden of the Barn Owl Trust in Devon hands me the first of six owlets.

In the morning they soon settled down in their new tea chest home up in the loft of my byre. When approached they swayed and hissed but never tried to bite or clutch me with their talons.

When they first began to fly they hid from my approach in the 'cubicles' made where the roof rafters met the floor of the loft.

So the owls could fly in and out of the loft easily I propped open a dormer window and made special pine pole perches.

Surprisingly, Small Chick was the first to fly beyond the bird table. She got her wings wet in a rain shower but managed to make it back up to the loft without help.

Cheeky colourful jays were also bird feed table robbers. I did not begrudge them, they lightened up the place.

The 'paradise' farmhouse I found in a huge Borders forest, with its own salmon burn.

I fixed a big black plastic barrel in a lodgepole pine near the house and Browny and Blacky took to it at once, as a nest box.

When I spotted a rare pine marten (not supposed to inhabit this forest) I swiftly removed the barrel and installed it in the loft, as a second nest box.

After seeing three golden eagles on the eastern end of the forest I climbed the hill beyond and found not an eagle eyrie but a lone peregrine chick in a high nest up a narrow gorge.

Swallows raised two broods in the byre below the owls' loft, undeterred by my constant comings and goings.

I learnt to drive a digger and dug out a 70 yard lake, then stocked it with trout.

The main eyrie of five in Haweswater, strangely quite near a public footpath.

My 'paradise' farmhouse in the Borders in winter snow. At 1,100 feet it was often over a foot deep in snow, yet not a flake was to be seen in my shopping town of Hawick.

From a town flat, and largely due to my eagle enthusiast pal Steve Phillipps, I launched my most successful eagle season ever. And on the way, we filmed otters.

We first filmed what we called the 'windy glen' pair, male on left and the female trying to incubate a single egg, lying low, on the right. She was a tolerant bird and did everything at the nest I could have wished for my film.

After Steve carried the hide up the steep buttress, a climb I might have funked had I been alone, we set up my kind of 'invisible' hide overlooking the best of three eyries. It is just left of centre in the photo.

The kind of moorland and peat bog country our best pair of eagles hunted.

The mother eagle, having fed her chick until its crop was full, prepares to guard it all night.

*She feeds it beak to beak with the utmost delicacy. I once
counted 173 slivers of meat tendered in one feeding session.*

During the day, when the eaglet is well grown and fed, she often perched, and sometimes slept, on a bow shaped branch not far from the eyrie.

The whole eagle family. Male on the left, larger female on the right, and below her the well grown young female.

Another fully grown eaglet watches with apparent envy as its mother flies away.

Steve Phillipps, who has worked with Mike since the early 1990s, filming on Snowdon for the ITV series Wild Islands *in which Mike helped to film golden eagles.*

Golden eagle hunting its typical terrain, and banking to its right.

The huge nest in a larch tree.

The female eagle from the sea cliff pair at sheep carrion in winter snow. She was the biggest eagle we ever filmed. The pair used the carcass as a meat larder, returning to it if hunting was not successful in the mornings.

The peregrines in the Welsh quarry. This is the male with his chicks.

After a long search, we finally found twin chicks in a new eyrie for our favourite pair. They gave me a wonderful 70th birthday, one feeding from steak in my hand as the mother watched, preening quite unconcerned. She knew me of old.

Another eaglet two years later was not so friendly when Steve went near to toss in some meat and she tried to bat him away with her wings.

body a good swab down in Mi Caballo but after I'd taken Steve home to Kilchoan, I found a foreigner in a red car in the wee quarry. I lied that I had permission from the owner but said that he could stay there too, if he wanted to. He said there were far too many 'midgets' for him and in a few minutes he left, leaving me in peace once more.

A more restful two days followed and I filmed damselflies laying eggs in a pond, the male clasping the female round the neck with their anal claspers and seeming to dash them down time after time to deposit their eggs onto reeds at the water's surface. No female emancipation in the damselfly world! Attempts at adders resulted in just one shot of one zig-zag patterned tail vanishing into the grasses, but I did get a superb sequence of a buzzard flying, hovering, flying, hovering again and diving to catch a vole, then swooping back up with it and eating it on the wing while holding it in its right foot's talons... a large herd of red deer stags on the skyline, all shaking their heads to drive off flies, hinds flicking their big ears on a ledge overlooking Eigg and Skye... an eagle flying over the tops of the windiest glen, landing in a cleft and preening for over two hours... perhaps best of all, though, two ravens flying to a sheep carcass then one repeatedly jumping into the air from the ground, teaching her youngster: 'This is how you fly, this is how you do it!' for it copied her actions and yet it had seemed to fly well enough before.

On 8 August we had one more stab at 'our' eagles. We slogged up, had a fruitless two-hour wait, then spied a herd of red deer moving on the highest crest to the south, some walking, some running, with three of the hinds hurrying over and down a steep slope, almost a cliff. As I got the camera going, we saw the cause – soaring high above the deer was the big eaglet, her white immature wing patches showing clearly, and just above her was her mother, who may actually have shown her the deer. I wondered if at this stage, the young eagle would recognise the deer as prey. It seemed, at any rate, a lovely ending to that season's eagle saga and would surely be an end, or near end, sequence for my film.

15

A HOSPITAL NIGHTMARE BUT
MAKING THE EAGLE MOVIE

Most of that autumn I spent going to and from the Highlands, trying to find a new wild home and doing serendipity wildlife filming as I went, such as an oystercatcher showing her chick how to find and prise open mussels on Loch Duich. I entered into negotiations to buy a sweet little cottage in very Spanish-looking country on the edge of Loch Kishorn, where I also filmed a black-throated diver chick swimming along beside its mother, then climbing on her back. The cottage fell through when I found the local farmer driving his tractor through its garden to reach a cowfield behind, and that he had rights to do so. After several meetings, some new reader friends near Drimnin on the west coast offered to rent me an isolated cottage above the sea in an oak and birch wood. It seemed ideal and I spent two weeks there working on my eagle film script which was now called At Home with Eagles. But the Drimnin dream ended during two rainy, muddy days when local crofters drove a herd of cows right up to and around the cottage and said they would be over-wintering there – as usual. Now, I have nothing against cows; I like milk in my tea and am very fond of minced steak, but I could not put up with their methane stench and stinking dollops so close to the cottage and often in the porch itself, not to mention their frequent, loud and inane bellows when I went in and out.

Back in the little High Street garret, I worked on the eagles material and kept the filming side alive by shooting river scenes like little dabchicks diving, huge salmon migrating up a long concrete weir and spawning, a heron grabbing a small duckling in its dagger beak, turning it upside down and swallowing it head first, its little paddles going down last. I had now decided to make a film about all life on a river and Hawick's River Teviot seemed a brilliant starting point. At Drimnin, too, I had filmed Atlantic seals diving in the sea and hauling out onto rocks, which would fit in to where a river ends. It was when I was driving back from Drimnin on a dark and rainy day, the track out so long, almost interminable, with three gates to open, that I realised that this had been the tenth time I had tried to rent or buy a last wild place in the Highlands since returning from Spain. Why did my love for the Highlands make me keep bashing my head against brick walls? (I'd had a fainting spell on one hard trek at Drimnin.) I had wanted only to get great eagle sequences this year and had succeeded beyond my wildest dreams. I had often written that part of loving is knowing when to let go so now, maybe, I should love and leave. As the ferry ploughed across to Corran and the mainland, I said my adios to the western Highlands. And as I worked on the eagle script over the next few weeks – difficult, as neighbours below were moving elsewhere and were banging about - I began to think of returning to Sussex, the gentler South Downs where my love of nature first began. That retirement flat on Worthing seafront and a walking stick suddenly seemed attractive options. I even rang an old school pal who ran a campsite, who told me that I'd be welcome any time and could camp free as his personal guest until I found a new home.

By 15 November I had worked out 150 sequences on the eagles film editing script and a week later had it basically finished. Now all I needed was for Steve to visit and help me with the editing machines, because with modern technology I had proved to be a total dinosaur. A bill for £967 to get Mi Caballo through his MOT was a shock, but nothing compared with the nightmare that followed when, at the end of the month, I went to the loo and saw a splash of bright blood over the bowl and seat. At the local cottage hospital a fine doctor called Pat Manson examined me, found nothing wrong but said that I would have to undergo some tests. On 5 December I went back for a colonoscopy by consultant surgeon David Bremner, who said he would pump air into my bowel and shove a telescope up me. 'Better than binoculars, I suppose', I replied, which raised a laugh from him and the nurse. He found nothing significant but said he would send me to the Borders General Hospital near Melrose for a barium enema, which would tell 'the full story' of my bowels. At least there was no need for medication – yet. I hiked back to my flat in a snowstorm, feeling like Dr Zhivago towards the end of his life. The radio said the snow was everywhere, even between Bognor Regis and Chichester where I would have been had I had obeyed a desire to go south before my gut problems began. Alexandra Bastedo and her husband Patrick Garland had written offering me the use of their annexe near Chichester if I wanted to hunt for a new home in Sussex. 'I often wish you lived nearer', she had written. Well I would head down, but needed to get these pesky medical tests completed first.

I spent a lonesome and freezing Christmas in my poky flat, not turning up the gas fire too much because of the cost. 'No one wants a sick old man', one of my favourite older readers had once written to me. How utterly true, I thought, but I've usually been on my own at Christmas and I'm on me tod again now! It's just not so easy when you're getting older. I felt dispirited and that I'd come to the end of my real life, my active life. It wouldn't be any different in Worthing, just lonely walks along the promenade or beach, and it would be the same wherever I went, probably worse than along the Teviot River! That thought forced me out and I soon felt that there were worse places to be than Wilton Park at Christmas. Beautiful crystals falling like tinkerbell mist from the thawing branches, swirls of sunlight on serene surfaces, two mute swans in the upper pool and the gulls, ducks, dabchicks all in motion. I had the camera on the tripod as a resplendent goosander drake drifted by with two females who swam and dived all round him. Then I filmed some of about twenty salmon spawning under Lawson Bridge, three with whitish fungus on their torpedo bodies, and the ducks which kept comically falling over as they scrambled for my tidbits on the icy weir.

I got back to find the film *5 Card Stud* on television, and it had just started, the western starring Robert Mitchum and Dean Martin which I had visited on the outdoor set in Durango, Mexico, with my Canadian wild dog Booto some thirty years earlier. During a tense scene Booto had escaped from my truck and run across the set. I had feared a public lambasting but tough director Henry Hathaway had declared him the best thing in the scene. Now, for the first time, I saw it on the screen, and watched Booto run and give a little bark which I did not recall hearing at the time. I was copying the film onto the VHS video so it was wonderful to have at last a record of old Booto's cameo role.

The best and most exciting time now was when Steve arrived by train and bus to help me make the master Hi 8 tape of At Home with Eagles from the six full tapes we had shot, using my shooting script as a guide. It was a hard, nerve-racking, brainstorming period but by 7.30 p.m. on the second day we had it licked. It came out at one hour and 42 minutes, a little shorter than Eagle Mountain Year, but it looked fabulous. Next day I hiked Steve round the Laurie bridge, he amazed at the close salmon still spawning and the tameness of the mallards and other birds as I fed them. I gave him a cheque for £150 plus a fiver for his bus fare to Carlisle, and he deserved every penny, the wee genius. There was no way I could have done it alone and it was far cheaper than hiring a studio. The amazing thing was that the Canon camcorder held out all the way, through multiple windings and re-windings. Steve said all I had to do was to watch the program and make my own commentary on Hi 8 tape which we could transfer onto a special track on the master any time we liked. Next day I watched our film and knew it to be the best I had ever made or ever will make.

My euphoria was brief, though – my medical nightmare was about to start.

A packet dropped on my mat saying I had to go for a barium meal (a euphemism for 'enema', no doubt) at 2.30 p.m. on Thursday, 25 January. And I had to starve myself for two days first to clear the gut. And I had to arrange my own transport, as most patients were unable to drive afterwards. It sounded horrendous. A snow blizzard was blowing when the day came but I reached the Borders General Hospital safely, rather dismayed by my first sight of it as, with its huge chimney, it looked like a giant charnel house or as if it had its own crematorium. The doctor, though, was reassuring as he laid me down naked, let the barium into my rear and took photos with the machine while turning me this way and that. Some barium leaked out when he lowered its bottle, then he blew me up for more photos and I had a job to retain the air, but he congratulated me for doing so, I didn't like the look of a black triangle that almost filled one part of the bowel, and he took several photos of that area but said nothing. It looked like a blockage of some kind to me. It was all over in twenty minutes. I wanted to question him about it but when asked if I could get off the table unaided, I managed to vault off, still retaining the air and barium. The nurse quickly said 'Aye, you're fit' and promptly ushered me into a loo where I had left my clothes in a basket. She added 'You can escape through that door ahead,' and shut the door I'd just come through which, when I turned, had a big sign on it saying 'Do not re-enter'. So I didn't get the chance to question the doctor about the black triangle. I guess they didn't want patients farting barium all over the place.

I felt fine despite the sedative, just a bit blown up, and I drove myself home, but I had to stop four times for noisy expulsions of air and barium into plastic bags, bunging them into roadside bins. Snow was still falling but not settling. I celebrated my safe return with a few drams. As the doctor told me: 'As long as whisky is well diluted, it's OK.' I had replied 'Churchill drank wee diluted drams most of his working life, he was fat, he smoked, but he lived to over 90!' I was told I would hear the result in ten days if all was well, or if more tests were needed. I feared the worst, in fact, but it would be good to know if I was doomed. It would concentrate my mind (or what was left of it) on making speedy provision for my 'estate' and what to leave to whom.

I mooched about on salmon treks, nursing a sprained hip incurred when putting my clothes back on in hospital, wrote many business letters, and then, on 3 February – plop! A thick envelope landed in my hall. I read that the X- rays had revealed a growth on my large intestine and that – to my horror - I had to go into hospital in three days' time and have an operation. And I would be there for a few days. Don't panic! Don't panic! But I think I did. This was the most frightening thing I'd faced in my life. I always dreaded the surgeon's knife, my being put 'out' and at the mercy of others and, also, coming to in the middle of an operation yet unable to move or tell anyone. I was shivering and only partly from the cold, so I shoved on all the fires, heated up water… there was no point now trying to save gas and electricity, if I was to die on an operating table. I immediately consulted Dr Manson who said it probably was cancer but that David Bremner was a leading surgeon in his field and that I was in good hands. I was exceptionally fit and strong for my age, he said, and should get through it well enough. If an operation to remove the growth was necessary I would probably leave hospital in two weeks but it would take me six to twelve weeks to get back to full strength.

The news that day was that one of my favourite film heroes, the wonderful dancer Gene Kelly, had died at 83, as did another hero, Cary Grant. I'd always believed I would go at 83, but now it seemed I'd be lucky to see 68.

I have written ten thousand words in my diaries, detailing all my experiences over the following two weeks. From the time an ambulance drove me, alone, from Hawick Medical Centre to Melrose Hospital I was starved, shaved and emptied and on 8 February came the most terrible day of my life. The nightmare began. I was first in theatre so was given an early injection and, as two theatre nurses wheeled me in, they jollied me along with bright spirited conversation, apparently fascinated by my wild life. I kept saying that the injection had had no effect. Then the anaesthetist came in, made two tests, came nearer... and I knew no more until I came to in a public ward of six beds, with a big orange tube sticking out of my stomach, a catheter up my dick to drain my bladder, and a saline/glucose drip in a vein on my left hand. There was a huge ten-inch wound in my left gut. All the tubes and drain tank were held on a wheeled gantry by the side of my bed and it was painful to move an inch in any direction. One of the beds contained a nutcase returned from failed 'community care' who raved through most of the night, adding to the nightmare.

Next day I was wheeled away for a bath and bang went my modesty. When I insisted on walking back to the ward under my own steam, the nurses said that no one had ever done that before, the day after such an operation. In my drugged state I felt childishly chuffed. Tough guy again!

For two early mornings the night nurse came in, emptied all the urine bottles of the men with prostate cancer irrigation problems, but forgot even to look at my full one. I had to struggle up, shove the catheter up and down and try and pee round it into a hand-held bowl. Damn nightmare! In the end I had to gather all the tubes into one hand, hobble to the loo and empty the bottle myself. I had to take great care as any sharp movement of these tubes hurt like hell. However, after three awful days and nights, I prevailed upon the nurses and doctors to let me pay for an 'amenity room' and be on my own, which at £23.50 a day seemed cheap for comparative paradise, and from then on my recovery was fast. Nicky, the very pretty nurse who had bathed me and washed my hair, was most influential in getting me the room, especially when I lied about needing to get on with my eagle script as I would lose £3,000 if I didn't finish it inside three weeks! As I worked on it, everyone was nice. Surgeon David Bremner popped by several times to see how I was and Alexandra rang a few times, again offering me her farm annexe near Chichester as 'It would be ideal for you to convalesce and Patrick wants you to come down too.' She also sent me some property pages.

My Edinburgh solicitor came with my new will, which I signed. He said I ought to give his firm Power of Attorney because if I died, there would be a lot of money to worry about. I said I intended to get a small seafront pad down south, leave just enough for my bequests and blow the rest myself. He laughed and said that was a good idea. Once the tubes had been removed I took to marching up and down the corridors and stairs, in a lovely blue dressing gown brought to me by a nurse when I said I didn't own one, and I stuck to a tough regime - 352 steps up, two at a time, matched with 352 steps down. Once an orderly came up and said he thought I was overdoing it. I replied I'd been a cycling champ and had trekked round mountains on my own with hefty packs for over thirty years, so perhaps knew my own body better than anyone. On 20 February two nurses took me into a treatment room and, relatively painlessly, removed my stitches, twenty nine of them. Next day, twelve days after the operation, I was released. They said they were sending a car ambulance for me but I replied that I didn't want any special treatment. In the end an orderly came to help me down with my gear and I was driven back to Hawick in a routine Patients' Van with four other geriatric occupants. My wee flat was untouched and the driver helped me up with my case, then dropped me back to the supermarket at the other end of town. After getting two bags of groceries I suddenly felt terribly lonely, almost abandoned, and in the rain now falling found myself shuffling along like an old man. I felt I had been suddenly catapulted into old age.

The operation site still hurt, of course, and was most painful when wind built up. Mr Bremner had told me I still had the top half and bottom quarter of the large bowel – it was the third quarter that he had removed. There was no chance that either wind or constipation could blow the join apart, as it stretched in the same way as the rest of the gut. It was still too early, however, to know whether or not I was cured. When I was a show business reporter I had the last interview with the great Gary Cooper, who shortly before had undergone the same operation, with only ten inches removed – and he had lasted only another six months! I felt reassured when David Bremner told me he had the laboratory report on my piece of gut. It was cancer, but only a large malignant polyp which had not penetrated the bowel wall and my recovery chances were 97%. 'You'll live another fifty years!' he quipped. I still felt I could die tomorrow but now each day proved better than the last as I made small river treks and finally finished the commentary script for my eagle film. But I could still hardly believe it – cancer? Me? The hard facts stared me in the face: it had been an awful shock and my whole outlook had to change. There was no question of returning to a life in the wild, such as I had endured for more than thirty years, with no utilities and only small boat access. Neither could I think of returning to Canada as one would need a clean bill of health, and permanent residence in Spain for an old man living alone might be unwise. I kept thinking of a small seafront flat, about all that I could afford, down south among my youthful nature haunts.

On 8 March my old trekking pal and fellow wildlife enthusiast Jim Crumley came to visit and with his keen interest to goad me on, I showed him the eagles film and managed to record the entire commentary onto three Sony Walkman tapes. Jim said he was very impressed, that I had some amazing material, the best eagle film he had ever seen! Such praise from Jim – without doubt the finest nature writer in Scotland - meant a great deal to me and further inspired me to have videos made so that others could enjoy the spectacle, drama and beauty of these great birds' lives. 'You need never climb those mountains again!' he said, and echoed my own thoughts precisely.

In late March my publishers Jonathan Cape booked me into a Hampstead hotel for two days while I made the At Home with Eagles master tape at JBF studios, had a hundred videos produced and attended to other business. Then I drove down to Alexandra's little animal sanctuary where she cooked me a super fish meal and I moved into her annexe. For the next two weeks I chased around looking at potential flats in the beach areas of Bracklesham, the Witterings, Clymping, even that seafront in Worthing. By far the best seemed to be a small flat on the beach at Seaview Court on Selsey Bill, right near the Pagham Harbour nature reserve. Alex and I twice walked her two big Doberman dogs around East Head and there was a dream-like quality among the sand dunes; we even sunbathed briefly and I liked the area more and more. In the end the flat project fell through, due largely to restrictions imposed by the geriatric mafia of the Residents' Committee: 'No boat on the beach' and the like. A super top-floor flat on the seafront at Littlehampton also fell through when I saw the sleazy stairs and hallway, many low-life youths with guitars sipping beer cans in corridors and alleyways, and was told the area held much of the overflow of DSS cases from London. A drugs dealer had just been evicted from the flat below the one that would have been mine. After lunch with Alex and Patrick at the Chichester Yacht Club, I even looked at some houseboats, but they were a bit ramshackle and over-priced, the canal was full of lily branches, making a rowboat impossible, and it would be fetid in summer and damp in winter.

A two-night business trip to London proved poor business as my editor at Cape told me they did not want to buy my autobiography, my archives, reprint my Canadian book or do a book that he had suggested. Moreover, my royalties for six months had gone down to £163, the lowest ever. My mood did not improve when I went to pick up my At Home with Eagles master tape and a hundred video copies. The tape had already cost £588 to make and the videos now came to £705. I doubted I could sell the videos for more than £9 or £10 each, so wouldn't make much profit, if any. Added to this was the fact that Steve had advised me to get a new fluid head and tripod for my camera and had located a firm in Feltham, Middlesex, who sold good ones at the cheap price of £119, so I drove there and bought them. My savings were taking a real bashing. After a farewell supper with Alex and Patrick, who said they would keep looking for a new Sussex base for me, I drove back to Hawick.

In early May I drove up to Perth to start negotiations to sell my archives to the fine A.K. Bell library and met the head archivist Mike Moir. En route I visited Jim Crumley in Stirling and he took me to the Lake of Menteith to try and film fishing ospreys. No sooner had I set up my new gear on the lakeshore than one sailed over from behind us, diving into the water with talons extended, and I just got onto it as it struggled out with a fish. I filmed it flying along, labouring a little as the fish was almost as long as itself, and shaking a little shower of water from its wings as it went. We then hiked and climbed to a fairly hidden spot not far from a big nest and I got great scenes of the male coming in twice with a fish, the pair changing guard duties, the male eating a fish on a branch peeled white by his constant perchings, the female on another branch. I had a fine lunch and two-hour talks with Mike Moir and his assistant Iain Macrae at Perth library and in the end they paid me £6,000 for my full archives, some seven boxes of diaries, letter, wildlife files and photographs, freeing up space and relieving me of much weight. As I told Mike at the time, they had thrown a very large lifebelt to a man about to drown.

On my 68th birthday, for once not spent watching nesting eagles, I put my garret on the market and started doing it up. No-one came to see it for ten days so I decided to head south again and make another stab at finding a new home in Sussex. On the way I met a reader of mine, Peter Woods, who had a 5-acre patch near Carnforth. He took me to the edge of a huge limestone quarry where I filmed three peregrine falcon chicks on a ledge just below us, and their parents flying in with food.

I next headed on south to meet a reader called Val who had offered to let me use a room in her large, airy flat on the edge of Lewes while she went on a week's holiday to the Appleby Horse Fair. My rent? I had to feed her three parrots! As an added inducement, she added that she had a family of foxes visiting her garden every day. By the time I had reached Lewes and carried a few valuables and essentials from Caballo up to my room I was good and tired, so after an early supper and chat with Val, I went to bed early.

Just after dawn there was a furious knocking at my bedroom door. It was Val, yelling, 'They're there! They're on the lawn, the foxes.' I jumped out of bed, pulling on just my underpants, grabbed my camera and dashed to her bedroom window which, luckily, she had left slightly open. A large vixen was standing on the lawn, letting two cubs, who were almost as big as she was, suckle her teats. Next day, with Val now away at the Appleby Horse Fair, I got up at 4.30 a.m. There were now three big cubs suckling the vixen and I got superb material with close zoom-ins as she stood there, legs straddled, letting them pump her all over the place. I had put out some food - bread with tinned dog food - and twice she ran off under some trees to the left before coming out again and gingerly eating some bits. I had a quick breakfast of tea and raw tomatoes on toast, and when I got back there were five foxes, the others obviously having been joined by the bigger dog fox. Some were looking for small bits of food which I had scattered in some bushes, obviously having been joined by the bigger dog fox. My diary from that day shows how excited I was: 'I'll never get better fox stuff than this!' Four mornings later, the cubs gave me a great display of fighting or, I suppose, of play fighting, because they often reared up, cuffing each other round the ears with their paws, bowling each other over and then diving in, taking mock-bites at the downed ones' throats. Sometimes they would stop suddenly, their ears back, and look all around as if sensing danger.

Of course, during the week Val was away, I dashed around looking for that elusive new seaside home in Sussex. It was when I was filming Canada geese and swans on the beautiful meanders of the river at Cuckmere Haven that I met a friendly coastguard, Alan Godwin, who told me that the best places for possible beach houses were Norman's Bay, Pevensey Bay and Birling Gap. I went to search those areas. I checked many coast road houses for sale but most were very costly - £89,000 being the cheapest - for what were basically shacks, although they had the rights to have boats on the beach. They were also too close together, often only a metre apart. One had three kids' mountain bikes next door, with a large boat with a 60 hp engine on the other side. There'd be no privacy of any kind there. I little realised then how grateful I would come to be to Alan Godwin, and not only for concentrating my property searches in this area of Sussex.

One good thing did happen at that time, though. I was passing through Polegate when I spied Jamie Wood's outdoor shop. I went in and bought a new green Fensman hide with light aluminium poles for just £98. 'I thought you were supposed to be retired!' I said to my reflection in Caballo's mirror as I drove off. When Val returned I spent two more days looking at flats without success, then returned to my attic flat in Hawick to take up an unusual invitation from a man who was becoming Scotland's leading wildlife photographer, Laurie Campbell. He had written that he liked my books and would like to meet up and asked if I would like to film his family of 'fairly tame' badgers? Well, would I! I reached his home near Paxton, Berwickshire in early evening, as dusk was approaching, and when Laurie said we could start right then and there, I wasn't sure what to expect.

16

HAND FEEDING BADGERS, A HUNTING WILDCAT AND A VISIT TO EAGLE ISLAND

Laurie drove us to the grounds of Paxton House, over a field and to within fifty yards of the badgers' sett in a small wood. He had built a small, rickety wooden hide between two small trees and he put me in it before heading eighty yards higher up the wood to read a book I had lent him about badgers, written by Ernest Neal, by means of a miner's torchlight strapped to his head.

I was all scrunched up in the hide and had to sit too near the edge but he had said I could dangle my legs over it if I was too uncomfortable. I figured that was probably not a good idea because of the scent, if not the sight, of them so I stuck it out as I was. I was soon rewarded with my best badger film so far. One cub came out, then another, and in the end I had four fairly well grown badger cubs running about, knocking into each other, rooting about for grubs and going in and out of both major holes of the huge sett. After two hours the light was too poor for my camera, so I shoved a white bag through a slit which Laurie had carved in the side of the hide, to tell him that I had filmed enough.

He came and walked me out and I thought that would be that for the night. Instead, he took me back to where he had been lying to read his book, told me to sit down and whispered that the cubs would come up the track towards us. And, sure enough, they did. By shining a rather weak torchlight regularly he had habituated them to come for food. One at a time, two cubs came cautiously, noses lifted to sniff the air, and I filmed him feeding one with his fingers. Then both reared up and climbed a sloping fallen tree trunk, scratching for bits of dog biscuit which Laurie had set out earlier. It was the first time I'd realised that badgers could climb, and climb almost as well as cats. Then a third cub came and ate from my hand, but I couldn't film it because any movement with my other hand could have scared it. We spent half the next day filming sea birds at St Abb's Head. When I got home to Hawick, I found that heavy rain had forced the top front gutter to overflow. My neighbour below refused to help me clean it as he was busy in his own flat, so I had to do the best I could on my own. There was still not a single potential buyer showing any interest, so I realised it would take me a long time to sell up. On 30 June I was back at the badgers with Laurie, this time sitting on a tuft downwind of the sett for a different angle. The sow only showed her head and neck once but the cubs were all over the place, including over my boots. With Laurie's miner's torch strapped to my head I managed to use a hand-held camera to film myself feeding them. I was lucky again next day when we went to film swans on the Whiteadder river, for as Laurie waded round the far side of their nesting islet, the mother swan tramped off the nest, followed one by one by the little cygnets for their first walk-off and swim. Then two climbed up between her wing and her body to sit on her back. The whole scene was so charming that I later used it to open my film about the life of a river. I noticed Laurie kept taking his still photographs long after I would have stopped, not heeding that his Wellingtons were full of water, obsessively trying for the right shot, the true shot, cygnets on a rock parallel to the camera, the pen coming towards him with a chick's head sticking out above each wing, the same shot from water level. Modest, quietly spoken though physically powerful, he thought of shots that would never have crossed my mind. No wonder he is now Scotland's top wildlife photographer, bar none.

In mid-July I was back in eagle country with Steve, who had already told me that the sea cliff eagle pair had been robbed of their eggs, as had our favourite pair in the lowest nest. We set off on a six-mile trek but while we saw the Glen More pair flying at a distance, their two eyries had not been used. When we got back to our vehicles a callous on my left foot had split and was bleeding. I told Steve that was, for sure, the end of my eagle work.

We went to a wood near Loch Mudle where we had often seen wildcats, set out rabbit bait, draped a loose scrim hide between two high rocks, sat down on mossy boulders and kept watch. By the end of a three-hour vigil, in near dark, no wildcats had turned up and the midges were so thick and ferocious that we had to give up. Next morning our bait was still untouched so to stay would have been a waste of time anyway. One consolation came when we walked the fields opposite the windy glen looking to film adders. Steve stepped over one, then another wriggled off into cover. Steve prised the bracken away with his tripod legs and I got a super sequence of the adder coiling back, hissing, then sliding out of sight into a tiny gap in the sheep wall. Another positive was that I sold a lot of my videos to various outlets on the journey up and back, most of them to a tourist shop in Fort William and to the Glencoe Visitor Centre. The most popular, apart from Eagle Mountain Year , was the new one, At Home with Eagles. Yet more proof that I need never 'work' eagles again.

By now Mi Caballo was looking really shabby, his paintwork poor and rust patches showing. I took him to a garage and was told it would take about forty hours and £1,000 to restore his looks. The mechanic looked him over. 'Why don't you just go to Woolies, buy a tin of Dulux and a wire brush and do it yourself. It will last just as long anyway.' So I did exactly that, adding rust remover to the shopping list, found an isolated forest glade and over three days got him gleaming again, though it took all of five big cans of paint.

At the end of August I met Laurie Campbell in my old hunting grounds at Lochailort as we had planned to try and film the magnificent sea eagles on the Isle of Mull. First, though, we had to go to Glenuig and meet a lady called Anne Mungin who, we had been told, owned a fairly tame wildcat. We rang her but got no reply, then found her in the Glenuig Inn. Laurie got her out and we drove back to her house where Anne let the wildcat out of its luxury box home in the porch. It was called Pringle, was a magnificent specimen - and was tame! It immediately wound itself round Anne's ankles, padded over to inspect me and, before we set off on one of its regular 'walkies', it wound itself round my wellies too! It was wonderful to see a female wildcat again, so close, so tame and so like my own wildcat Liane, although this one had a far better tail, long and thick and bushy with wide black rings. She was really splendid and did everything I could have hoped a wildcat would do for my camera. She walked about, giving me super zooms in and out, disappearing through rushes, bushes and clambering over dry rocks in a flowing burn. Once she sat down and groomed herself extensively with her tongue, working it down her flanks, along her tail, down her chest fur. She ran at great speed after Anne who had walked on and was over a hundred yards away. She even climbed a tree right in front of me and I filmed her scrambling all the way up and down again too. It was all superb material and I told Laurie and Anne that it had been worth coming up all this way just for that alone. We took Anne back to the Inn and I bought a round of drinks, but after a while I couldn't stand all the smoke and chat so left, followed soon after by Laurie. As we camped overnight off the road to the Lochaline ferry he said he would show me a good place for sea eagles on Mull and was sure we would get them. He confessed, though, that he had spent the best part of seven weeks in hides and not got them at all. 'Och, we'll get them in three days!' I joked.

We caught the ferry to Fishnish next day, drove to Loch Don and scanned the coast and sea from Grasspoint but saw no eagles. We drove back to Gorten and hiked the shore, and there we did see one on an isolated rock but too far out to sea. We were debating where to put a hide when I stumbled on what I felt was the very best place, behind a big rock and turf wall on each side of a boulder, ready for my new Fensman hide, the roof of which would only poke a foot above it. Laurie then took me a lot further to see a BBC cameraman's hide but other naturalists had used it recently and he felt the eagles would be spooked from going near it again. He showed me his own hide but I didn't like it much as it was in a cold, wet windy spot and bits of plastic and corrugated iron were showing. He thought it was the best bet, which I couldn't understand, as it had failed him so far.

Next morning we hiked out from our camp and set up my hide, arranging plenty of foliage to break up its square top outline. I got in, sitting on a small cushion on an upturned bucket, and read some documents relating to a seafront Sussex flat I was thinking of buying, sure that no eagle would come down. I looked up in less than an hour. A huge white-tailed sea eagle was perched on a big rounded rock only forty yards away, its yellow grapnel talons biting into the rock as it steadied itself against the buffeting winds. Man, did I move fast! In the end, I filmed it and its larger mate on another rock further away, him flying to her with slow ponderous wingbeats, then the two of them apparently kissing, twiddling their great beaks together, stroking each other's cheeks, as it were, in what must be part of pair bonding. Then he flew off, over the sea and the far beach on the other side of the loch, and landed in a tree.

For nearly two more hours the female just stayed where she was, turning her head from side to side at times to scrutinise the sea and horizon. I was getting bored, my backside aching from my awful seat, and was thinking about quitting the hide when she suddenly thrust her head and neck forward as if seeing something significant and launched into the air. She flew to a long, flat, rocky islet about three hundred yards away and as she landed I saw a small animal, an otter, was already there and appeared to be eating a fish, to judge by the tail which kept bobbing up as the otter pulled at the body. The eagle watched this for a minute or so then made three big bouncy hops with uplifted wings, and the otter backed off and dived into the water. The eagle then grabbed what was left of the fish, flew over the sea towards where its mate had landed in the tree but landed on the shore at least fifty yards from him. It was as if she was saying, 'Here it is. If you want it, come and get it!' The male took his time, though, and didn't fly down to join her for a good three minutes. It was obvious they would share the stolen fish but they were now too far away to film clearly.

What a fabulous day! I felt alive again. It was as if the wilderness gods, the Great Spirit, were telling me, 'It's all up here, pal, not in bloody Sussex!' I had a few too many drams that night but Laurie was tolerant about it. He went out later to spend the whole night in a new bivouac hide overlooking a regular roosting site, but he got nothing.

When I hiked out to my hide next morning, both sea eagles were on the nearby rocks. I had got them well the day before so I just marched on and got into the hide, sending them up into the air. I was sure they would not return and just hoped I'd sent them up to Laurie's area. They did, though! In two hours, one had landed a little further away than on the previous day, then the other flew in to a rock four hundred yards away. More filming followed, including a truly superb long flight of the female in a semi-circle right over the sea, then turning amidst a flock of curlews and landing on a gravel spit. I had won again. Surely I should be living somewhere like Mull? When I left the hide I rang my Sussex solicitor who was most understanding and said that he had felt all along that a little retirement flat, with all its restrictions, would not suit someone like me. Laurie, a real glutton for punishment, changed the position of his bivvy hide and went in for another night.

Next day he had again got nothing. I showed him all my footage and he was very nice about it although I could see that he was both amazed and a little hurt. Seven weeks for him and I'd got them inside an hour! He did say, however, that for still photos he needed to get them much closer than I had. I helped him set up in a new position then had to dash for the ferry as I had arranged to hand in the last cartons of my archive to Perth Library. It still baffles me today why Laurie failed when I was working with him, for in the years since he has taken better still photos of Mull's sea eagles than anyone. On leaving Perth I had dinner with Jim Crumley and he said, as had Laurie, that I 'belonged' back in Scotland, not in Sussex. And, of course, Steve had said the same.

Mid-September found me back on Mull, but there were no sea eagles on the rocks where I had filmed them. I'd just got back to my van when a female hen harrier came winging up the hill. I filmed her as she winnowed her wings above the ground, hunting along, head bent down, dark eyes staring at the ground for small prey and twice making pouncing dives, but coming up both times with empty talons before vanishing over a ridge. That was nice footage but I was determined to get more sea eagles, as I now realised they would make a superb ending to my river video, the river ending, naturally, in an estuary and with the stars of that estuary, sea eagles. I badgered the estate agents in Tobermory but there were only three houses for sale. Even so, I drove all round the island to look at them (none fronted the sea) noting the fabulous views over Inch Kenneth and Loch na Keal and finding many wildlife habitats in an island paradise. No wonder everything was so expensive. I also noticed that most of the accents were English. 'Ay, 'tis full of English settlers now,' said one local. English settlers! I hadn't heard the phrase since I lived in California. I got back to the quiet of the Loch Don campsite, grateful that it was empty.

I trekked out early towards the sea after seeing the huge female sea eagle on a far spit. As I came round a sheep wall - woof, woof, woof – and, from a thick oak branch up to my left, away went a big, brown, speckled juvenile sea eagle! I saw the branch bouncing up and down, so powerful had been the downthrust of the eagle's feet. She flew with steady, slow wingbeats towards her mother and landed near her. I was unable to get the camera set up in time to catch the flight, but I filmed the two together. Somehow I had to get closer. I hiked back, to get out of their sight, followed a far fence, then went behind a hill full of bracken. I showed myself climbing the fence, showing the eagles that I was going away from where they were perched, but once I was behind the bracken I ducked down and crawled alongside it, then forwards through it, until I was almost out the far side, closest to them. There I found a natural grass stool, gently parted the fronds of bracken, little by little, and set up the camera. I felt there was no need for a hide and all the palaver involved in setting it up, because I and my camera were well-hidden and low down, concealed by the bracken. I had sneaked in and felt sure they had not seen me.

A truly wonderful five hours followed, and I got just about everything I hoped for. Mother with chick, both flying about, the mother landing on a nearby hill next to a sheep, showing she was the same size, then flying off again, diving at some small prey, missing it, flying on and landing near the chick which was feeding itself from a fish on the far spit. Later I took a dramatic sequence of the female launching off and flying towards me and landing on a much closer rock, where she preened herself and posed in several nice positions for me. Apart from the sea eagles, and the super hunting and pouncing flight of the hen harrier earlier, I even saw and filmed a red kite hunting. What a day and what a place! Again I thought I'd like to live there. Only three houses for sale? Well, I would return and look again. I had also seen ringed plovers, wigeon, flocks of sandpiper , many herons, ravens, mallards, kestrels and golden plovers.

When I called on the local RSPB warden and told him all I'd seen, he said the red kite sighting was very rare; he had only seen one himself. It had probably wandered off course on its normal migration south from Sweden. When I broached the possibility of getting a licence to film sea eagles at the nest, he was not negative and said it might be possible, but warned me that the sea eagles had not accepted the BBC hide this year. I said I was not surprised if, as I understood, the crew had put the hide up and taken it down on every visit. The eagles should not know a hide is there and I explained my methods. Putting up and taking a hide down on every visit was bad work. I had been watching, photographing and filming eagles for thirty years and had not lost a chick yet. He was friendly but didn't invite me in or to visit later.

Back in Hawick for the rest of the autumn, I met one of my most loyal readers, Annemauraide Hamilton, a violinist with the fabled Hallé Orchestra. I showed her my video At Home with Eagles and she said it lacked the drama of music. She thought she and two friends in the orchestra could enhance its final sequences with a special music track. Oh sure, I thought, and forgot about it. But in the end, Annemauraide, on violin, her Hallé pals Wilma Patterson, on oboe, and Jinny Shaw, on oboe d'amore, got together in a church hall and recorded three different themes – gay and bright, slow and dramatic, and soaring and lyrical, which when fitted into my video sound track improved the second batch enormously. What's more, the three ladies wouldn't charge me a penny. Think of it, the Hallé orchestra for free! I will forever be grateful to them.

At about this time, Steve landed a permanent job as wildlife cameraman with Performance Films in Wales. This was fulfilling the destiny I had always envisaged for him, for he was a brilliant talent, although I realised I would now work with him less and less, if at all. As if to confirm this notion, after a hard trek round Alemoor Loch in Craik Forest, my old stamping ground, I developed severe pains in my left hip which I presumed were arthritic, so bad that I couldn't disguise a limp when I went out to ring both Steven and Laurie. What with the foot callouses which had again opened up, and for which Dr Pat had prescribed new ointment, it was very clear that the great eagle treks were now finally over. Alexandra had been exhorting me to come back and use her annexe for another new home search. Maybe a peaceful old age in Sussex – in the Friston and Cuckmere Haven area – was, after all, the answer.

I did go back, staying with Alex and two other friends, and chased around seeing flats and cottages, but it was an office with outline planning permission that finally took my fancy. It was a small, two-roomed former postal sorting office at the foot of Friston Hill in East Dean, the road quite noisy, with a lot of traffic, but it was set well back from the road. It also had a fallow acre of walled land behind it which, if I could rent it, would make a fine vegetable garden. I drove the 1 ½ miles down to beautiful Birling Gap and the sea and realised I could enjoy really super bike rides to beyond Beachy Head and back, while the walks in the area were some of the best in the county. I took Val there who thought, at £28,000, that it was a bargain for Sussex. Well, I went through all the hoops – architect's drawings, council regulations and finding and commissioning the right builders to install a kitchen, shower room and back door. I contacted a solicitor and the owner of the fallow acre, who said I might use it as a vegetable garden if I made a good neat one but that I could not buy or lease it officially. I'd made sure all was going ahead before shooting back to Hawick where a new examination by Dr Bremner proved that my hip and recent left side pains were muscular rheumatism rather than a return of the cancer. As he said, I had no bowel left on that side anyway! I was totally in the clear. I had more nice news when I happened to meet Laurie and his family in their motorhome on the road to Galashiels. He promptly handed me the book Golden Eagles, for which he had provided the photographs and which Roy Dennis had written. The book had been my idea in the first place but I hadn't liked the advance the publisher had offered. I was surprised and more than gratified to find he had mentioned me as one of the few folks he wanted to thank for their help and encouragement. I'd done no work with him in the field, so I assume he meant from my own three books on eagles.

17

A MOVE TO SUSSEX BUT AT THE EYRIES AGAIN

At the end of March, on the very day I finalised moving into the East Dean cottage, Steve told me over the phone that he had secured a government licence to film our favourite eagles at the nest. All he had to do was find out which eyrie they were using. Would I help and put him into the hide? Inwardly, I groaned. Had I not done more than enough of this? But my love of eagles reigned supreme and I said I would – I could always sit out on the hill and get the birds hunting and going in and out at a distance. Next day I did my first bike ride, down to Birling Gap and on to beyond Beachy Head and back, a good ten miles, with some hard climbs which would have tested any cyclist. Such rides would keep my legs 'in' for the eagle terrain without jerking and shocking my knees and hips.

By mid-May I was filled with doubts. Why do eagles again? I'd already got the best nest stuff and I could have pegged out then and there with a heart attack and been content in the 'happy hunting ground'! The eagle area was 600 miles from my new home, very costly in petrol alone, but when Steve phoned on 22 May to say that if I couldn't help, he would ask a chap I didn't like … 'I'm on my way!' I said. He added that he had found that eagles were nesting in their highest eyrie: he could hear chicks calling but couldn't actually see them.

'Naturally,' I replied. 'Eagle chicks are ventriloquists!'

I entered my seventieth year, not with eagles, but with nesting peregrines, filming with Peter Woods near Carnforth. The birds were on a new ledge 250 yards across the quarry but even though we could have posed no threat at that distance, the female came yelling over our heads. Later, I walked through his orchard for a super shot and zoom-in of a young tawny owl on a low tree branch. I joined Steve two mornings later after talks with my Hawick solicitor about selling my old flat. We set off early, as he wanted the sun on the eyrie and it went off it at 10.30 a.m. I was dismayed, as the trek up was horrendous and the high nest was a mile further on from the one we had filmed so well two years earlier. It was tortuous, tussock-filled, steep terrain most of the way. I pleaded for a brief rest to get my breath back, then Steve spotted an eagle perched on a square crag on the skyline almost two miles distant. It was too far away, but I got the camera ready on its tripod. 'It's gone!' called Steve. We waited, then to our surprise saw it beating towards us, just left of the new eyrie cliffs. I got onto him and he came on and on, sailing past only about fifty yards away, but I lost him briefly as I had to twist round 180 degrees. I got him back in frame as he soared round a bluff two hundred yards further down. I was just packing up when we saw the eagle had turned south out of our sight and was now circling over herds of red deer on the skyline. I got four complete circlings, all in frame throughout, without having to pan the camera at all.

I followed Steve up to near his hide but found I could not go the final ten yards. I was traversing a narrow heather-covered ledge behind him and found it far too dangerous as I couldn't see where I was putting my feet. I stopped, perched above an 80-foot drop, and waited while Steve set up his camera and got into the hide, which seemed to take ages. How dared I even think I could work with eagles like this again, on this terrain, at my age? I thought, as I held onto heather stems for dear life, catching glimpses of the drop below me. And yet I'd wanted to help Steve, for he had helped me often enough. How I got off that ledge without falling, I don't know, but with hips hurting again I made it back to old Caballo. I knew that one day I would be 'done' on the hill and that this was the day. The midges were terrible at dusk and I had to shut all the windows. It was then so hot I took off all my clothes while making a meal.

We had a day off the next day, trying only to film four young stonechats being fed in a nest. The chicks, though, flew off as soon as I'd got into a hide we'd set up. We got supplies in the village and I bought some steak and lamb flank as well as my usual mince. I felt there had to be a shorter route up the eyrie cliffs and as its gate was unlocked, we for once took a chance and drove up a private Tilhill Forestry track. A left fork, I thought, pointed in their direction. Steve was not so sure as he had tried it once, turned off to the left and ended nowhere. I suggested we go right to the track's end and we found ourselves in a clearing. I felt sure by compass reading that we were going the right way. We crept along a tiny deer path, had to climb a high fence when the trees grew too thick ahead, and came out by a forest gate which we had seen when coming down from the eyries. We had cut off a lot of distance and would have saved a lot of hard labour if we had used the Tilhill track on every trek over the years.

We hiked on and on, striking out to the left to avoid a daunting row of sheer peaks, before seeing an eagle turning towards us from the direction of the eyrie. This time it came even nearer and, as she swept past and I zoomed in, I could clearly see her beak and glaring golden eye. I managed to keep on her for a full four minutes non-stop. It was my best ever flight sequence in thirty years of studying eagles, including the bald eagles in Canada in 1967.

Before I saw Steve into his high hide again, he threw the pound of steak and the lamb flank into the nest. He had told me the eaglet had not had much to eat on his last stint, just a piece of decaying lamb leg on the nest. And it had not excreted or moved about much. If true, the new meat should ensure its safety. Before leaving, I showed him a high spot behind a sheep wall where we should put another hide, as it was opposite the eyrie face, so allowing us to get a good side-on view and shots of the birds flying in and out, and he agreed. I doubted I would get anything better than I had that day but I did want an actual kill, and that would be a good vantage point from which to see one. I hiked out the new route, sure I'd get lost, but I'd marked it well and was back at Caballo in record time, not at all tired and for once with no hip pain at all. I felt I had somehow been rewarded.

Next morning Steve reported that the mother had flown in at about 7.30 p.m., had left almost immediately, then come back in and fed the chick from our steak. Then she had rended and eaten a lot of it herself. As she had brought nothing in on either visit it was gratifying to know that we had fed them. I didn't want any strenuous foot treks that day so, as we both wanted to film rare chequered skipper butterflies, we drove to a woodland nature reserve where I had seen some. These species of flying sunshine are about the size of a 50p piece, bright brown with chequered gold patterns on their wings, and now endangered. This area of the Highlands was one their few strongholds and at Wildernesse I had grown their food plants, increasing their numbers over a dozen years.

We hiked along the track between the oaks and I stopped at a likely open spot while Steve trudged on. I sat behind my camera for half an hour, seeing not a single skipper and becoming a bit paranoid that he would be getting great film. I wearily trudged after him. After half a mile I found him set up beside the track, focussed on a blue bugle flower, hoping that one would land on it. I set up too and within minutes I was getting my best ever chequered skipper film. One flitted along, settling on the dry mud track here and there as I pressed the button. Then it landed more positively, probed its proboscis into the wet ground and began ejecting moisture from its rear, small globules which glittered like diamonds in the sunlight. I even managed to switch to macro and get all this in close-up. I guessed this was some kind of mechanism to rid itself of excess liquid from the mineral nutrients it had imbibed. To my annoyance, I found the play back button on the camera had stopped working , so I wouldn't be able to check on this or the great eagle material until I got back to East Dean, I had not, of course, brought the Hi8 editing machine with me as that needed mains electricity. Not wanting to risk losing any footage, I put in a new film. That night I found a tiny and superb new campsite well off the road near Salen, between small trees and shaded from the sun all the time.

I had time on my hands the next day, as Steve didn't want to go into his high hide until 3 p.m., so I paid a visit to the old jetty in the Castle Tioram area from which I used to launch my boat when I lived on Eilean Shona. Horror! The quiet little car park, which had never contained more than two or three cars, had been widened and now held twenty four! And there were tents all over the sandy beach, with yelling tourists and kids running in and out of the sea. Good for them, bad for me, as I'd often had vague dreams of going back there. I learnt, yet again, that ye canna go back to women, and ye canna go back to places.

In the afternoon Steve and I made the new, shorter slog up to the eyrie, he carrying two rabbits a friend had brought us, and I set up in my new spot by the sheep wall using only scrim as a rough hide as I needed to see all round me. After a long wait, I filmed the female sailing along at a fair distance, then she landed on a ridge of thick heather, tugged a few sprays with both beak and talons and carried them back to the nest. It was interesting, but further away than I'd hoped for. Later, Steve told me she had fed the chick well on one of the rabbits. After promising him I'd be back in a month for the last of the eagle season, I hastened back to Hawick to meet a man interested in buying my flat and to load up Mi Caballo with as much gear as I could carry to take down to East Dean. The potential buyer caught me carrying my desk top down the stairs but had a good look round the flat and offered me £7,500. I said I'd paid £8,000 for it and had tarted it up, so had hoped for a small profit. 'Tell you what,' he replied. 'I'll give you seven and a half and pay your legal expenses!' We shook hands but he still wanted a survey done. Back in my little East Dean cottage, I checked all the new eagle footage, playing it from the Hi8 machine direct onto my big screen TV. All was perfect and I could never hope to get better. No need to go back now, I thought, and yet... my love for, and fascination with, eagles was unquenched. Maybe they might still need our help in feeding them?

On my return, busying myself with building chores such as making a shingle path on the mere metre of land I owned around the cottage, I noticed that Alan Goodwin hadn't done much to his allotment while I was away. A few days later I bumped into him on Friston Hill and asked if he could do with some help with the gardening. To my amazement and delight he said he had been so busy lately that he was thinking of giving up the allotment altogether and wondered, if he did so, if I would like to take it over? It had been my dream from the moment I bought the place. Almost a whole acre of secluded, walled garden! Alan said he would talk to the squire landowner and that, meanwhile, I could do what I liked with it. I ended up with full control of what became my 'garden' and when, a few days later, Alan showed me how to work the mower and rotavator, I went a bit mad and had my hardest working day for many a year. I mowed all the grassy areas, rotavated the last two of six furrows and planted all the seed potatoes and most of the leeks, cabbages, courgettes, broad beans, carrots and even tomatoes he had left me, making the heaped banks for the tatties with my spade and staking all the tomatoes with small, defunct branches from my two ash trees. It was gone 11 p.m. when I finished, sweating like a horse. That garden became my favourite hobby at East Dean, so successful that I often handed some of my crops to passers-by for free, startling some with my 'Would you care to take a leek, sir?' before handing over vegetables that were often three inches thick at the base.

Another hobby began at this time when I renewed acquaintance with an old schoolfriend from Steyning Grammar, Peter Spear, a former farmer who had become a brilliant wood turner. He had made a name for himself and had once sold a large wooden goblet of burred mulberry, so fine you could almost see through it, to an American collector for £1,000. Peter's hobby was target shooting: he had been a battalion shot in the Army and had a collection of over a hundred guns. I had done a great deal of shooting myself, in my youth, and Peter soon revived my interest, to the extent that I bought my own guns and at least once a fortnight drove over to his beautiful, isolated Harwoods Farm, two miles outside Henfield village, where we held competitions, shooting at various complicated targets with both air rifles and air pistols. I little knew then that I was to spend ten years of my old age in that lovely place, lonesome and rather dilapidated though it was.

By late June problems were accruing with the Hawick flat. Some of the roof fell into the bath and the neighbours below complained that rainwater was leaking into their flat from mine, so I dashed up to sort things out. En route I camped near Abbeystead in the Forest of Bowland and filmed curlews flying, calling their shivering piping songs, landing and giving courtship displays. Using the van's window frame as a tripod, I also got a kestrel hovering closer than ever before. Back in the flat I sorted out the problems, spent four days doing my yearly accounts then carried more gear down to Caballo for a full load to take back to East Dean. I still had a lot more to take but that could be taken after I had fulfilled my promise to Steve to work eagles with him for the last time. By then, I hoped, the flat would be sold. I got rid of some items when, on the way back to the eagles in mid-July, I called in on Jim Crumley in Stirling and gave him my old swivel chair on which I wrote all my books and which he had always coveted.

On 13 July Steve and I stormed up the Tilhill Forestry track, which we now had permission to use provided we gave the company a final copy of the video. We carried my hide, its poles, cords and film gear and after much trekking and searching found an ideal site between two small bushes from which to view the eagles' nest from 250 yards. This would give us good flight shots in and out of the nest and, I hoped, the eaglets' first flight. I got in, set up the camera, lining it up on the nest, and it began to rain. We could not film in bad weather but I left the tripod fixed so that I could just shove the camera on and still be in line. We hiked back to my new camp site at the end of the forestry track, my hips hurting but my knees feeling fine. Steve drove back to his mum's house, and a meal, in Kilchoan. He wanted to go into his hide early on the morrow, so would drive back and meet me at 4.30 a.m. He hoped I would be up! I poured myself my usual dram and said that I would be. I glanced at the milometer – 646 miles since East Dean. Cripes, I must be nuts! Poor old Cab, who would have to do it all again when I took the last of my gear from the flat. Maybe after that he could retire.

I woke at 4.15 a.m. anyway and was half-dressed when Steve arrived, looking most surprised that I was even up. We hiked up and split, he into his high hide and me into my new one. It was bad luck day for no adults came in or even showed themselves. But I took five minutes of Steve throwing some meat in which the eaglet, now fully fledged, grabbed with one set of talons. It just held the meat for several minutes while looking all about it as if wondering where it had come from. Then it fed well and I filmed it trampolining round the nest to exercise its wing muscles, excreting over the edge and 'attacking' the nest twigs with sharp, sudden grabs with its talons. All good stuff, but only as useful fillers.

Two days of foul weather followed, but on the third I bought a large slab of meat from the local butcher. It was deep frozen so I cut it into two, not only to allow it to defrost more quickly but to give Steve a second chance if he missed the nest with the first chunk. We slogged up and Steve set his gear in his cliff top hide before going over to just below the eyrie as I got into my hide. I got a fabulous section of the eaglet showing alarm at Steve's approach, trying to drive him away with furious batting of its wings. I filmed him throwing the two chunks of meat up and into the nest. The eaglet grabbed one and held on to it for dear life. It took its time to start eating and didn't do so until Steve was back in his hide. I filmed the female eagle flying in from the north then passing down to the right of the eyrie as the chick called to her, then more nice footage of the chick eating more of our meat, trampolining around the eyrie and almost flying off the edge but for a last-second grab at the nest sticks. When the eaglet lay down, lowered its head and neck over the nest and went to sleep, I could see the weather worsening and left the hide.

Two days later, the weather hot and sunny, we hiked up again, Steve carrying one of his hides for me to my first spot as he was going into my distant hide for in and out shots. The eaglet was still in the nest and I filmed it jumping about, peering longingly out and over the void and calling loudly to its parents. By now, though, they were trying to starve it out, tempting it out by flying past with food in their talons, so yet-a-bloody-gain they didn't come in. Steve cut short his stint as he was running out of petrol so he borrowed my spare can, under strict instructions to bring it back full as I, too, was running short. I felt strangely at peace at 6 p.m., having swabbed myself down and washed my hair in a burn as I sat amid the pine trees in my remote camp spot. This definitely was the last of eagles. I have to stop some time. There was no need to do them on my seventieth birthday next year. No, I would instead go to Spain and do the mighty – and much harder - lammergeiers!

I prepared myself a meal of stewing steak, leaving plenty to give the eaglet tomorrow, although I was no longer sure I should if the adults were trying to starve it out. When we trekked up again next day we saw half a rabbit in the nest so we didn't throw in any more meat, not even scraps, for fear of interfering with the adults' natural behaviour. I frequently filmed the young eagle flapping out of the nest and back and out again. These were really its first flights but it never went beyond the next rising ledge of ferns and grasses. Later I told Steve I thought we had here what I called a 'brancher', an eaglet that would not take a big chance and fly out directly, a sort of 'cowardly' one that would leap from branch to branch, to tuft, to rock, to ground and sort of climb-flap up the hill – and certainly wouldn't fly finally until way out of sight of our cameras! He thought I might be right. I recharged the camera's two batteries by running Caballo's engine for five minutes while tending a paella meal cooking on a little campfire. I looked at patient old Cab just sitting there, my faithful horse, my shelter, my 'home' for years. Battered old van, battered old man – we will never part!

It was hot again next day. The little bread I had left was mouldy and the last of the milk had gone sour, as had the orange juice. Breakfast was the remains of last night's cold paella and black tea – ugh!

Steve hadn't shown up by 9.05 a.m. so I set off alone, leaving a note that he could catch me up. I was just halfway up the steepest section when he did just that, storming up and carrying nothing at all. I had told him his hide was in a pretty safe spot and so he'd left his camera in it – his £20,000 camera! My 'lucky' eagle trews snagged on a bramble and I silently promised them this would be their last eagle trek. As we went over the top of the steep bit and were going up the long, uphill, boggy-tussocky, also hellish stretch, Steve, who had borrowed my binoculars, said 'I thought it was a deer up there but it's an eagle!' I saw it too, with the naked eye, and yelled 'Kneel down!' He did so, fast. I set my pack on his back, got down myself and got the lens onto the male eagle, perched on the skyline ridge. I filmed it shaking all its feathers, like a big, wet dog shaking itself, and finally jumping up and flying off. It came towards us, the auto focus working well despite the open sky, then veered off. The auto focus suddenly went awry so I pushed the switch onto manual and got more fab footage of it flying around in wide circles. Oddly, it showed no fear of us, coming quite near at one point.

We hiked on and decided to take down my main, closer hide rather than leave it until later, when the adults might be wanting to come into the nest and would be disturbed. I carried the rolled-up hide to my far one by the sheep wall. Just after I set up, the eaglet leapt to the left and got its talons stuck into a piece of red deer leg. I filmed three sessions of it feeding and one of a dramatic flapping trampoline from left to right across the nest, the eaglet landing in a small cliff-side bush beyond the nest ledge. That really was its first flight and I waited with baited breath, sure that, finally, it was going to leave altogether. After a few minutes, though, after scratching a fly off its neck with just one talon and shaking its head, it just sort of belly-flopped back onto the nest. I knew then it wouldn't fly that day either. At least the adults were again feeding it, which meant for sure it wouldn't leave until it was again hungry. Adults will try to starve an eaglet out but if it won't fly, they feed it again, not wanting to lose it to starvation, and hope next time they can succeed in starving it out or tempt it out by flying close with food in their talons. I'd had enough by 3.30 p.m. as I was sure it wasn't going to go and I had arranged to meet Jim Crumley and spend two days filming the nesting ospreys at the Lake of Menteith. Steve had said he would stay on for two more days, so I hiked out and down with camera pack, tripod, main hide, scrim hide and the metal poles. It was a heavy load for this old man. I reached Cab totally knackered and told the old horse, 'That really is the end of my eagle filming in the Highlands!' I thought I almost heard a sigh of relief.

There was great news when I got back to the village to stock up with food supplies. I rang my Hawick solicitor, Charles, and he said he had received 'a cast iron offer' of £7,700 for the flat. When all was cleared, I could pick up my cheque inside a week.

After a convivial evening in our favourite bar in Doune and some rather awful pistol target shooting at a forestry campsite near Callander, Jim and I made a pleasant little trek the next day through broadleaf woods and up a short but almost sheer ridge to give us a perfect view of the of the osprey nest. It was at the top of a Scots pine, about eighty yards away, and the same distance from the shores of the lake. We didn't even have to set up a hide as we were surrounded by a natural one of bracken, six foot high. For most of two days I filmed the ospreys coming in with fish to feed their two well-fledged young, much bigger birds than they look on TV screens and the same size as buzzards.

18

Ace Gardening, Peregrines and a Ghostly End to Biking

I spent five days back in my Hawick High Street flat, with much business to attend to because, after all, I had lived in this area for six years. I sorted out final gear (what to keep, what to give away and what to dump) and loading it into Caballo. Jim came on 30 July to help me carry down the heavy sea and pine chests which held all my copy diaries, notes and photos and my few valuables. After camping overnight in my old Craik Forest site, I picked up the cheque from my solicitor for £7,314 (more than I had expected, with all fees paid), bunged it into the bank for special clearance and began nursing poor old Cab, carrying his heaviest load ever, back to East Dean. I was glad to leave the grotty flat and so-so neighbours but sad to be leaving Hawick and its lovely river.

I got back to my little forecourt without any trouble, apart from two madly-hooting truck drivers who felt I was going too slowly, and found the wee cottage untouched. I was surprised to find my garden a riot of weeds, though, as I had only been away a month. I spent two hours unloading most of the gear from Cab but was too tired to sort any of it out, so heated up a tin of soup and crashed into bed.

For weeks I slaved away on the garden, sorted the cottage interior, got a telephone and cable TV fitted, annotated and edited all my video tapes and Steve came down to help me buy the right Sony Hi8 editing machine for a whopping £1,750. I also went on more tough bike rides, down to Birling Gap to beyond Beachy Head and back, and it was on one of these that I had a strange experience. I was no slouch on a bike, had won several cups and medals in my early twenties and, even for an old man, felt I was going really well as I laboured up the two-mile hill from the gap. Suddenly I heard again the once-familiar 'grind grind grind' of the chain over the chainwheel as the rider puts on real power on the sprint track, and saw an old man with greyer hair than mine and far huger thigh muscles go past me as if I were standing still. He wore an old-fashioned white racing helmet as used in the late 1940s and early 1950s. As he swept past, I shouted, 'You must have been a champion!' His head turned and I could hardly see his eyes but he shouted,

'Once was!' and churned on, up and away. I reached the brow of the hill about two minutes later and could see the road clearly for the next mile. There was no sign of him. He could not have covered that distance in that time on a damn motorbike.

Back home, I kept thinking that there was something familiar about the whole form of the cyclist, the position on the bike and, from what little I'd seen of his face, the small eyes. Then I remembered... In my early twenties I had just started being successful on the sprint track and, with other members of the Chichester Cycling Club, once cycled the 120 miles to Herne Hill and back to watch in action the only sporting hero I've ever had. Reg Harris was five times world sprint champion and he came back at the age of 54 to win the British pro championship, a feat I confidently claim will never be matched. We were seated near the entrance where the cyclists and their trainers entered the velodrome, and I was thrilled to watch my hero defeat the great 'Flying Dutchman' Arie van Vliet over three matches. As we were leaving, I noticed some middle-aged men were looking over the wall at a white racing helmet lying on the ground at the entrance some eight feet below. One of them said that Harris had removed it from his head as he was leaving and just dropped it there. This was long before the days when sporting heroes threw their balls, shoes or shirts into the crowd but I was over the balustrade in a trice and retrieved the helmet, surprised that no-one tried to stop me. Now, did I still have it? I sorted out the little cardboard barrel containing redundant cycling, fishing and other gear which I had lugged around for years, unscrewed the lid and there, at the bottom of the barrel, was the old helmet. As I dusted it off and held it up to the sunlight streaming through the window I had a strange and disturbing thought – had I seen the ghost of Reg Harris?

Between long bouts of gardening, writing scripts and editing footage for master videos of barn owls, the river, Spanish wildlife and the eagles, I kept up the regular bikes rides to keep my legs strong but, still feeling rather humiliated by the defeat by 'Harris', I didn't push myself too much. One fine October day, though, the sun beaming out almost summer heat, I felt full of energy as I came to the top of the two-mile downhill to Birling Gap and decided on a long sprint, to see just how fast I could still go. Down on the pedals, heave up with the arms and off I went. I passed two cars and halfway down the hill I must have been travelling at about 45 miles per hour. Suddenly I was into a terrible wheel wobble, the whole bike shaking, and felt the rear wheel hit something small. I knew I couldn't control the wobble, let out a terrified scream and the front wheel hit into the raised bank at the side of the road. The left handlebar hit the ground first and over and down I went, striking the hard grassy bank with my left forearm, somersaulting sideways and as my right shoulder hit the ground hardest of all, I heard a loud crack by my right ear as if I'd broken something in my body, yet felt no pain. Instinctively, I must have tucked my arms and legs in for a couple more sideways bounces, and it seemed a minor miracle that I sustained no cuts, just two small bruises.

I picked up my bike and saw that the rear tyre had been punctured, probably by a sharp stone, and that the left handlebar was bent slightly downwards. I walked the bike back home and never again took it on a public road. Later, I mounted it on a Tacx machine that allowed you to pedal indoors against a heavy flywheel at differing pressures. I kept my leg muscles strong but got nowhere. The dénouement of this story came many weeks later. I was tending my runner beans when I noticed that one of the long bamboo poles was thicker than the rest, almost the size of a javelin. I'd been quite good at throwing the javelin in the army, so I went to the bottom of my garden and hurled it, hoping to reach the top some eighty yards away. To my surprise, my arm could not move fast enough and the 'javelin' came down after a mere 30 yards. In the shower later, I saw in the mirror that when I moved my right arm the end of my right collarbone that should have been joined to my breastbone was loose and poking in and out under the skin. It was clearly broken, and yet I had felt no pain at all at the time and never have, even when doing fairly strenuous work, so I've never bothered to have it X-rayed or checked by a doctor. If it was Reg's ghost, maybe he was warning me that I was now too old and saying 'Get off yer bike!' Well, I had now obeyed him.

Early in the New Year, Steve came down for three days, showing me some of the more complicated capabilities of the editing machine and helping me finish the master tapes of My Barn Owl Family, River Dancing Year and, after we had added a long new ending, At Home with Eagles. I dubbed on a few changes to the commentaries and a week later drove the masters to a huge video duplicating factory in Mitcham, Surrey, to have fifty copies made of each, at a total cost of £1,066.32. Phew. By now I had sold most of the previous stock of videos but considering I never paid a penny in advertising - they were just listed at the end of my new books - I was doing quite well. It was, of course, time consuming and occasionally seemed pretty inefficient to pack and post only one or two videos at a time, but I wasn't working on a book at the time, wanted to keep my readers happy and was at least earning enough to keep going.

I kept filming, too, even in my little garden – a large dog fox I tamed by regularly putting food out by the back door, a red admiral butterfly driving off flies with fast uplifts of its wings, jackdaws bashing holes in my growing apples, nesting magpies feeding their young and goldfinches on the teasels I'd planted. I came up against a problem when making the Spanish wildlife master, though – I had no film of griffons and rare black vultures decimating a goat carcass, only still slides. By cutting the right-sized hole in the lid of a sweet tin, which I then fitted over the end of my long photo lens, I could film the slides against bright daylight. I kept in touch with Steve all winter and wrote glowing references for him to the Welsh authorities to help him get licences to film goshawks, merlin and peregrine falcon at the nest, but when once he rang to ask if I wanted to film eagles on my seventieth birthday, I was able to say with certainty, 'Aw, come on man, I've done enough of all that! We've made the movie anyway!' Even so, I went to Travis Perkins and bought an 8ft by 4ft

Stirling board, and hand-sawed it to the right size to make a single wooden bed for him to sleep on when he visited.

On 18 March, an old Worthing pal, Bill Baldwin, who was managing director of a large joinery and a keen birder, drove me to some chalk cliffs between Arundel and Storrington, where his son had seen peregrine falcons. We parked, hiked to the edge of the cliffs and, to my astonishment, found ourselves on the edge of a terrifying sheer drop of at least 200 feet. The great white cliffs ran for about 300 yards and had several little ledges on which grew small bushes. We hiked round and down a huge semi-circular staircase of broad, earthen, boarded steps leading onto a public footpath that ran right below the cliffs. Bill said that a TV programme had shown that peregrines had nested there the year before but that the exact location had not been revealed - only his amateur detective work had got us this far. Looking up, I was amazed how vast the cliffs were, ranking alongside anything in Scotland. They faced south-southeast, were fringed by trees that ran alongside the River Adur and the land above them dropped away from the road no matter which direction one was taking.

I was disappointed to see two hippy-type tepees in the brush below the cliffs but I knew that peregrines are not too bothered about humans, provided they are high enough above them. This is why they frequently nest on high city buildings. Near the foot of the staircase I looked up and saw a male peregrine launch itself from near the cliff top, swinging and soaring as it headed further and further away. For once, I had not brought my camera. I started looking for a place for the hide but the two tepees put me off, even though they were empty with no sign of habitation apart from a small, dilapidated canoe. Maybe they were birders' hides, I thought, although some daft druidy signs suggested otherwise. Suddenly I saw the larger female peregrine flying – hurtling - down from the cliffs to my right, soaring along to my left and landing again, although hazel and birch bushes prevented me from seeing exactly where. We were ambling past the tepees when she jetted out again, calling 'raich raich raich' but quite quietly, travelling off to the south with quick, lightly-flapping wings. Bill saw her too. 'Fantastic sighting,' he said. I raked the cliffs with the bins and finally found what looked like a small eagles' eyrie but it could only have been a cliff-side crows' nest, with plenty of biggish sticks protruding. This was where the female had initially come from, so she could have been using that ledge or the tough old nest for laying. It was very interesting for tame old Sussex! Going back out and up the long high staircase, I had to stop twice to catch my breath and ease my pounding heart and aching hips, yet I was carrying a mere 5 lbs of camera gear. Had I really climbed all those mountains in Canada, the Scottish Highlands and Spain, sometimes with 60 lbs of filming equipment? That day my latest idea – to do a survey of peregrines, goshawks and buzzards in Sussex, mostly on foot - went out the window.

In early April, Steve rang to say our favourite eagle pair were on eggs and back in the lowest nest, the one I had filmed two seasons running some twenty years earlier, but with the increasing number of tourists and hill walkers we both felt they could be robbed this year. The 'windy glen' pair were in their highest nest, on a ledge not far above ground level, so easy for humans to reach. And the sea cliff pair were again in their high eyrie on the sheer cliff face, with nowhere to put a hide. They had failed for the last two years anyway, with not enough wild prey on the mountain to feed a growing chick. We found out that in order to decimate the rabbit populations which were eating the grass for his sheep, a local crofter had released a rabbit diseased with myxomatosis. The plan had worked, to the eagles' detriment, although the crofter later wondered why a wildcat was suddenly raiding his chicken runs. I'm rather ashamed to admit, though, that the poor news about the eagles brought with it, for me, a sense of relief. I now had a good excuse not to make those long slogs again, especially as Steve later told me that four of the eyries around my old home were dead and unused.

By early May, I began to have doubts about staying in East Dean. Plans had been posted that the busy garage almost opposite my house was to be demolished to make way for a block of luxury flats. The garage and the often fast through traffic at the bottom of Friston Hill were noisy enough, even though I'd installed double glazing, but a building site? There were also rumours that some locals were planning a gardening club and as I had no official authorisation to run the garden, the squire could easily please the local community and hand it over to them. Nevertheless, I kept working on it.

One night Laurie Campbell rang me for a long chat. He said two pairs of sea eagles on Mull had been robbed; they had not been protected well enough. I wondered why no-one ever asked us? We could have done it. He was looking for a new place to live himself but felt, as did I, that the western Highlands were now overwhelmed with tourists and that rare wildlife was in trouble, with coachloads of folk looking for otters, driving them into more nocturnal activity, and private wildlife-watching firms taking trippers to strategic spots to see sea eagles and the like. I agreed with him, though, that the eastern coasts still had many fascinating environments which were not swamped by tourists. We agreed to meet soon. (Laurie did eventually buy a new home in the east).

Over the next few days, apart from battling the armies of snails and slugs which were attacking my new plants, I dithered about going back yet again to film eagles on my seventieth birthday, especially as Steve said he was going up there anyway. I rang a local landowner called Sarah who not only gave us permission to use her own private track, which would cut even more off our trek, but who said she had a friend who would be willing to sell me an old croft near Ockle at the far end of Ardnamurchan. I could have it for free if I did it up enough to live in and left it to his estate on my demise. I decided I would make just one more visit – just one - to the eagles, and arranged to meet Steve at a small ford over the burn at the start of Sarah's track the day before my birthday.

On 15 May, after a hard day of digging and scything my borders, I woke up with awful hip and lumbar pains and could only just move enough to switch on the radio, to learn that my favourite popular singer Frank Sinatra had died of a heart attack at 82. I recalled how kind he had been to me in Las Vegas in my reporter days, giving me a free ticket to his show.

I rubbed Powergel from my Hawick doctor into my left rear lumbar and hip region, took a pill he'd given me for such pains, felt a bit better and did a foolish thing. I volunteered to cut the tall hedge of my next door neighbour, a lovely old lady called Madge, as she knocked on my door saying walkers had complained it was blocking off the footpath. It was much harder work than I had expected, standing on rickety steps and sweeping up the hedge trimmer with one hand. I hurt my back more and she urged me to give up but I said I would finish the job, or else it would look awful. I then did another two hours' work planting all the young sprouts a local had given me and watering many other plants, wilting after the recent dry weather, reflecting all the while that a local allotment group could move in and my privacy would be totally gone. I decided I would like to return to the Highlands and would look at the Ockle croft. Surely, though, I was too old to start the real 'wildernesse' life all over again, with no mod cons at all?

For two days my back pains seemed to be getting worse. I could hardly put on my socks and shoes, or even gently swing the scythe. Cutting Madge's hedge when my back was already bad was a philanthropic but foolish move on my part; I had just made it worse. Now I feared I would not be able to drive the 640 miles to the eagles and climb the hills for them on my seventieth birthday. I took it easy the next day, rubbing on Powergel, letting the sun get to my back, doing no gardening at all. On 18 May the pains were worse than ever. I woke up at 5.15 a.m. and could not turn in bed one way or the other. I rested, half awake, dozing, until 8.15 a.m., then had a terrible job even to sit upright. It took two hours to do that and get my vest on... then my underpants... my socks (worst of all) and my best trousers, as I knew I would have to get the local doctor in, if I could locate one. When I tried to walk, even using my old Wildernesse staff, every movement was painful but I managed to make a breakfast of toast and plum tomatoes. I then weakened, struggled to the far end of the living room for the phone book and rang the local surgery, which to my surprise was just behind the garage. A very nice lady said the doctor would actually visit me, as I couldn't even walk that far, once surgery was over. He did come, at 12.30 p.m., and I managed to unlock the door for him. He was none too pleased that I hadn't registered with him when I first came to the area, but he had a good look and probe and thought I had pulled a series of muscles. He produced some painkillers, told me how many to take and when and said that the condition should improve in two or three days. I rang Steve and told him about my back. He said that if I wasn't going up, then neither would he, as he had plenty of work on his plate with goshawks and peregrines in Wales. I was to ring him on 20 May with my final decision.

The day before I was due to phone, my pains were a little less severe, but getting out of bed was no easier. I wrote in my diary, 'For sure as hell I won't do eagles on my 70th'. At about 7 p.m. Alan Goodwin turned up, insisting on doing some much-needed work with his mower, and bringing me a litre bottle of Famous Grouse whisky for my birthday! He said he felt he owed me something as I'd clearly wrecked my lumbar region working hard on the garden. This may have been true, but it was an extremely nice and thoughtful gesture. We had a good chat and he did an hour's sterling work, acceding to my request to leave 'natural grassland' around the pear trees. Two hours after he left, all my pains suddenly ceased and I could move my whole body and all my limbs in any direction quite normally, without any discomfort anywhere. Even today I can't explain or understand this, but it seemed a minor miracle. Next day I rang Steve in Wales to say I was on my way, and we agreed to meet early on my birthday at the small burn ford at the bottom of Sarah's private track. When I told Alan I was off to film eagles yet again, he wished me good luck and said that he would water all the plants while I was away. After that, though, the garden would be all mine - unless I needed him in an emergency - as his workload had increased.

As I set off in old Caballo on the 640-mile drive to the eagles' site I told myself I must be nuts. We arrived in Ardnamurchan half a day early so drove to Ockle on the north coast to look at the 'croft' I had been offered. It was a totally derelict site, with only the foundations of the walls showing, with no electricity or even burn water nearby. And it was a mile from the sea when I had wanted to be near it. I drove to the ford campsite well before dusk but was dismayed when lots of tourists kept hiking past. I counted eight groups in all before dusk fell and a visit to my old village on my way through showed the whole area to be buzzing with them. My old world really had gone.

19

BEST EVER EAGLE BIRTHDAY

Steve arrived dead on time and we drove up to the end of the forestry track and the quiet, isolated campsite of the previous year. We hiked on up and I felt fine; although my back still hurt a little, it seemed to ease and get better the nearer we got to the eyrie ledge. We were both sure, as these eagles were using their lowest nest, which had been robbed two years ago, that they would have failed. We split up when 300 yards from the cliff, Steven tramping off to check the nest while I laboured to erect a 4-pole double scrim screen/hide on the opposite hill. After half an hour I heard the clumping of boots beside me and Steve's indignant voice saying, 'Didn't you see me signalling?' 'Nope,' I said, 'I had my back to you while putting up this scrim, and there is no hope for that nest anyway.'

'Well you're in for a shock,' he said. 'They've got twin chicks!' I nearly had a heart attack from sheer joy. Never, in the twenty two years I had been studying them, had this pair raised two chicks! I just had to film them now. We sat behind the scrim for a while, then Steve located what looked like a fox hunting and foraging over a large, bright green, grassy triangle on the distant hillside. Or was it a fox? It looked too big, had a thick bushy tail and seemed black in colour. Could it be a wildcat or even a black panther? I shot some footage, the camera working superbly although recently it had been a bit hit and miss. Steve wanted to get nearer to the animal and we also reckoned that if the eagles had seen us behind the scrim and then saw him walking away, they could be fooled into thinking the coast was now clear, would swoop into the eyrie and I could film them.

No sooner had he set off than a great mist came sweeping in from the sea to the northwest. The wind became so cold that my hands went white and I began to shiver. After about half an hour I began giving occasional shouts so that Steve would have a reference point. To my great relief he finally appeared out of the mist, saying it had been a near thing - he almost did get lost - but that he had not seen the strange animal again. We both agreed it was now too cold to sit and wait for filming, so we hiked over to the eyrie. I wanted to climb up, leave some meat that I had in my pocket for the chicks and get my own footage. It was not the same having Steve do it with my camera. Seeing the daunting cliff again, though, I was sure I couldn't repeat my feats of more than twenty years ago. The trees and branches supporting the nest were, at least, thicker than they had been then, though, so I got my right leg up onto a branch, almost as high as my head, put my left elbow on a rocky projection and, with one great heave, found myself up, my head level with the nest.

The two chicks were lying asleep about two yards along a left bend of the ledge nest, so I had to heave myself over and onto the old part of the nest and inch my way towards them for filming close. As I put a piece of the rump steak I'd brought for them in front of my face, the far eaglet, its big white head lying sideways on the sticks, opened one eye. The eye focussed on me and zip, up came the head, now with both eyes goggling away at this strange apparition. They were both fat and healthy-looking. This was my seventieth birthday and, on impulse, I decided to take a chance. I reached over, slowly worked my hand under the nearest eaglet, and lifted it up. It was very heavy for its size, I noted. It showed no fear, didn't struggle or peck or clutch with its already big talons. It seemed totally trusting and oh, how I longed to take it, how I would have loved to own it. I had never held an eaglet in my life but now, on this special day, it seemed hugely appropriate that I should lovingly hold one of the birds to which I had devoted most of the last thirty one years of my naturalist life.

I gently put it down again, tweaked off a small bit of the rump steak and held it out between the ends of finger and thumb. To my delight the eaglet looked at it, made a grab with its great beak, and jerked it back. Nothing had ever been more gratifying to me than that one brief movement, its total acceptance of me. How easy it would have been to tame it, how wonderful to have a great golden eagle as a friend.

There was a sudden movement, and Steve was up beside me, taking a few still photos. We then realised we might be putting too much weight on the nest structure so he got back down fast. I was glad he did. Not being able to see where my feet were going and no longer being agile, I found he was able to guide my lowered feet so that I didn't fall and go bouncing down the near- sheer ground below the eyrie. By now the mist was really bad and we got lost temporarily on the trek back but nothing could shatter my enormous happiness. Luckily my compass readings were successful and although we had to stumble down a new and steep rocky section, we came out above the forest where Caballo was parked. I checked my new footage on the van's twelve-volt system and all seemed well. Steve then left to check the 'windy glen' eagles before driving to his mother's home in Kilchoan If he was not back with me by 11 a.m. the next day, I was to join him there.

At 11.05 a.m. I was preparing for another darn drive when up chugged Steve in his little red car. The 'windy glen' pair had nested but had been robbed, the eyrie empty and deserted, so he had come back. He had brought two huge chicken thighs with him. Should we feed our eaglets again? 'You bet!' I said, and off we went again, my hip hurting a little more than yesterday. When we were a few hundred yards from the eyrie cliffs we saw the female slip off the nest, fly along the ridges and land about half a mile away. We were sure she was going to watch us so we climbed up and filmed the eaglets again and, as we did so, Steve nudged me and pointed. The mother was preening herself. We fed them but only for a few minutes, then we got down and out of there fast and as conspicuously as possible, to ensure that she saw us go. Sure enough, we were only a quarter of a mile away when we saw her soar back to the nest. I was certain she knew we were helping her feed her young, as I had done on my own so many times before. We sat for a while in the warm sunshine, looking back at the eyrie cliff, the pristine scene, not a tourist or hill walker in sight. Then, from the southern summits, came the male. He flew towards and round us in a semi-circle on the high winds but not near enough for me to get better film than I already had, before going to join his mate. As we tramped down the last of the hill, the inevitable happened. 'That really is the last time!' I said. He laughed in friendly derision. 'Nah, you'll want to see if they fledged won't you?' I said maybe I would, and left it at that. I stayed in my forest campsite, ate well, finished off the lovely bottle of whiskey Alan Goodwin had given me and went to bed early. Tired, yes, but happy. Oh, so happy...

On my way back to East Dean I was passing Loch Dochart when I saw a wildly gesticulating figure in a layby. It was Jim Crumley who had just moved into a cottage down the road and had recognised Caballo. We waded out over boggy tussocks in almost knee-deep water and I filmed four whooper swans which surely should have flown north to breed in mid-April, a raft of wigeon and - my luck was in again - a super sequence of a hen harrier hunting the marshy edges. I called in at my dentist's in Galashiels and next day had lunch with landowner Sarah at her Warwickshire home. By now she and her sister had given me permission to camp on their land but they had no properties to sell or rent. She told me she was friends with a new landowner who had bought the estate next to hers with plenty of sea frontage, and she would ask him if he had something I could rent. I survived the exhausting final miles, the long jams along the M25, irate truck drivers hooting slow old Caballo, and found my cottage untouched. As I unloaded seven lots of gear and food into it, I found I had driven 1,365 miles and, along with the hard foot treks and climbing twice up to the eagles' nest, felt that this old man had maybe taken on too much. Knackered as I was, though, I was still so happy. What a seventieth birthday that was. I could not have imagined it better, and it was worth all the effort.

I took a break from constant gardening in mid-June to check some extensive woodlands near Patching with my old Worthing pal Bill Baldwin, as we had seen buzzards there. We trekked around to see if any had bred successfully that year. It appeared they had not. We found seven nests, quite new and all in larch trees except one, which was in a tall fir. There was no sign of recent life, though, or of white splashed on or below them and we saw only one buzzard, gliding high through a glade of oaks. I had just filmed the best nest, panning up the trunk of a huge larch, when I noticed something browny-grey out in a field of barley which flanked the wood. Through the binos, I saw it was the head and ears of a red deer hind, which are not common on wild land in Sussex. We bent down and stalked a few yards, I started filming and then she saw us and bounded off, making great kangaroo leaps above the tall barley so that she could see to reach a wood on its other side, a neat and rather comical sequence. We drove on to check the peregrine falcons in the chalk cliff, trekking in, and it seemed they had failed too, if they had laid eggs at all. Their ledge was overgrown and despite a one-hour wait we did not see the birds.

Through early July I kept in touch with Sarah and, on and off, with Steve but he was busy filming sparrowhawks and goshawks at the nest for Performance Films, using complicated tower hides, and didn't think he could get away to check whether 'our' eaglets had fledged or were ready to fly. I agonised for days – I just did not want any more long drives, and certainly didn't want to make those hard treks on my own any more. Then Sarah rang to say that the new estate owner reckoned he had just the right place for me. It was remote, isolated, had electricity (allowing me to edit and make my videos) and, above all, it was on the sea. He also wanted someone to keep a check on that part of his estate. I told Sarah I was on my way. She said she would have some public schoolboys with her and asked if they could come and see the eagles too? I groaned inwardly but because she had been so helpful I agreed, fairly sure that I could prevent them from going too close. When I reached Sarah's house in the village, I found she had seven boys with her, aged between nine and twelve, and public schoolboys or not, they were as rowdy a handful as any, shouting, knocking each other about and enjoying general horseplay. Oh boy.

I was mightily relieved next morning when Sarah said she only wanted to take one boy, a sensible lad I'd noticed called Edward. They followed me in her argocat to my old campsite at the end of the track. Sarah suggested the three of us could go up to the eagles in the argocat but I explained that its noise, its strangeness and our sudden fast appearance could 'explode' well- grown chicks from the nest prematurely and if that nest failed, as had others in that region that year, it would be a major loss to the wildlife heritage in the area. She agreed and so we hiked up cautiously in my normal way, and stopped about 200 yards away from the eyrie cliff.

Through my glasses I saw the twin eaglets were still there, and fully fledged. They were perfectly framed between small rowan and birch bushes. I handed Edward the binoculars and saw his jaw drop as he saw them closer. As we stood there, the eaglets began their squeaking calls and in swept the mother, right over our heads, dropped some prey, turned and took off again. It was a shot I would have loved to take but, distracted by my company, I wasn't set up. 'You'll never be closer to a wild eagle than that!' I told Sarah. It was only the fourth time that had happened to me in thirty two years of eagle watching. We moved closer, quite safely with the mother gone, and I filmed several minutes, but the shyer eaglet had retreated into a deep crevice on the far side of the nest. I wanted to stay longer but Sarah was worried about her friend who was looking after the other six boys. As I'd checked and got all I wanted, I hiked back out with her. Her argocat had a flat battery and wouldn't start so I carried my spare over and off she went. I was tired after the drives and decided to stay in my wood campsite and not go to dinner with her and some influential friends which, looking back, was probably a big mistake.

Two days later I met the new estate owner, who proved to be charming and very much on the ball regarding Highland matters. He drove us out to an old fishing station at Fascadale which, I now realised, I had seen once before. It was remote and right on the sea with its own jetty but was certainly not deserted. There were two camper tents nearby and as we were talking, up drove a large truck with eight kayaks on a special towed rig and ten healthy, hairy young men reached into the rig, seized paddles and noisily contemplated their forthcoming outing. The owner explained that he liked to let campers, hikers and various clubs, like this kayaking club from Glasgow, enjoy his bays and beaches.

As for the house, the roof was of corrugated iron, a bit rusty in places, and some of the timbers were rotting. There was no mains electricity, only an old generator. There was a huge cattle shed nearby and the owner said that they wintered a herd in that area and calved them in the shed in spring. As close-bawling and dung-dropping cows had driven me out of the nice cottage at Drimnin, I sure wasn't going through it all again in this even more remote spot, especially when the mains water supply would be the doubtful burn, so easily polluted by free-ranging cattle. My heart was sinking and I really began to feel it was not 'meant' for me to return to a Highland wilderness after all. What would I do all day, anyway? I no longer wrote books, my eagle studies were over, my videos were all but complete. No, the place was not for me. I thanked him for his kind offer, gave him my best eagle book and started on the long drive south. At a campsite halfway home, old Caballo broke down, refusing to start in the morning. I got the AA to tow me to a garage where it was found that my starter was kaput. It was a Saturday and there were no stores open. I took a big chance – I got the lads at the garage to push-start me and managed to get the old horse back to East Dean without stopping and without stalling the engine. If that feat was mainly due to good luck, the trend continued. On my doormat was a letter from the Inland Revenue containing not the demand for money I half expected but a refund cheque for £688.80! I immediately rang my accountant, checked it was correct and said I was going to write and thank them. No need to do that, he said, it's all done by computers now.

Next day Steve rang to say the sparrowhawk chicks which he had been filming from a tower had all died in a freak 24-hour rainstorm and as the weather forecast was good for the Highlands but still bad for his area, he had dashed up to join me at the eagles and had missed me by hours. He wanted to know all I had seen at the nest because when he got to it there was only one eaglet left. I told him, and added that as both eaglets were capable of flight when I left, the bigger one had probably flown just before he got there. He said he did see a floppy, awkward-flying eagle on a ridge not far from the nest but it had been cloudy and he couldn't make out any wing markings. I felt this to be good news.

Back to gardening now, and my days were filled with digging, watering, thinning, planting, re-planting, mowing, hoeing and all the rest. One Saturday, though, when I bought the newspaper that contained the best weekly TV magazine, I had a shock. The famous actress Eva Bartok had died at the age of 72 and it said that she had ended her days in a Paddington hotel. Eva and I had been very close once, almost married at one point, and she had been extremely influential in my life, urging and supporting me to give up my life as a reporter and to make a stand to fulfil my initial ambition to be a writer. Ended her days in a Paddington Hotel? I could hardly believe it… what a tragedy. If I had known I would have tried to spend some of those days with her, maybe all of them, being somewhat lonesome myself these days. The secret she told me and which I had kept all these years - that Sinatra was the father of her daughter Deanna Grazia - must have been out for some time as the short obituary said she claimed this. The main obituary was in The Times of 4 August, so I just had to get a copy.

I hiked over to the paper recycling bins behind the garage and started raking through the discarded newspapers, ignoring the stares of passers-by to whom I was obviously a down-and-out vagrant. After twenty minutes I found the right paper, carried it back, reverentially cut out her obit after a tearful reading and filed it in a special box. This box already contained obits of 'the world's most beautiful animal', Ava Gardner, who had also been influential in my life and who had died at only 67, and also of John Wayne, Robert Mitchum and Elvis Presley, who all had been good to me in my reporting years.

By the autumn my vegetable garden was in such good shape that I no longer had much to do. I wrote in my diary on one particular day that 'this is the day I dreaded… An old man with nowt to do but sit on his bum in easy Sussex and watch telly and videos… as apparently Greta Garbo did in her last years in some New York apartment…' I just couldn't think what nature project to attempt next. I did make a few half-hearted treks around the South Downs, finding rare orchids and spying what looked like an osprey on a platform at Arlington Reservoir, although it turned out to be a cormorant through the binos. I filmed Canada geese waddling about and grazing on the wetlands below Friston Forest and swans and mallards at Cuckmere Haven on my way to do some shooting at Peter's farm near Henfield.

I often thought I ought to return to the Highlands, despite my failures on my last visits to find anywhere to live, and then saw a Highlands Holiday programme which indicated tourism there had greatly increased. If I went back to live there I'd have to be part of tourism (after all, many buyers of my books were tourists) unless I went further north to the wilder, more barren lands of the Flow Country where there was less tourism and also less wildlife. Yet to try and start again in the wilds at my age might be rather foolish. After one of the Sussex treks, I again had painful hips, having to be careful even when stepping on and off kerbs while shopping in Eastbourne! I was sure now that I was 'done' on the hill.

It was the foxes that helped change my mind. I had a few glimpses of a vixen with a cub in the near dark at the top of my garden, and had filmed her crossing the road and into a neighbour's garden up the hill. I began setting out food by my back door but for three days it was not taken. On 14 November I was shining a weak torchlight through the rear window when it revealed a big, fat, old dog fox eating my mix of old bread and dog food. I switched the torch on and off but he seemed so hungry he just kept eating, as if knowing I was friendly. Next day I set up for him fully – twin studio lights and video camera on tripod, and even rigged up a screen to keep cooking steam off the window, but for two nights I failed, once I think because the neighbours' big Doberman kept barking at crucial times, and because I switched on the lights as the vixen came. She darted in fast, grabbed a chunk of chicken and legged it. I moved one light indoors and taped red plastic over the outer light hoping to make it less scary for the foxes.

Before eating my supper, I checked out back by switching on the lights – and the big dog fox was there! He flinched back at first but then just kept scoffing all the chicken and meaty bits I'd spread out. He was quite fat with a broad head, and as he moved from piece to piece the black oval pupils of his amber eyes reflected flashes of the light back to me. I filmed him for over four minutes and as he finally reared backwards and slunk away into the gloom. At that moment I decided to make a Sussex wildlife video. I had some fairly good material already and it would keep me officially 'in work', allowing me to charge some expenses, such as petrol, against tax.

No foxes came for four nights in a row but I rigged up a weak light through the bathroom window which I could keep on all the time. On the fifth night I found they were getting rather picky. They took the liver bits and the remnants from a soup can but left twin slices of wholemeal bread with the last of a tin of mince spread thinly on them. It rained heavily all next day. I bunged out some food at 5.40 p.m and by 6.15 p.m. it had gone. To my surprise the rain stopped and I put out a meaty white bread sandwich at 6.20 p.m. Five minutes later the big fox was at it. It seemed he came faster after bad weather, when hunting would be poor. He again impressed me with his size, weighing a good 20 lbs, I thought. He took the sandwich two yards to the left and ate the bacon scraps in another bowl, then went back to the crust of the sandwich he had left. Because I'd found a faint animal trail through fallen leaves leading up to the far wall that held up Madge's fence, I was sure that was his exit, as a fox has no difficulty in scaling a 5 ft brick wall. But he waddled off to the right, towards the top of my garden, and went out of view. (In winter I discovered he did exit into Madge's garden too, as many time I found his footprints in the snow atop the wall.) On 29 November I filmed him on my very doorstep and I felt I could now leave him alone, just putting out food without the bother of keeping watch. I had more than enough footage of him in that one situation.

Although I was no longer writing books (my editor at Cape had retired and no-one else there wanted my writings) I had plenty of indoor work as, apart from video scripts, diaries and voluminous correspondence, I was also typing out a précis from all my books of the new facts I had discovered about golden eagles, which took several weeks to complete. And the more I read those facts, the more I realised I need never work with wild eagles again. I was reading them when the water meter man knocked on the door. They took a reading and said it was so low that it wasn't worth bothering with. 'You must be the lowest water user in the UK,' said one. 'Yes,' I replied. 'I was brought up in the desert – by the Bedouin!' They laughed. 'Can I have a medal?' I asked. They said I probably could, and left.

Around Christmas some pals and I rang each other with the usual good wishes, Steve saying he was heading home to Kilchoan to be with his parents and two brothers. Jim Crumley said he was also spending Christmas with his family, his three children and his daughter's partner. Both asked me what I was doing. I said I was spending it alone, as I had every Christmas Day for some thirty years. I told him what had become a kind of truth for me. 'I don't even like folks visiting me on Christmas Day,' I said. 'I'm the prisoner who fell in love with the jail.' Before this, Alan had completely given up his interest in the garden and told me I should negotiate my own annual rent with Jimmy, the land owner. 'Oh, a fiver a year will do it!' said Jimmy, when I rang. 'Bung me a note whenever you see me. Not a cheque, they're a bother to pay in!' I'd never met Jimmy in the two years I'd lived there but I hate owing money. That day I didn't have a fiver in my wallet, so I posted him a tenner.

While to many it would seem a gift from the gods, I was now finding the garden hard work, self-inflicted as it was. On 24 December I put in two hours of double-trenching, which is hard digging indeed. Next morning the back pains were so bad I could hardly get out of bed, and I had to take one of the pills the doctor had given me more than a year before. I began to feel increasingly trapped – the gardening was causing me pain, even injury, but if I gave it up, others would doubtless take over and I would completely lose my valued privacy. Add to that worry the constant traffic noise outside, occasional accidents, the air pollution, attempts by a few local organisations to enrol me into their activities - I'd never been any good at 'community' - were getting to me as well. When permission was granted to knock down the garage opposite and build a block of luxury flats on the site, I began to think about selling up and returning to somewhere wilder.

20

TRAGEDY AT AN EYRIE, OTTER HAVEN AND FAREWELL TO SUSSEX

Early in the New Year, Steve rang to say he now had a job with a new film company, was being paid £400 a week and wanted me to work with him again on the Highland eagles in the spring and summer. I said I didn't need any more at-the-nest material, maybe just a better hunting sequence, but if he needed my help I'd see how I felt nearer the time. While I was now filming birds on a large 'natural' bird table, water birds at Cuckmere Haven and on a nice easy trek around Abbotswood Lake and some rare circular holes in oaks made by sap-sucking woodpeckers, all this was a far cry from wild eagles in the Scottish mountains.

Because I needed to finish off my film about the rare wildlife of Spain, I had already planned to return there for a three-week filming trip in the spring. While it might seem a trifle foolhardy, as the Spanish mountains are higher and tougher than Scotland's, most of them have innumerable tracks, or caminos, cut by foresters, and if one can get the necessary permisos, driving up them makes the work much easier.

Another problem was that I was booked into Eastbourne Hospital in late February for both an endoscopy and a tracheoscopy, in which they push one camera on a tube up the backside and around the bowels, and another down the throat to check the oesophagus and stomach. While this was a routine check-up after my colon operation three years earlier, I dreaded it and, of course, was not sure how it would end. If the result was bad I would obviously not be able to help Steve and would also have to cancel the Spanish trip.

From the time a taxi came for me until another took me home, I had the most enjoyable experience I had ever had in a hospital! Everyone was so kind and patient, the nurses asking thorough questions, checking blood pressure, fixing saline drip and throat spray, giving me semi-sedation and wheeling me into the operating theatre. I watched everything on a little colour TV by the bed and felt no pain at all, just a little bloating when they pumped in air. I saw them snip off three small oval polyps, chasing them over ridges in the bowel before pulling them out. They told me my throat was clear and normal. The bowel was in good shape, the old operation site barely detectable, and although the three neat little polyps might be cancerous, they would be sent for analysis and I would hear about them inside two weeks. The whole operation took only half an hour and Michael Rakon, the enormously kind and efficient male nurse, told me there had been five patients before me that day and that they get through twenty endoscopy cases a day! Heavens, I thought, they do work hard. They would not just let me go afterwards but insisted I wait half an hour, have a cuppa, then another, and were most concerned that I had no-one to look after me at home. They wanted to keep me in overnight, I started dancing about like Muhammed Ali to show that I was fine and really not dizzy at all. In the end a nurse escorted me to the taxi phone and even waited with me until I was actually being driven away. Back home, I felt like I had enjoyed a short stay at a luxury hotel. Even so, I was naturally worried about the results of the polyps' analysis and rang my Sussex solicitor to meet in three days' time so that I could make a new will.

On 3 March a letter from Eastbourne General Hospital seemed to say that the polyps were benign but as I couldn't understand some medical terms, and still a bit fearful, I rang up. I was right, though: the polyps were not cancerous but some dysplasia in one of them meant a future check would be a good idea, and they would let me know when it would be. 'You're in the clear,' said the nurse. What a relief! The Spanish wildlife trip was now definitely on.

I sailed Brittany Ferries from Plymouth on 24 March and for three weeks charged all over Spain filming (in daily order) nesting white storks, griffon and Egyptian vultures, flying golden and short-toed eagles, red kites, Montagu's harriers, black kites and even an eagle owl feeding two chicks in their nest. I filmed imperial eagles turning over in the air and touching talons and, near Villafáfila, some great bustards feeding, preening and giving magnificent long displays. I was lucky at the Mallos de Riglos to get a rare lammergeier on its nest in a high grotto on the great sandstone cliffs there. On my last day at Escalada, one of my favourite places in Spain, I filmed a male golden eagle bringing food to his mate in a small cave eyrie, the female feeding herself and a chick, and her leaving the nest – a best-ever last night in Spain. Poor old Caballo covered just over 3,000 miles on that trip and before our last camp, up a high, sandy hill overlooking Santander and the ferry, he gave out an odd, roaring, grinding noise from somewhere underneath and a smell of burning wafted up. I stopped, topped up his oil, as the indicator said only half full, and nursed him down to the ferry. It was almost as if he had been voicing a protest, but we covered the last 256 miles from Plymouth to East Dean without further trouble.

I had only been back two days when Steve rang to say that 'our' eagles were back at their best eyrie in the Black Rock cliff and would I come up again? I said I might, if he and I could rent a cottage together, but after twenty one nights out in Spain I was fed up with camping out all the time. He said he had tried but that rents were far too high, and that he would probably be based at his mother's house in Kilchoan. I bore in mind that I had helped him in and out of hides two years ago yet had only got about a minute of useable film myself, and that he was now earning £400 a week, more than I earned in a month. It would cost me a lot in petrol alone to go up when I didn't need any more eagle film. I suggested he might be able to get someone else reliable to help him but, if not, I would reconsider. I reminded him I never worked an eagle nest until any chick was at least ten days old anyway, and then only on a dry, bright day when the parents would spend hours away from the nest. By the time Steve rang again a week later, I was once more getting bored with life at East Dean and said if he got all licence permissions I might come up for a week or two around my 71st birthday!

I must admit that I was not at all bored with Sussex wildlife on 4 May when I went to check the peregrines' cliff near Amberley with my long-standing pal Bill Baldwin. After the long climb down I set tripod and camera, soon spotted the nest ledge and was filming it when the falcon, the female, poked her head over the edge, looked both ways twice then stood up and flew off downwards and away over our heads. Next, Bill located the tiercel, the male, perched in a tree on the cliff face and I managed to film him there and shaking his feathers out. Twenty minutes later I was too slow to get onto the falcon as she swept back into the nest but I filmed her shuffling back onto either eggs or small chicks. After a few more minutes she stood up and began feeding herself from a cock blackbird. I even had time to put on the X2 extender and get some of that up closer.

A pretty woman with a dog came by and said the tepee men had been ejected by court injunction but that Saturday nights were hellish below the cliffs as 'louts' came with booze, lit fires and barbecued there. I was glad the tepees had gone but realised if the peregrines could put up with such festivities, they certainly wouldn't be bothered by us, as we were right down at ground level and kept quiet.

Another good thing at this time was that on my return from Spain I had put Mi Caballo into Skinners garage in Eastbourne to ascertain the cause of the loud grinding noise. Although they had kept him almost a week, they put in a new clutch assembly, charged a very reasonable price, paid for my taxi home and sent a driver to take me to the garage to pick him up. It was good to have my 'wheels' back but not so good when I got in to hear on the radio that Dirk Bogarde, another star who had been helpful to me in my reporter day, had died at the age of 78.

By now I was torturing myself mentally, debating whether or not to make the 1,300 miles return drive to help Steve with the eagles and make those long hard treks again. My anxieties ended on 13 May but with a big shock. Steve rang. 'The Black Rock eagles are finished, finito… the male came in and ate the chick.'

I could hardly believe my ears and asked Steve to repeat what he'd said. 'The male eagle flew into the nest and killed and ate the chick!'

Never in my life, in the thirty two years I had by then been studying eagles, had I even heard of an eagle killing a chick. Steve said he had done everything by the book, by our book, had been put in and out of the hide by a mutual friend, also a nature photographer, and had been in the hide when the incident happened. I had an immediate paranoid thought: maybe the two men were saying this to keep me away, to keep the eyrie for themselves, and said that I was coming up to check the nest.

'Do what you like,' said Steve stoutly. 'You'd be wasting your time. I filmed everything and will send you a VHS copy right away.' He added that he had thought something was wrong as on his two visits to the hide the mother had tried to feed the chick but it had not responded or taken food from her. He thought she had deserted.

His tape arrived three days later and, sadly, his story was true. I saw the white downy chick lying on its back, showing poorly-developed toes and talons, even looking slightly deformed, and apparently hardly breathing. Maybe the mother had finally deserted knowing the chick was a runt, that it was dying, and in later discussions Steve and I agreed that this was probably the case. The male eagle flew in and landed and looked down at it for a long time, his head twisting from side to side, as if making sure it was dying. He walked towards it and looked again for many careful seconds. The chick did not move, apart from sporadic weak breathings. When he picked it up with his beak its deformed feet showed more clearly and its beak, too, was abnormal, sparrow-like, when even young eaglets have big hooked beaks for their size. He put the chick down then stood with his left foot on its neck for a long time as if to make sure it was dead, or at least beyond sentient feeling. He looked at it again several times from different angles. Only then, when all movement had stopped, did he bite into and pull bits off its head and neck and swallow them until both had gone. Then it flew off, leaving the rest of the little carcass on the nest.

Needless to say, my 71st birthday was a damp squib compared with previous ones, spent finishing my yearly accounts, repainting bits of Caballo and battling snails in my garden that were trying to scoff the new runner beans I had planted. In a way, though, that male eagle had done me a favour. While I would only have gone up to help Steve, all that driving and the hard treks would have been tough on this old man! The year before with eagles had been so fabulous that it was surely time to end my love affair with Highland eagles?

In early July I again headed north to see if I could find a new wild home, this time up around the Moray Firth which I had often been told was less touristy than the Highlands. On the way I camped at landowner Sarah's Warwickshire farmhouse, had supper with her, cleaned her little wild pond of weeds, swam in her pool and promised her I'd nip over to the west after my Moray search and take her new party of teenage boys to see otters. And while I was away, she would consult her sisters about renting me a piece of pine-covered land on the sea which I coveted and that they all owned. I drove up to Moray and from the factor of Seafield Estates in Cullen obtained details of several properties. After three days of chasing around, though, none were what I wanted. I kept my promise to Sarah to take her teenage lads to see otters and was somewhat surprised to find they were all Eton pupils and in the same class as Prince Harry. It was also a surprise to find two girls among the group, one of whom, Charlotte, seemed a quiet, thoughtful lass, in contrast to the cheeky boys.

Naturally, I didn't expect to see any otters at all next day when I took them to Kilchoan and down the long trek of the burn gorge on the west side of the eagles' sea cliff. The boys were talking too loudly, leaping about and wanting to go too fast, but they did obey my order not to go past me. Round a bend we startled two huge red deer stags, and I filmed them running away over the hills. We came near to the beach and darn me if it wasn't the lovely, quiet Charlotte who first saw an otter. Then we spied two. Incredibly, we watched the otters for almost an hour. They ran about with ungainly little leaps, lifting seaweed fronds to look for tasty invertebrates, holding butterfish and crabs in their claws and chewing them. They swam through little pools in the sand, played about, performed some mock mating (maybe it was real mating?) and I got more than ten minutes of great film, my best ever otter material.

Some of the brats - er, boys - got a bit restless, said they were bored and wanted to go back. One of them, the one who had said, 'This van stinks' as soon as he'd got into Caballo, kept leaping about yelling my name and being extremely cheeky. I could have clouted him. On our way back in Caballo, Charlotte asked if she could live with me in the van? Sure she was joking, I said, 'Of course, but bring your grandmother with you.' The boys laughed but when I looked round at her she seemed to have been serious.

Back at Sarah's, some of the boys were even cheekier and I decided I couldn't trust them enough to camp in Caballo on her forecourt overnight so drove to my little campsite between the trees near Salen. Before I left, Sarah imparted some bad news. She said that while she wanted to help me, her three sisters did not want anyone on the southern seafront part of their land. I then found a local shop was still advertising my videos in the window, yet had only bought a few copies a year before. Were they selling pirated copies? I decided not to try and find out and also, now that I had all the eagle film I ever needed, never to return to live in my old area of the Highlands.

I spent four more days searching properties on the Moray Firth from Buckie to Macduff, had two near misses but no luck at all. I did have a lovely letter from Lord Seafield, who had read my book *Golden Eagle Years* (which I had given to his factor as a sort of glorified visiting card), saying he hoped I would take over a certain farmhouse. But the place was well run down, far too large for one person and not near the sea, which I wanted most of all. It was when I took close looks at the beaches around Cullen and Portknockie that I felt this area could just be a great, free, forgotten paradise of the UK – miles of golden sand and hardly anyone about, and the little harbours were also fine, with few boats in them. I could have my rowboat here, with plenty of rocky islets to row around and fish among. I redoubled my efforts and found a super house for sale by the sea at Auchintae but the agent said the price was £129,000, beyond my purse. A little white lodge opposite the sea and inside the Seafield gates was for rent but the new factor, a woman, told me there had been a closing date and that they were now taking up references of the interested folk. If things went wrong, she said, she would let me know. Yet again, no damn luck.

One Saturday I hiked out to the picturesque Bow Fiddle Rock and filmed eider duck families, great black-backed gulls, fulmars, kittiwakes, cormorants and even a pair of peregrines. I had the place to myself for two hours, on a Saturday. It seemed almost to be a tourist-free area. On my way back through Cullen, I met a chatty fisherman on the seafront who said it would be easy for me to have a boat in any of the harbours and that it was a great place to live, 'even if it is a long way from anywhere!' On my return to East Dean I wrote in my diary 'Target now – sell up here and go back to Moray Firth.' I then picked up a thick letter lying on my mat. In it was a nice note from Sarah and from three of the boys, all thanking me for taking them to see otters, and the nicest note was from the cheekiest boy! I thought from the way they were behaving that they just didn't like me. Shows what I know about modern youth.

I was now back facing the twin ordeals of gardening and of cutting Madge's hedges and lawn too, allowing me to dictate the times of such noisy work rather than have them forced upon me when I was trying to write. When there were two traffic accidents in a week right outside my front door, I finally decided to sell up, and began frantically redecorating the cottage. Three estate agents came to see it, one valuing it at £80,000, which I thought unrealistic, one at £25,000, which would have lost me money, and the third, the youngest, called Nick, at £60,000, an estimate which tallied with my own hopeful one. Nick made extensive notes and took photos of the exterior and interior. I decided on another ten-day trip up to Moray and to try harder to find that elusive new home on the sea as, if I sold quickly, I'd have to bung all my gear into storage and be left wandering around in my old camper until I did.

On a very hot 4 September I trekked all the beautiful Cullen beach and sat under the superb arch of the Bow Fiddle Rock for over an hour. The sun, blue sea, golden sand could almost have led me to believe that I was in the Caribbean, and I saw only three couples. I again dashed about looking at cottages and farmhouses and, after many complicated enquiries, finally settled on what seemed an idyllic farmhouse, in a totally isolated location less than half a mile from the sea. It was in fine condition, with three bedrooms, a living room, a study, kitchen and bathroom. I could just move in. There were twelve outbuildings and it took me three hours to check them all. I could have a garage for old Caballo, a workshop, a loft for barn owls and an indoor rifle range to which I could invite old Peter for target-shooting holidays. The garden was in good shape, too, the tatties not harvested, so I filled a bag. I dashed back to the Seafield office just before it closed and told the factor I loved the place (I had even performed my wilderness prayer on its doorstep: 'I will love and look after you, if you will love and look after me') and as it was being advertised at 'Offers over £40,000' I said I would pay £45,000 and give her a cheque right then and there. She said they might be able to take it off the market but as so many folk were interested in it, they would probably have to let it go to 'offers' and set a closing date. But that could take weeks.

Back in East Dean, glad to see a 'For Sale' notice on my forecourt, I kept in touch with the factor, who said £45,000 had not been enough to take the farmhouse off the market. Interest in it had increased so they were going to advertise it widely before setting the closing date. When I said it would probably go for £60,000, she agreed. About two weeks later I put in an offer for £48,000. On 18 October my solicitor in Hawick rang to say I had not, after all, bought the farmhouse. There had been a higher bid, not much higher but high enough to make a difference. Damn hell! I had my heart set on that place. I could not avoid a sneaking feeling that someone, somewhere had thought they didn't want a single, sad old man there – and they certainly didn't want him if he was going to start a shooting range in the barn.

In all, eleven lots of folk came to view the cottage, mostly couples who said it was too small. Finally, on 20 November, a youngish couple called the Browns came to see it, having just sold their big house in Seaford and bought a plot on the Isle of Mull. They needed a small Sussex base while building a new house on the plot. The mere mention of Mull got us all going and I told them of my adventures with the sea eagles there. They loved wildlife too, had actually read some of my books and insisted on buying my video which featured the sea eagles. They did not want the garden; any local man or club could work it. They stayed two hours, we sank plenty of coffee and when they left they said they would definitely make an offer 'soon.' How soon was most unexpected. I had just eaten lunch when my agent Nick rang to say that the Browns had made a firm offer of £49,500. Feeling greedy, I said, 'Try them for £50,000 and they've got a deal.' Nick said he would. I dashed off to Safeway to buy a lamb joint and some whisky and had just got back when Nick rang again – the Browns had agreed to the fifty thou! When all formalities were completed, the Browns wanted me out by 14 January, which meant I would be drifting around Scotland in old Caballo in mid-winter. A neat profit of £20,000, though, would give me enough 'fat' to hole up occasionally in a comfy hotel while on yet another search for a new wild home.

Naturally, now I had decided to leave, my wildlife filming began to improve. On a bright, sunny day in mid-December I drove to Cuckmere Haven, trekked along the banks of the meandering river to the seashore and filmed redshank, white egrets flying, a dabchick frequently diving and swans with cygnets as big as themselves but still in their immature grey plumage. A hunting kestrel came flying along until very close and then started hovering – the very sequence I had wanted for ages. Through the telephoto lens, I could see her whole body quivering with the beating of her wings yet remaining motionless like an anchor in the sky, her dark piercing eyes glaring at the ground for tiny prey. Steve drove down from Wales to pick up a new film camera from London then, while I still had a roof over my head, came down to me and over two days we edited a new ending to my At Home with Eagles master tape, using the hypnotic music by the Hallé Orchestra ladies to great effect.

Final arrangements were complicated but by handover day on 14 January, all my gear had been taken by Stan for storage in Galashiels, the postmaster at Buckie post office had agreed to keep my mail, I handed the keys over to the Browns and old Caballo and I were on our way north - to a very uncertain future.

21

RUNNING EVEN WILDER

As soon as we again reached the Moray Firth area, fully-laden Caballo having slogged his way up in two days of sunny weather, it became clear that the uncertain future could become a very unpleasant future. At our last campsite in a forest at Deskford, heavy rainstorms lashed and buffeted us. Moving gear around so I could get the bed down was very difficult, as to keep it dry I had to do everything from inside. When I woke up next morning my hands were white with cold. There was no way I could live up here in old Caballo in winter.

I went to three estate agents, the last putting me onto landlord Alastair Scott from Turriff who showed me a detached house overlooking the sea in Harbour Road, Portknockie. It had three bedrooms, was luxuriously furnished, and I could have it for a minimum of three months for £360 per calendar month. That was £90 a week! I hadn't forked out that kind of rent since I'd left my St John's Wood flat in London thirty four years ago and at first my mind baulked at the idea. But earlier I had rung a hotel in Cullen which wanted £30 a night! When I demurred and said I had two other properties to look at, Alastair cheerfully offered to drive me to them, which I thought was astonishing. One was a grubby little flat above a chip shop, the other was a fine little lodge but in the entrance of a large hotel, and neither was near the sea.

Reasoning that I had made a fair profit from the East Dean sale, I agreed to take the Portknockie house. Alastair drove me back, we checked electricity readings, then he said it was normal in the area to pay one month's rent as a deposit against damage, so I had to write a cheque for £720. Phew. I wondered if I was being conned but later enquiries showed that rentals here were as costly as in Sussex, if not more so, and I would get the extra £360 back if I left all in good shape. Next day, when I was unloading gear from Caballo into the house and undoing everything from his roof, the strong gales were so bitter that I had to dash indoors twice to warm up my frozen fingers. I had found shelter just in time. At least I was where I wanted to be, on the sea and with a lovely view over the harbour, a nicer one than Cullen's whose few boats were always afloat, even at low tides. A few days later I met harbour master Bert Reid who came to join me for a few drams and on the spot gave me written permission to have a boat berth in the harbour for an £80 annual fee.

For the next three months I drove about the whole area looking at, almost buying and then rejecting what appeared to be ever-elusive seafront homes and, in between, trying to fit in wildlife filming. I got redshanks running about and feeding near the Buckie seafront car park and a curlew close to an oystercatcher, both lit up by the setting sun in Portgordon. When I discovered Spey Bay I thought I may have found my new seashore paradise. The mighty River Spey ends in a spectacular estuary about a mile across, with many spits and sandbanks holding flocks of sea birds and waders in both fresh- and sea water.

I turned, away from the sea, and trekked along the eastern bank of the river now fringed on shingly, sandy banks with willows and alder. I had been told that otters had been seen there. I avoided many sandy puddles and had to keep shifting the tripod and camera up my left shoulder; I was carrying them that way and not in their pack so as to be ready, fast, for action. Suddenly, just before a huge old footbridge, the camera snapped off its base clip, plunged into the only deep puddle in thirty yards and smashed open at the back, soaking the tape, lens and all the top working buttons. It was clearly done for. I dried it as best I could, though, and hiked on to the bridge and over its solid floor of huge wooden sleepers.

I was halfway along, surveying the river through binoculars from between the steel girders, when I saw on otter swimming, making a wide V in the water as it went. It scrambled out onto a sandy bank and started devouring something very small. Then I saw a much larger mammal form, a young, yellowy-brown, furry seal, hauled out on a shingle bank. I hastily set up the camera but, of course, it just flickered and dimmed and wouldn't film anything. As I was trying to get it working one of a group of five hikers saw my gear and said 'There is a seal out there sometimes... it was there this mornin'... but it's nae there the noo.'

'It is there the noo!' I replied, and handed him my binoculars to look through. 'Oh, aye, now I can see it too,' he said, and he and his dog walked on to rejoin the others. Even at this early stage I began to feel that this area, too, had many tourists and local walkers, and this was only late February. A few days later I repeated the trek to the footbridge, my camera working again having fully dried out, and saw a huge flock of greylag geese grazing in fields away to my left. I stalked, set up and got them feeding, walking about and suddenly all flying off and wheeling about the sky before heading south. I hiked to the Garmouth car park and back, filmed the Spey in spate looking like grizzly country in Canada, then saw the seal again. It was swimming and diving nicely as my camera whirred, then it hauled itself out onto the same shingle bank as before, but finding it hard to do so, with more caterpillar humpings than usual. On the way back I decided to walk down on the side of the river but it was rocky, although most of the stones were rounded and flat. I found that my feet didn't always go where I wanted them to, I lost my balance at times going up and down the banks, and I felt slightly dizzy too. For the first time, really, I realised that I was now an old man. Even so, I kept looking for my new home.

I found what seemed my ideal cottage had just come onto the market, at an ideal price and on the seafront, and I went after it. After employing a surveyor and talking to the owner, though, I found, among other problems, that the water supply was a bodged-up mess, that tinkers camped on the foreshore in summer, picking shellfish, and that there was a long-standing dispute over boundaries with a neighbour. I became friends with a couple who had a detached house, in a row of others, right on the beach at Spey Bay but they couldn't decide whether to sell it as it was or to do it up first and so make more money. I was in two minds about going for it but after the first weeks I'd noticed gales there were frequent, that heavy surfs seemed ceaseless and that the beaches were all large shingle, rather than sand. When the house next door got planning permission to build a huge new extension, that was another dream that bit the dust.

One sunny day, although there was plenty of snow inland, I went to walk the golden mile of the Cullen beach. It stretched out so invitingly, I broke into a jog, only to find myself pitching forward, my knees tending to half give way on every landing step. I had to stop. I said it aloud: 'Godammit, I hate getting old!' then realised that was the exact phrase the great movie star John Wayne had used to me when I met him while he was making The Undefeated with Rock Hudson near Baton Rouge in 1968. 'You just can't do what you used to any more. I hurt this damn shoulder when I fell from that horse out in Louisiana. In the old days it would have taken ten days or two weeks to heal up but it's now more than a month and it's still giving me hell!' At the time Wayne was only 61. But I knew what he meant. Recently, when my hips, back and/or knees hurt after treks, the pains took much longer to wear off than they had done in my 60s.

Although there were quite a few bargains in terms of property, I found the narrow streets and terraced rows of old fishermen's cottages somewhat claustrophobic, and as the weather improved, especially at weekends, the streets were often full of roaming, cheeky kids and teenagers, many on skateboards, yelling to each other. One sunny weekend in mi- March I knew, really for the first time, that I could not settle here. The road and area surrounding my seafront rented cottage swarmed with cars, walkers and kids who monopolised the harbour piers, the public seats in front of me, even the pontoons; voices could be heard everywhere. At dusk on the Sunday, small gangs of teenagers roamed past my windows with drink bottles in plastic bags, swarming over some boats in the harbour itself. One lot smashed a float from a small kind of lifeboat onto the mud and used it as a stepping stone. Was I glad I had not put a rowboat down there! They hauled a tangle of old electrical leads into the turning next to me and left it in the road. It might just have been general horsing about, but I realised that in summer this place could be hellish for the likes of me. That night, the TV news said that Fraserburgh, just up the coast, had the biggest heroin problem in the north of Scotland. Occasionally, two or three cars would pull up right outside my house at night and men would get out and talk for several minutes, often looking at the harbour. I wondered if they were drug smugglers or plain clothes cops looking for smugglers, but I lacked the courage to go out and enquire; they didn't knock on my door or bother me, apart from irritating me just by being there. Another annoying thing at this time was that my mobile phone kept losing its signal, so for much of the time it was impossible to make business calls.

I left Portknockie on 7 April. I had an interesting job to do now, having been hired by the Aberdona estate near Alloa to make a wildlife survey of 300 acres of its four wild woods and three large ponds. My practice on such a survey is to cover every square metre of land on foot, and as the Alloa area is not known for being mountainous, I thought it would be a doddle. The woods, in fact, had some deep and steep hidden gorges so it was occasionally hard going, and I made sure I took it easily, taking my time to save my poor old hips. I saw goshawks, found their kills and two huge nests, signs of pine martens and dens, and located the badgers' sett the owners desperately hoped I would find, a fine, well-used 4-holer. In my report I advised on best sites for artificial otter holts and where to put flat 'sprainting' rocks, I recommended that the owners plough a two-metre strip along all woodland edges and plant self-regenerating cereals for seed-eating birds, voles and mice, that they stock all ponds with fish such as rainbow trout, planting willow whips and alders around them, and advised them on where to put bird hides and where to set out marten foods. I listed all the species and where I'd seen them. Apart from common ones, these included sparrowhawk, buzzard, snipe, oystercatcher, goldcrest, kestrel, dabchick, roe deer and tufted duck. I made special mention of a tawny owl on eggs who saw me coming through her nest hole in an old beech tree and just sank down very slowly, as if in a lift, until her head disappeared completely.

On my way back to Spey Bay and the deserted old aerodrome which was to be my campsite for a while, Radio 4 said that the sea eagles' nest on Mull had been robbed again, for the second year in a row. The previous year, both nests had been robbed despite a so-called 24-hour surveillance guard mounted by two prominent conservation bodies and the SAS. Some daft eagle watch that, I thought. I knew I didn't want to live on Mull now. I immediately rang Steve, who rang me back from his film company's office to save me the mobile phone bill. He was not going to the Highlands until late April and would then be with his new girlfriend, taking her to meet his parents. I knew right then that there was no prospect of me working with Steve on golden eagles that year, and I felt a strange mixture of disappointment and relief.

After typing my 4,000 word Aberdona report, I drove from the aerodrome to the car park at Spey Bay and filmed a huge Atlantic seal sporting about in the sea end of the estuary and, further out, rafts of eider ducks frantically diving before the big waves hit them. They dived, resurfaced after the wave had gone past, then had to dive again before the next one. It was quite comical. I would have stayed all day but tourist cars and vans started to fill the car park, many disgorging noisy families. On the way out I saw a buzzard tearing at a dead rabbit in a small field but although I tried, and reversed twice, there was nowhere on the narrow road where I could pull up, stalk it and film it. After posting my report, I decided that as I was already so far north in Scotland I would take one really last look for a seashore home in the northwest Highlands. It would need to be a careful decision because if I found a home, I felt it could well be my last.

I made a four-day trip, ending the first by camping in a small quarry above Kishorn, but found no seashore homes for sale, although I filmed some wild goats in a small gorge. In the morning I turned west at Shieldaig, where I filmed an otter swimming in the sea, and drove to Applecross, hoping to find something on the beach along the narrow road. There were some alarmingly steep bits, then the road went well inland and the shore was nearly all cliffs. The weather worsened halfway – I had forgotten such stair-rod rains and mist. At Applecross I set off over the high, steep mountain pass to Kishorn but met a driver coming down who waved me to stop and said it was terrible up top. I decided not to put old Caballo through all that, and drove back the way I'd come, finding another small quarry in which to camp before Cuaig. Next day I drove up to Gairloch, sold six books to an outdoor shop and went along the narrow coast road to Melvaig but found nothing for sale. On my way back I paused for lunch on the shores of spectacular Loch Maree in, at last, blazing sunshine, and filmed the majestic mountain of Slioch and beside it a complete rainbow, a full semi-circle of blazing colours which I had never seen before in my whole life. All the driving seemed almost worthwhile for that alone.

I drove back to Kishorn to see a cottage I'd been told about but it was right in the village, so no good. I went down many tiny roads, even down to Achintraid and along Loch Carron shore, but found nothing for sale anywhere. I was nearing Craig when I saw scary lightning ahead and heard loud thunder, so I pulled onto a Forestry Commission track, hoping the storm would be gone by the morrow. As I shifted heavy gear from back to front so I could get the bed down and make a meal, I reflected how lonely life had become, with Steve getting married soon and all other pals with their mates. This feeling was enhanced by my final realisation that the west Highlands were now over for me. This was the fifteenth time I'd driven back here to look for that isolated seashore home and, yet again, it had not worked out. The message was clear. My spirits lifted when I got back to the deserted aerodrome where I had by now set up a campsite between pines where I could not be seen from the road. I saw a small car drive up onto the weed-covered tarmac and a woman get out, remove some packets, dump them down and drive off. Curious, I went over – and found she had dumped some wee trinkets, perfume bottles, lacy underwear and some great LPs by Ray Charles, Tony Bennett, Doris Day, Perry Como and two by Frank Sinatra! I have them to this day as all are among my favourites. I felt she must have been a luckless lover who wanted to rid herself of reminders.

All through my Highland drives my mobile phone had been unable to get a signal so it seemed a sad coincidence that when it did eventually ring, it was Steve with sad news. Our favourite eagle pair were back in their lowest, and easiest, nest and had laid two eggs, but both were stone cold and there was no sign of the adults. The sea cliff pair were flying about but their high ledge nest had been blown out by winter storms and they had not made a new one. The 'windy glen' pair had made up their nest but had not laid eggs, and it was now the end of April. Steve had seen neither of the birds. He added there had been a lot of hill walkers in that glen, and some had camped near the nest crag, probably not knowing it was there. Steve said he would do nothing further and would not try to film eagles this year but was returning to Wales with his girlfriend to find a new home and to get ready for their forthcoming marriage. Again I felt some relief, along with a strange kind of guilt for feeling relieved.

I've failed again on the west coast, so let's try the east coast, I thought. Pausing in Buckie to pay in the £250 fee for the Aberdona survey, I decided to drive up as far as Helmsdale and look along all seafronts. I went via Inverness to Munlochy and Avoch to Chanonry Point but the famous dolphins didn't show up – just plenty of cars and gawpers. On I went, up through Cromarty and Jemimaville and Balblair to the A9 and north to Alness. I then took the coast road through Invergordon and Barbaraville but there were no small homes for sale on any seafront. The Cromarty Firth looked rather hideous, filled with oil rigs, cranes and naval works, so I didn't want to live there anyway. I went past Tain and over the Dornoch Firth to near Skelbo, where I camped in a Forestry Commission clearing. That night I had a powerful dream that I should just go back to the Hawick area! My main bank was there, after all, and my best doctor, dentist and lawyer. And what about its fascinating river, which would star in the video I was still making about river wildlife? When I woke up, though, I felt I must still pursue my dream of a place on the sea.

I drove on up to Helmsdale but it was all very touristy, with golf courses and caravan parks at the end of even tiny roads wherever there was a sandy beach. Only the Embo area and Loch Fleet wildlife reserve had the terrain I liked but there were no properties for sale. Knowing I had failed again, I drove all the way back to Spey Bay by 7 p.m. and while I felt downhearted, I forced myself to cobble together a pressure cooker meal before getting the bed down and collapsing into it.

To cheer myself up next morning, after re-stocking Caballo in Buckie with groceries, water and petrol, I returned to my campsite below the pines and rang Jim Crumley and Laurie Campbell to exchange news. We agreed to meet shortly. I then had a 'Fleet Street bath.' This involved my standing naked in an empty bowl on spread-out sheets of newspaper and swabbing myself down with flannel and soap from a bowl of hot water. I could then change my underwear and socks, not before time, as I'd had them on for nearly three weeks. I felt a lot better. I was still thinking about a return to Hawick, but had to visit Laurie in Paxton en route. It was then that a memory suddenly came back to me - Dunbar! I had briefly visited the birthplace of John Muir, the first great conservationist, and had glimpsed in the park named after him many long golden sandy beaches. If the great man could be born there, maybe I could die there! And it was en route for Laurie's home anyway.

I had another long drive the next day and I ended up camping beside a ruined castle. As I cooked up, I reflected how urgently I wanted to find my little seashore paradise. All the long drives were killing me. Next morning, when I drowsily peeped through the side window, I saw many hares running about in the fields beside Caballo, some jumping on each other and actually boxing. This usually takes place when an over-zealous male is plighting his troth a little too strongly and the female is trying to stop him and drive him off. Naked or not, I grabbed my camera, by luck still on its tripod, slowly opened a front window and poked it through to get the best 'courting' hares footage I ever took.

Shortly after this, dawn turning into early sunlight, I was walking between the pines along the golden beaches of the Muir Park and, after covering almost half of the eight miles of sand and salt marshes, found myself really beginning to think that this was it! I sat on a dune for almost two hours, writing up my diaries of the last few days and looking out onto the small flocks of sea birds drifting on the blue sea. On the hike back, now on the well-used track further into the trees, I soon changed my mind. It was a Saturday, mid- morning, and walkers, many with dogs, were coming from the direction of the town, increasing in number near the end of the track. Some were none too particular where their dogs left their waste. Muir Park? More like Dog Poo Park, I thought. And the car park was filling up with cars, vans and mountain bikers. I did spend a day looking along the coast road and harbour and even viewed three flats in the High Street, but in the end knew I could not return to the kind of claustrophobic life they offered. I called in on Laurie in Paxton, enjoyed some good crack and a nice supper cooked by his wife Margaret. His wildlife photography business was going well and he told me he was not pleased about his tax bill of the previous year. He mentioned the amount, a higher figure than I have ever earned in a year, let alone paid in tax. I camped in the drive of his new house and next day he took me on a short but hard trek on which we found a new fox earth, and I located some scattered cub scats. Laurie offered to set up with me but I had an important bank appointment in Hawick next day and this old carcass needed a few restful days, so I had to forgo his offer and drive on to my old 'home' town.

In Hawick I visited my lawyer friend Charles who sent me to see the best property for me on his books, an old Boy Scouts' headquarters near the main bridge and on the banks of the River Teviot. It was not seashore but it was waterfront and in terms of film the river was always interesting. I investigated all possibilities but detailed planning permissions would be needed for all conversions and would involve a lot of hassle. Back at my Craik Forest campsite, I debated whether or not to give up and run back down to Sussex, where my love of nature began. I thought again of that dreaded retirement flat in Worthing or some such place, because that would be all I could afford. I then recalled an old friend of mine, Phil Corcoran, a former estate manager, who told me that he thought the most beautiful part of Scotland was Galloway: two pairs of golden eagles, plenty of red deer, pine martens, wild goats and not many tourists. Phil had been the man who arranged for the owner of the idyllic island of Eilean Shona to meet me, resulting in my living in an old croft there for three years, which I wrote about in my book Between Earth and Paradise. I valued his opinion, so off to Galloway I went.

22

ON THE BEACH AND GOSHAWKS IN WALES

Whenever possible I took the minor coast roads but, again, where there were sandy beaches, so too were the inevitable caravan parks and small golf courses. It was all very touristy. Through Annan to Powfoot ('Swimming dangerous!' said the signs), onto Bowhouse and up to Dumfries to visit four property agents. I took the Dalbeattie road, turned off at Beeswing and investigated Southerness – a huge holiday village – before heading onto Sandyhills, which seemed worse - like Cornwall, with free parking for only 30 minutes - down to Portling (yet more caravan parks), up through Dalbeattie and Castle Douglas and down the A75 to Gatehouse of Fleet, which Phil had told me years before was below a 'real mini-Highlands area.' I was running short of fuel so when I found the petrol station closed, I took the little road up to Laurieston and after five miles saw a ruined little croft in a wild spot, so camped there. I began to feel doomed. I would never find my Last Wild Place.

Bright sunshine the next morning lifted my spirits and I was filming old Caballo in his picturesque setting by the ruined croft when I noticed a large brown bird flying low and towards us. Just a buzzard, I thought, but as it went overhead I realised it was an eagle, doubtless a male. I tried to swivel the camera onto it but I was just too late and only got its vanishing rump. This incident was enough to make me feel that I may as well search a bit longer, as a return to Sussex was not yet a favoured option, so after getting petrol at Gatehouse I drove through the Cairnsmore of Fleet wildlife reserve to look at an isolated cottage. It proved to be very nice but too small, and too pricey at £70,000, but then I ran into my first piece of real luck in five months of searching. I met the Scottish Natural Heritage warden Kevin Carter, who said he had read most of my books, especially my three about my work (or should I say adventures?) with golden eagles, and that he was a big fan of mine. He added I could have free reign of the whole area.

Kevin also told me I should take a look around Wigtown, which was really Scotland's Book Town and equivalent to Hay-on-Wye in England. On the way there I looked for properties from Mossyard to Creetown and found none, but did find two long lay-bys, fringed with trees, just a pebble's throw above lonely sandy beaches. 'I could live here!' I said to myself. One lady who ran a specialist wildlife bookshop in Wigtown said that my books went out almost as soon as they came in but she did have one left, which I bought so that I could sell it on. She wrote down the names of three estate agents in Newton Stewart who, she was sure, would be able to help me.

Through Kevin I met the Forestry Commission's head land agent Stephen in Galloway Forest Park Centre. He immediately left his office and drove me to Glenhead House, which I had been told was on Loch Trool and for which the Commission wanted the right sort of tenant. He thought I might fit the bill, and they would charge a peppercorn rent. I looked over its many rooms but it was a full mile from Loch Trool and down a long and very rough stony track that would have killed off Caballo in two weeks. The house was in rough shape with many holes in the floorboards, broken windows and water off the hill. There was no electricity, just an old generator. Twenty years before I would have taken it on (the croft on Shona had been in worse shape) but it was beyond me now. As we talked, up came a shepherd called Willie who had found one of his ewe mothers without her lamb and had been looking for it all morning. I glassed the hills with my binoculars, saw some ravens moving and flapping on the ground, pointed them out to Willie and said that he would probably find the lamb up there, dead. He climbed up and returned with its bloodied corpse. He and the agent said they were amazed and, to be honest, I was kind of surprised myself.

I decided to head down to Sussex for a week to complete business, visit friends, put Caballo into the reliable Skinners garage for service and repairs, have his TV and video 12-volt system fixed and take one last look round the Worthing-Goring-Ferring area before heading back to Galloway, which I now far preferred to the Moray Firth region. I did all that and when I discovered that even grotty, sordid, noisy little flats above shops were going for over £70,000, my Sussex dream, fading as it was, came to an end. 'It's all down to wonderful Galloway now', I wrote in my diary.

I drove through the Lake District in mist and driving rain but at Gatehouse of Fleet all of Galloway seemed bathed in brilliant sunshine. I took a second look at a nice, isolated cottage near Port William but the title deeds revealed that a burn I had liked did not adjoin the property, the kitchen's flat roof had sprung several leaks, there was a dead and decaying mouse in the water well and the price had been upped by two thousand pounds. Back in Newton Stewart I had just left two estate agents who had nothing on their books that interested me when I bumped into the forestry land agent Stephen, who was heading into the off licence for some Jim Beam whisky. When I told him that I, too, was a whisky man, he not only invited me to share it but to go back with him to his super farmhouse, meet his family, stay for dinner and camp there too. What a nice and unexpected surprise! We had quite a party night: his wife Jane was charming, his three kids were full of life and we fooled around, with me even teaching 13-year-old Alistair a couple of boxing moves as he had a bag up in the garage (and a harder punch than I would have believed in a 13-year-old). I collapsed happily into my bed in old Caballo, knowing I had already made new friends in Galloway.

Next day I ambled into the third agent in Newton Stewart's High Street, C. M. Thomson, and asked, as usual, for 'Anything small, isolated and on the sea?' 'This has just come in,' said the agent and handed me details of a holiday cottage on the beach near Monreith which seemed fairly isolated. I took one look at the photos and thought 'This is it!' I took the details and drove down, turning left through Port William into Monreith, then right along a track. I could recognise the cottage, a bungalow, from the photos: it was out on a green, grassy spur, all on its own. I turned left at the end of the track and saw the first long, sandy beaches – it was a fabulous coast, even better than at Cullen or any I'd seen on the Moray Firth. I drove into the garden of the bungalow, got out of Cab – and fell in love with the place! It was perched on a bulging 50-foot cliff directly above the sandy beach and overlooking the beautiful Luce Bay. The nearest holiday cottage was sixty yards away but a thick gorse hedge hid most of it. The garden was large, nearly half an acre, and although it would need re-fencing to keep sheep out, that wouldn't be costly as I could do it myself. I drove to see two other cottages but they didn't compare.

I made lunch in Cab then rang Thomson's. I wanted to see inside as I was very interested and they sent a Mr Evans that very afternoon to meet me with the keys. I liked the interior, the two bedrooms, well enough, even though it was rather run-down and substandard, with asbestos in the walls. The sun lounge was huge and quite splendid with windows on all three sides. We found a steep, winding track down the cliff, leading from the garden to the beach, and I decided that if it was private, which Mr Evans was sure it was, I would buy the place. I told him to offer £500 above the asking price of £40,000 and he said he would put it to the owners the next day, as by then it was late. Next morning I hiked/climbed down the cliff footpath, passing under a large wooden arch into which I could easily fix a gate, and stepped onto the sandy beach. Again I had the impression of the Caribbean, the blue sea lapping the golden shore, the rock pools with small darting fish and the cliffs in which fulmars and gulls were nesting. I even managed a few jogging steps without pitching forward this time. I liked the place more and more and after climbing up the path again, I went to the porch and made my little Wilderness prayer. 'I will love and look after you if you...' But when I checked with Thomson's I realised I would have to be more patient. Mrs Robb said the owners were away on holiday in Greece and would not be back for ten days, but she was sure I'd get it with that offer.

As it was my 72nd birthday next morning, I decided to go up to Cairnsmore of Fleet, give Kevin what seemed my good news and go and look for eagles around the Clints of Dromore, the great 'dramatic' cliffs Phil Corcoran had told me about so long ago. Kevin was away for the day, so I went up on the top road and surveyed them from about halfway along. There was a large notice board there, showing the famed landmarks: The Clints, The Door and The Spout. I may as well have a wee trek, I thought, hiked over to a Forestry Commission fence and then just kept going. In the end I traversed the entire range of the Clints, first at low level then back again up but higher, right below the cliffs. It became a fab eagle day. I saw one eagle, far off, located two eyries, although they were old and had not been used that year, and a nesting peregrine. The nest ledge was too high for me to see if she was on eggs or very young chicks when she flew off. I also spotted three young ravens who had just flown their nest, and filmed them briefly. I covered five hard miles, with some climbing involved, so it was good to know that I was not quite 'done' yet! I then drove to Murray's Monument area where I had been told there were wild goats, I saw a small group but they were a long way off and I wasn't up to any more trekking that day.

At dusk I went back to camp in what I hoped would become my garden and had no sooner arrived than Jim Crumley rang to wish me happy birthday. It was most thoughtful of him and when I told him I was trying to buy in Monreith, he reminded me that Gavin Maxwell had been born there, which I had completely forgotten. It was Maxwell's classic book Ring of Bright Water and its descriptions of the Highlands that had brought me back from Canada in the very week he died. It seemed an odd and scary coincidence that I may end my life where he was born, not having remembered that fact when I came here.

Next morning Steve also rang. I told him of my eagle treks and how I'd missed wild goats yesterday and he said he had been trying to film wild goats in Snowdonia but that it had taken him over two weeks to get satisfactory film, of two big billies fighting. Two days later, after half-heartedly looking at other properties, my heart being set on the bungalow, I drove back to the Murray Monument and was amazed to find many wild goats down by the roadside, being fed by tourists! Out came my filming gear and I had a marvellous hour getting superb material – young kids suckling their mothers, goats browsing on the vegetation, butting each other out of the way in pursuit of a particularly succulent piece, and two balancing on high rocks, with all four feet close together. Best of all, I got some big billies fighting, rearing up on hind legs and coming down hard to bash their heads against their opponents', repeating the move again and again until one or other turned tail and fled. Sometimes just a turn aside was enough to stop hostilities but one billy walked after a defeated opponent and butted him up the backside to try and make him turn and fight again. I still believe my resistance to the idea of phoning Steve to impart this information was quite heroic. It might have slightly upset his mood for his marriage in two weeks' time. There was plenty of light left, so I had a nice wee climb up the Monument itself and spent a useful hour scanning the wide terrain of woods and cliffs, even locating two eagle eyries, although I didn't see any eagles.

Back at my Laurieston campsite next morning, I got a call from Jim Crumley who told me that he was using a Forestry Commission 'Keep Watch' hide over an eagles' eyrie at Balquidder and that if I arrived by 2 June he could put me into it. As we talked, I saw through Cab's side window that wheatears were flying in and out of some upraised turf only a few yards from the van, so I quietly lowered the window and filmed the nest as they took insects to their young.

The local Health Officer at Stranraer told me over the phone that the asbestos inner walls at the bungalow did not constitute a problem nor make the place inhabitable, and that I could live in it all the year round if I wished. 'Just don't drill into the walls or cut them up,' he said. 'You'll have no problems with us.' Sure now that my offer would be accepted, I drove over to Jim's cottage near Crianlarich, on the way dropping off the sales particulars to my solicitor Charles in Hawick and getting my teeth checked by my dentist in Galashiels ('How much longer can this old geezer hang onto his teeth?' I wrote in my diary). Jim drove us to Kingshouses as by then I'd had enough of driving, we had the usual great craic and I paid for the meal. Next day we were off to the Monachyle eagles.

It was a fairly hard slog up to the F.C's 'Keep Watch' hide which, as I had expected, was rather too far from the nest for really good film. I had enough close stuff anyway, so I filmed the pair flying and circling together over the eyrie cliff, a dramatic sequence of the female sweeping along the whole range of cliffs, the light and colours of the dark granite faces, the ash grey and light green lichens and the dark green of the heather all changing behind her as she passed them. The male also obliged me by flying into and out of the nest, presumably dropping off food prey, and half an hour later the female flew in and moved about, feeding the chick. I couldn't fit this new material into my main eagles video, which by now was selling well, but if I was going to continue filming them I could make a third new video, Last Eagle Years, which, eventually, I did.

On the way back from Jim's I called in, for once, at the Highland Wildlife Park at Kingussie , where some of the kittens of my own wildcat breeding project had ended up, as I had a lifetime free pass from the Royal Zoological Society of Scotland, who in 1988 elected me an Honorary Fellow. I was delighted to find the Park had a complete family of European wolves living on a wild-looking grassy hillock, complete with a small cave den, in a large enclosure. It was easy work, of course, but I took the precaution of making myself inconspicuous between two small trees so that they would relax as much as possible. I filmed the big male walking over to the female, who was lying down with her two cubs, and giving her a lick 'kiss' on the side of her head before walking off a few yards and lying down himself. I got the cubs walking in and out of the den, frisking and bouncing about and shaking their heads, and the she-wolf playing with them. Once, she gave one cub a cuff round the ear, which sent it roly-polying a few yards down the incline. All nice wolf material which would fit neatly into my Spanish wildlife video.

Back in Newton Stewart, Joy Robb said the owners were back from Greece and let me use her phone to ring the owner, who agreed to sell me the bungalow for £41,000. I rang Charles to get my official offer in fast. I camped around for a few days doing my yearly accounts, which were complicated and very tricky on a small rickety table in Caballo, the papers strewn across the seats and floor. I was just finishing them at my Laurieston campsite when a dainty little roebuck emerged from the trees and I filmed him walking about and grazing. On 7 June I camped by the bungalow and walked the entire beach, finding a ravens' nest on a crag and nesting fulmars, while gaudy oystercatchers and little turnstones, along with gulls, probed the rocky pools. I fell in love with the place all over again. I decided to stay all day and see what human disturbance there might be. I was walking back to the bungalow when an osprey flew past, quite close, and began its fishing hoverings over the sea. By the time I got the camera from Cab, though, it had gone. I measured the outside window frames, noting repairs that needed to be done. As I worked, I kept glancing around, and saw gannets, shelduck, ravens, swallows, crows, blackbirds, song thrushes, chaffinches, house martins and goldfinches.

The next day, on the way to Newton Stewart to post my accounts, I found at the side of the road a roebuck that had been killed by passing traffic. I rang the Forestry Commission but Stephen was away. Another official said that they didn't want it and put me onto a man who was part of the RSPB's Eagle Watch team. This man said they had been helping to feed a local eagle pair but that they had stopped once the eaglets were well-fledged, so he didn't want it either. I took it to Kevin and his boss at Cairnsmore but they didn't want it and seemed alarmed that I wanted to set it out for eagles, or even buzzards, as the public might see it and kick up a fuss. I said I wouldn't put it out where any humans could see it but, to pacify them, I said I would take it back to where I had found it. I must say I felt all this to be rather strange, not to mention faint-hearted. A whole roebuck would be an excellent food source to help eaglets keep strong for their first flight. I suppose, though, that one does have to be ultra-careful when dealing with the public. In the end I took it back to my Laurieston campsite and, after some searching around, left it where I could see it from Cab but no-one could from the road. Good news came, though, when I did speak to Stephen for he'd had a talk with Chris Rollie, the RSPB's chief officer for Dumfries and Galloway, and said Mr Rollie would certainly want to use me on their Eagle Watch.

A setback came when I drove back to Hawick to check all the sale documents with my solicitor Charles and conclude the deal. He said that one of the owners wanted to set back the entry date to 21 July as she wanted to spend 'a last sentimental week' at the house when her husband came out of hospital. She would not budge on this. That was a whole month away. I told Charles I would not camp around for another month and instructed him to pull out of the deal unless it was agreed that I move in within ten days. So sure was I that I'd lost out, I wasted a day looking at two High Street flats, both of which were unsuitable. Charles could not contact the owners' solicitor before lunch next day so I said I would leave it to The Fates: I would drive south to Langholm, poised to head west to Newton Stewart if the owners gave in, or south down the M6 to Sussex, and maybe on to Spain, if they did not. Half an hour later I parked for a quick lunch by the beautiful river in Langholm and rang Charles.

'Head on west!' he said.

Victory! The owners had agreed to a 4 July entry date, the lady didn't need a 'sentimental week' as her husband was still in hospital, and she would meet me the weekend before and show and explain everything. On the way back I managed to ring Chris Rollie, who was on his holidays at home in Castle Douglas, and he said he was sure he wanted me to help with the eagle pairs and with peregrines too, and would visit me in Monreith later in July. I arrived back at my Laurieston campsite to find the roebuck untouched but a barn owl flew a complete circle round the old camper van. It seemed a good omen.

I now had a few days spare so, after taking more measurements of the bungalow, I drove south - to see my London accountant and to camp at Peter Spear's and have a weekend's shooting (he even offered me a bath: greater friendship hath no man). I also wanted to take Bill Baldwin to lunch, check the peregrines (the chicks were flying) and buy some essential cheap timbers at his joinery, have Caballo serviced and see to some other business. Top of the list on this trip, though, was an offer from Steve to put me in a hide he had up on a goshawk nest. I drove from Worthing to north of Abergavenny, took a side road from Llanvihangel Crucorney and could find nowhere to camp but a small, muddy access to a sheep field. As I ate a sandwich and got the bed down, an awful smell welled up from some decomposing animal dumped nearby, but I was too tired to shift all the gear from front to rear to allow me to drive, so I just had to endure it.

Steve was dead on time at the Crucorney Inn and I followed his new Jeep along many miles of small roads, a route I would never remember, until he parked below a small forest track. We hiked up to his goshawk hide, a full 100 yards with a last 20-yard scramble down a steep, bushy, muddy cliff, and there it was. I had never had an easier trek. Steve put me in and it was hard setting up as the slope was very steep and I had to scrape my sitting-down hole deeper than it was to avoid knee strain. Steve freshened the small sprigs of greenery around my lens, then left.

A fabulous goshawk day ensued; the parents came in four times, but mostly just to dump prey. I saw a hen blackbird brought in by the male, and the larger female actually came in with a young but fully-fledged pheasant which must have weighed as much as herself, plucking the feathers until the pale pink skin was revealed, then ripping off bits of flesh and feeding the two chicks. Like most goshawk nests, this one was in a very dark wood and up a larch tree so it was not easy to get good, clear film. Goshawks seem to prefer finishing off their huge nests with larch twigs as, because they are clubby along the stems and at the ends, they grip each other and hold together better than do the twigs and fronds of other trees. By 3 p.m. I had all I wanted and, with the parents long gone, I left the hide. I'd only driven a quarter mile when I realised I'd left my mobile phone in the hide. Back I had to go, and make the mad, muddy scramble twice more to retrieve it. On my way north I saw a kestrel fly into the bell tower in Storridge. I braked, got out and filmed it peering from the nest edge. As I set off again, Steve rang, so I told him that all had gone well, thanked him profusely and added that I had also just filmed the Storridge church kestrels. He said he would set up for them too.

Over the next three days I met the lady owner, who showed me everything at the bungalow and said she would leave some keys in the house but that I'd have to pick up the main key from my agent once my £41,000 had been paid. I dumped all the timbers I'd been carrying on Cab's roof since Worthing, then drove to Hawick to complete documentation and arrange for Charles to pay my money over. Then I drove slowly back to the Laurieston campsite, where I found that the roebuck carcass had been turned round, but that no flesh was missing and nothing had fed from it. It was stinking and covered with flies, and I realised I'd wasted my time bothering with it at all.

Hiccups next day included having to wait two hours at the agent's office as my money had been paid late by a courier service, and the local sorting office saying they couldn't deliver my mail to the bungalow as there was no letter box. It was normally delivered to an old lady who had a cottage below my cliff, they said. 'No!' I said, loudly. 'Put it through my camper van's open window until I get one!' I dashed to the nearest hardware store and bought a new letter box and two Yale locks, so that I could change the locks on the two outer doors. I drove back to Monreith, entered the bungalow and spent the rest of the day unloading everything from Caballo. First, I hung up the five sets of red deer skulls and antlers that I'd found during my trekking years in the Highlands, then the huge oil painting of myself and my tracker Alsatian dog Moobli, and then some special damask curtains. I made up the best bed in the seafront bedroom, got in all the food and cooking gear, and even got a new video/TV set-up working. As the sun began to set, I looked out through the sun lounge windows, saw its last rays glimmering a path of gold across the tranquil waters of Luce Bay and thought, 'At last, I have my own little paradise!'

This concept seemed confirmed next morning when a nice young postman came right to my front door as I was drilling holes for the letter box, handed me some mail and said he was glad he could now deliver to my actual house 'as it is so beautiful here.' That was one of my main worried overcome. I spent three more days painting, puttying, hammering and sawing, wanting to get the place more shipshape – and rainproof – before relaxing enough for another walk along the beach. When I did I hiked the full mile, found again the ravens' nest and the fulmars, still nesting with grown young, and at the end I discovered a wee kirk in the rocky cliffs with a 19th-century graveyard, where some of the stones were in disarray but whose grassy paths were well mown. I wouldn't mind being buried there myself, I thought. The sea pools, lined with colourful stones and weeds of varying greens, were again entrancing, as were the little burns rippling down from the cliffs and through the golden sand to the sea. Yes, this was a fab place and I was dead right to buy it, despite all the doubts and small complications. This will do me for the rest of my life, I thought.

23

BEACH NIGHTMARES AND ME –
IN AN EAGLE TEAM?

It all began to go wrong in mid-July with the shrieking children. I was trying to repair the broken fence and had torn my fingers when curling back barbed wire without wearing my thick gardening gloves. Then, using five thick wire coat hangers from the house, I had it all done in two hours. It was then I heard the yelling. There was a large party of children on the beach, about a quarter mile to the west. Oh well, I thought, probably a school outing, a once- a-year disturbance, and I could hardly hear them inside the house when I shut all the doors and windows.

The next thing I heard was the loud slamming of a truck's door. Stan Purves, the removal man who had shifted all my gear on my last four moves (including to far-away East Dean) had arrived with it all yet again. During the three days it took me to sort out the chaos and stash everything in place, Steve rang, asking how my move had gone. He was fed up, as he had gone into the goshawk hide himself ten days after I'd left, although he'd meant to leave it only two, and all the chicks had flown. At least he had got good material on his first two visits. Shortly after putting the phone down, I heard a dog barking. I went out, looked around and saw it in the garden of the old lady who had a cottage below my cliff, on the far side of the track in. I had met her twice (she had warned me the council tax would be high, and it was - £809 a year for a sub-standard bungalow) but she had never had a dog with her. When I next climbed down my steep cliff track I found a full blue bin and some rubbish scattered on the very end of the track, opposite her house. I pushed it all off my track and knocked on her door. She said she had not put it there but thought I had, to deter folk from going up my path. Who was doing it, then, and why? Half an hour later I was painting my exterior walls when a white-haired old crone with false-teethy smiles and a wee dog marched in and handed me a letter of welcome signed by fifteen Monreith residents, inviting me to take part in their communal activities. I thanked her but told her I was a writer who came here for the privacy and needed to get on with my work. As she walked away, I reflected that communal activities were the last thing I wanted. The truth was that, at the time, I dreaded friendship thrust upon me more than a clear enemy.

Next day there were more kids yelling on the beach, nearer this time, so I couldn't do any writing. It was a hot, sunny day so I walked all along the beach, well past the noisy families, and had three short swims in the sea, the first sea swims since ones in Spain 12 years earlier. As I was drying off, an old man, whom I'd met briefly with the old lady opposite, headed straight towards me and said 'I wondered who was the brave one. How d'you like your new home up there?' Not wanting to encourage him, I laughed and said loudly, 'Fine, just fine!' and walked away. I was painting outside window frames next morning when another old woman walked in, collecting for the Lifeboats. I gave her 50p and went indoors. It was all far busier here than I'd expected. As I surveyed all my possessions, almost doubled by the furniture, curtains, kitchenware and other gear left by the owners, I felt, for the first time, that I had to get rid of the clutter if I were to be free. This feeling increased over the next few days with more families shouting on the beach, sea fishermen parking their cars, the old lady's dog barking more often and even a small camper or two blocking the track that I had been told was private and not open to the public. I wrote in my diary. 'I was wrong! This place is not quiet, is not a paradise, so start getting rid of everything.' I drove to Wigtown and met bookshop owner Margaret Hosken who said my books were popular and promptly bought £72 worth from me! That was a good start. I rang Stephen to come and collect free items for his holiday cottages, which he did, but took only cutlery and things that were easy to carry, still leaving me with four beds and other large items. I rang Mike Moir, the head librarian at the A. K. Bell library at Perth who, four years earlier, had bought my first archives and he agreed to buy the up-to-date ones. One day I filled Caballo twice with unwanted items and drove to the main dump at Whithorn where a nice young (and tough) lad helped me unload and said I could bring anything else I wanted rid of.

On 22 July I woke up to see shadows moving over the bedroom walls. There was a herd of heifers in my garden! They had already made a mess of my small lawn. They had not busted through my newly-repaired fence but must have come up the lane and through my gateway as there was no actual gate. I dressed fast and shoo-ed them out, whacking the odd rump with a walking stick, and blocked the gateway with Caballo turned sideways. Next day, a Sunday, the noises from the beach were hellish, shrieking kids all over the place, one family with German accents, fishermen blocking the track below and talking, the wind carrying their voices up to me. I'll never forget the sound of one father, sounding very Cockney, yelling, 'Come on in, Angela. It's not cold!' I heard it clearly, yet all the doors and windows were closed. In the end I had to put in ear plugs. I wrote in my diary, 'I cannot live here the rest of my life. The sooner I do it up and sell it, after getting rid of most of my gear, the better. I did not have that awful long search to end up with a place in which I have to wear ear plugs! I know it's only for two months a year but even that is too much.'

Once, after seeing lots of left-over logs lying around after forestry operations, I tried to get permission to cut a few for my wood stove, offering even to pay for them. Stephen had told me I would need a 'firewood licence,' costing about a fiver. When I investigated at two separate offices, I was told I would also need a chainsaw licence, which was hard to obtain and involved an examination. I didn't argue but did point out that I'd been a logger in Canada and used a chainsaw for 32 years with no problems. A plump fellow in the office said, 'So have I. But I still don't have a chainsaw licence!' After all the racket from the beach I decided not to pursue the matter any further.

The only good experience at this time came when Chris Rollie, the local RSPB boss, drove in to see me. Big, bluff and jovial, he and I hit it off immediately. He said he did want me to help with Eagle Watch next year and to work closely with himself and his two-man team, Ian Miller and Charlie Parks, who would be glad to have me work with them. The main work would be on the southern pair of eagles and he showed me where their nest was on his map. To my utter astonishment it was the very nest that Dave Walker had marked for me on my map, a map I had not even looked at during my search for a seafront home as it hadn't been during the eagles' breeding season. Chris said the team had seen an old guy with a backpack, binoculars and dark hair beneath the nest tree in April and they had all been sure it was me. I, of course, denied it but when he saw my map he took a step back and said, 'It must have been you. You've marked the nest!' I explained everything, that I had never been in Galloway in April and offered to show him my diaries to prove it. Chris said no, it was not important as the nest had been robbed before then and they had found the marks of the climbing irons. He said he was 'only too glad' to get my expert help and that I would receive money for petrol and a key to the forestry track that led to the nest. What was more, Ian and Charlie would meet me and show me the nest in the next week. What was most astonishing was that my little campsite at Laurieston had been quite close to the nest tree, yet I had not known it as I had not looked at that map. However, it did explain my first sighting of the eagle flying there.

I cooked us a fine lunch of ham and mushroom tagliatelli before Chris drove us to St Medan golf course. From there we hiked a fair way and over some rough rocky cliffs for him to show me where the only pair of choughs were breeding in Scotland. We peered into the dark cave and blow me if we didn't see both of them! They left their two well-grown chicks in the nest, flew out and dived about the sky giving out loud 'schriiaw' cries, which took me back to the mountains of Spain. Chris insisted on driving me all the way home, even though I offered to walk the last rough track. As chairman of all Scotland's Raptor Study Groups, he invited me to give a talk, or show one of my wildlife videos, at their next conference in

February. I said I would but asked him not to tell me the exact date or my knees would start knocking!

Although Chris Rollie's visit perked me up considerably, things took a turn for the worse next morning. The family in the nearest holiday home turned up and the man began work with a strimmer. More families with yelling kids came onto the beach, stopping right below my cliff as if hitting an invisible wall, and the second holiday home now had seven youngish folk in it who started barbecuing on their patio, some with binoculars pointing my way, though probably just looking over the sea views and not directly at me. I knew it now – I had stepped into a nightmare! I rang Mrs Robb at Thomsons and said I wanted to sell up! She was rather surprised but knew of two couples who were looking for my kind of place and said she would send them round. I worked feverishly to finish on the bungalow, hiring a long ladder to repair barge boards, flashings and gables on the roof and by 1 August had completed all the exterior work. I hoped to sell for £42,500 and recover all my costs. I still very much wanted to do the eagle work but that would be in the spring, and I would surely have found a new, quieter, more private home by then.

I had some complications arranging to meet the two eagle workers as Ian worked full time in a carpet factory and Charlie was retired but running some holiday homes, but we finally met in a Forestry Commission car park at Mossdale on 4 August. At first I thought they were a couple of hard, tough old guys but Charlie at 62 and big Ian at only 46 were both considerably younger than me, and I feared they would find my trekking abilities wanting. They led me and Caballo to the Loch Trool car park and from there we hiked in to the Galloway eagles' nest. It was a darn sight longer than the mile or so it looked on the map Chris had shown me – about three miles of hard terrain, with awful deep tussocks up to the conifer forest rides towards the end. But it was well worth it.

I had never seen a more magnificent setting for a golden eagle eyrie. It was a huge, broad nest up in the main crotch of a large Scots pine which looked as if it had been designed by some divine artist to emphasise its aesthetic qualities and spectacular beauty. My heart began to pound at the thought that I could be filming the kings of birds flying in and out, and landing and feeding their youngsters in such a glorious setting.

The two men let me prospect around for the ideal hide site, even beating down some 7 ft high bracken as I wanted to get one up on the south side of the clearing, where the light would be better all day. We checked various sites and they said some 'gardening' could be done, meaning that they could cut back any branches, or even a bush or two, that were in the way. I said we could not really decide until the tall, thick bracken had died down – there might be a wee hillock here, or a small fallen tree there, which could be best for a hide site. The trick was to outwit the eagles with an 'invisible' hide so that they would never know we were there, and neither should they be able to see us coming in. It all had to be planned like a military campaign, the eagles being armed 'snipers' who would shoot you if they saw you! The men said it sounded good but that they didn't operate that close.

Both had a great sense of humour and the longer we were together, the more I liked them – especially when they said I moved well for a man of 72. The fact was that after the six miles my hips were rather painful and I made no effort to hide or disguise my slight limp. If in the end I decided the treks were all too much for me, as a good eagle watch lasts a minimum of ten weeks, I would have a reason to duck out.

Back at the car park we had a fruitful discussion. It turned out that Ian had to look after (watch) 30 peregrine nests and two hen harrier nests in the region, so didn't have all that much time for the eagles, even though they were the most important. I, on the other hand, did. 'Here I am, born to do this kind of work and I'll help all I can as I have time on my hands!' I said. They seemed happy with that. I added that I thought the most important thing was to protect the eagles to allow a chick to fly, which meant stopping folk from going near the nest. They said there was no way they could guard a nest; they only had time to check from an opposite hill once in every ten days, or at most once a week. I thought it small wonder they were robbed, then, but didn't say it. I did point out that there are ways of stopping folk who go too close without being belligerent, as it is illegal intentionally to disturb a Schedule One bird while it is in, on or near a nest containing eggs or young, or to disturb its dependent young. Anyone disturbing the nest could be told as much. Ian gave me a cuppa from his flask and Charlie offered to share his sandwich lunch which I declined, saying that I needed to slim down! They told me there was a shorter route to the nest tree but that it was over a Miss B's private land, and she was an ogre who ordered trespassers off. The situation with the keys to the forestry tracks sounded complicated and I felt it would be easier to gain Miss B's co-operation, but these were early days...

I got back to my home intent on two things – selling up, and getting rid of gear, so I set about both in earnest. A couple came in and offered the £42,500 which meant, after all costs were included, that I would lose £920. It was well worth it, to get out of this nightmare! Margaret Hosken and her husband Mike came and bought all the books and two bookcases which I wanted rid of for £200, leaving me with only a tiny wildlife reference 'library' and hardly any personal library at all. I got back from Wigtown, after driving the bookcases to their shop, to hear that Alec Guinness had died at 86 and Robin Day at only 76. I always considered Guinness the finest character actor Britain ever produced and I was sad about Robin, as he and I had had enjoyed some memorable times on the French Riviera when I was a celebrity reporter. (We once went to a nudist beach in St Tropez but were too scared to get our kit off!)

Two days later, Mrs Robb rang to say the buying couple could not, after all, raise the money, so my home went back on the market. Stephen was interested in buying it but, after discussions with his wife Jane, felt they could not really afford to keep their big home and three holiday cottages, of which mine would have been the third. I told him I would soon need somewhere to store my dwindling possessions and lay my head, and he said he would try and find me somewhere.

At this time Chris Rollie told me over the phone that Ian and Charlie liked me very much and looked forward to working with me, and he approved of my setting an 'invisible' hide somewhere safe south of the nest. They would work out where I could park and camp in Caballo on a forestry track nearer the nest tree. If it turned out that I could only get to that spot by going along Miss B's track, he would send me all the information on her he could find and leave me to try to get her to co-operate.

24

No More Golden Beaches. Back to Town!

On 16 August, the sunshine was blazing outside. I was typing out some personal philosophy, having had had an argument with one of my readers who had said, 'Everything born is entitled to a good life.' I had argued, 'No! Everything born is not entitled to a good life – it has to earn it, by working hard, as wildlife has to, to survive.', when I saw two people standing on the cliff in my garden, gazing rapturously out to sea. I wasn't fully clothed but by the time I was and had got my shoes on, there came a light knock on the door. The man was clutching my sales particulars. They had been sent by Mrs Robb. I showed them round outside, pointing out new work I had done, then showed them around the inside, and the smiles never left their faces. When he said 'Could we look.. er.. perambulate alone outside?' I said, 'Of course, go anywhere, take all the time you like.' They walked around for a quarter of an hour and, peeping through the windows, I could see they were enraptured. They came back. 'We want to buy your house!' said the man.

The couple turned out to be a Philip Berkeley and his partner Kay from Ditchling in Sussex. He ran a property investment business which he could run, via computer, from anywhere in the country, and intended this to be their main home. Kay said that they'd been looking for somewhere like my house for years and would never find a better place. They didn't have to get a mortgage, they had cash waiting. When I told them that a price of £42,500 would mean my losing £920 on total costs, Phil immediately said, 'Oh, we can't have that. We will cover your costs too. How about £43,000?' There and then, we shook hands on the deal.

Phil and Kay came back the next morning and I showed them more: the private footpath and the beach, and they brought with them a super local painting of my view from the bungalow. I said, though, that it would mean more to them as I was leaving the place, and swapped it for a bottle of whisky! Mike Hosken turned up, too, and said he and Margaret had 'fallen in love' with the large, heavy beech table which I'd made myself with chainsaws and asked how much I wanted for it. '£200!' I said, by now acutely conscious that I needed to shed more weight, although I'd turned down an offer of £300 in Sussex. Mike produced the notes and he, Phil and I loaded the table into Mike's car, the boot sticking open.

I now needed to find new accommodation fast and, over a drink with Stephen, discussed my possibly renting under some kind of licence a well- presented hut with all utilities at the Commission's Talnotry campsite. I could stow my gear there and have the right to camp too. It was near the Murray Monument where I had seen an eagle and located two eyries. Stephen knew all about my meetings with the RSPB team and was glad I was 'now aboard', as the Commission also worked closely with the RSPB and local authorities for the eagles' welfare.

I spent days packing, selling and dumping gear and on 28 August, my removal man Stan came to collect about two-thirds of what I had come with for his cheap storage in Galashiels. The noise from the families on the beach was getting worse and I began wishing for rain to help keep them off. In early September, Phil wrote that he had now paid the money, confirmed by my solicitor Charles in Hawick, and he would take over the property on 15 September. On the eleventh, I drove to Hawick, met my old doctor in the street, who said he would take me back on his panel, signed final documents and bunged a sack of worn clothes into a friendly laundrette. Next day I delivered all the hefty cartons of my new archives to Mike Moir in Perth Library, who had agreed to pay £800 for them.

On the way back I called in on Chris Rollie at his home, who again confirmed he wanted me in the Eagle Watch team. I told him my ideas and said I needed to see all possible tracks in to the eyrie. He immediately rang Charlie Parks and arranged that we all meet the following week, to take me to the tracks and allow me to assess the true situation, including Miss B. Before reaching the bungalow, where I could never get a signal on my mobile, I stopped in Newton Stewart for groceries and to ring Stephen. Had he got the Forestry Commission hut for me or not? So I could be near the eagles? To my intense surprise and disappointment, he said no.

'Everyone wants to support you, Mike, and they're sympathetic to what you are doing. But we've talked to everyone involved and as it used to be a campsite, if you camped there now, many folk who used to do so will say 'Who is he?' and 'Why him?' The hut is not secure anyway, and it's not really suitable for living in.' My heart sank. If I had got that hut as part shelter, somewhere to store the hide and a few other valuable bits and pieces, I would have been far surer that folks were on my side and happier to do all the eagle work for nothing but petrol money. Now, however, I was not so sure. My doubts increased when I found out that no-one involved knew who owned the piece of land on which the eagles' nest tree grew. It was believed to be a famous actress. The actress was one whom I had interviewed early in her career, but she had proved so difficult that I never wrote the story. If it were true, what a strange quirk of fate that would be. If I were to do this work, I would have to find out and try to get her co-operation. Further enquiries revealed that, in some ways, the various authorities like the Forestry Commission, Scottish

Natural Heritage and the RSPB seemed at times to be at odds with each other. It was also a hotbed of minor intrigues, I now realised. There was the grudging landowner, some stalkers who had been annoyed at having to shift a high seat which was too close to the nest tree, and about a hundred folk who knew the site, some of whom liked to hike in and visit it. I could be a fool to build a hide nearer the nest, stay in it on my own and attempt – also on my own - to deal with any husky lads with climbing irons. Also, I would have to comply to some extent with what the rest of the team wanted, and I had never been a team man. Neither did I see the point of watching a nest from a kilometre away. I always worked best on my own or, at most, with just one other person, like the gifted Steve Phillipps. The truth was that, to date, I had photographed and filmed nesting eagles twenty times, and every time the chicks had flown. I had never lost a chick or caused any disturbance. In the end I decided I could not work in this situation unless I was put in complete charge and that, I knew, would not happen.

The day before Phil Berkeley was due to take over, the bungalow's bathroom floor was flooded by a leaking pipe. I struggled to repair it but in vain. I dashed to the home of a plumber in Port William, who wasn't in. I pinned a note to his front door to come to me, fast. He arrived early next morning, we both dug feverishly near the outside stopcock and found that a pipe had rusted through. He replaced it with a new polythene pipe, by midday the job was done and, with all doors open on a hot sunny day, the bathroom floor was dry by nightfall. When the next day I handed the keys to a smiling Phil. I somehow forgot to mention this incident but told him, 'Be happy here. It's your paradise now!'

As he waved me away with a kind invitation to 'Come and visit any time!' I felt I was yet again driving off into oblivion. I really had no idea where to head next, except back to Hawick, to collect my money and pay it into my bank there. When I stopped halfway to make lunch, Steve rang me on my mobile, inviting me to his new home in Llandeilo to meet his new wife Delyth, and promising to take me to a fab new site where I could film all the red kites I wanted! He and the boss of the film company where he worked also wanted to make a film of me going about my wildlife work in Spain which would a) be a fab holiday and b) get me a substantial fee. I said 'Yes!' on both counts, just as soon as I had got a new base in which to stow my gear. Caballo was yet again groaning with weight.

In Hawick I took Charles to lunch after he had given me a substantial cheque for £41,790 which meant I had not lost money on the bungalow deal but had actually made a profit of £384. As I came out of the bank I almost literally bumped into my wonderful former Dr Pat Manson, who again said he would gladly take me back on his panel if I came back to the area. I suppose it is a sign of old age when one picks one's next accommodation with a view to the medical care available nearby. I went back to Charles' office and told him that I wanted a small, quiet flat, maybe for just a year or so, as long as it was not in the High Street! He laughed, and handed me some particulars. I looked at two places that very afternoon, both of which were unsuitable, then drove to camp by the river at Tushielaw, as my old Craik Forest site was now gated.

I spent most of the next week looking at properties, finally settling on what was, to me, a luxurious 3-bedroom second floor flat in an extension of the High Street but in a quiet residential area. I even managed to beat down the purchase price from £27,000 to £23,500, and the surveyor I employed said I had got myself 'an absolute bargain.' It would be easy to sell on, too.

During this time, Chris Rollie rang me asking when I was going to meet him and the team to go and look at the tracks into the eagles' eyrie. I had to break the sad news that I would not be working with them on the eagles after all as I had a lucrative offer to make a film in Spain. It was rather a white lie but I felt that if I told him the whole truth he would be very hurt, and he had been extremely nice to me. It really was, after all, an honour that he should want me, a complete outsider, to help. He just wished me well in Spain and hoped that we would meet again soon. As an afterthought, I later rang him to say that the other reason I had pulled out was because the Forestry Commission would not let me have the hut. I would have had no close base from which to operate with the team.

All the tramping around Hawick and up and down stairs to look at flats, and the new days of camping wild, were giving me painful hips again as well as odd pains between my ribs. When I registered back with Dr Manson he laid me on a bench, prodded all round my gut and declared, 'Nothing wrong there!' He pulled my legs about, up and down and sideways, and the only pain I felt was in the main groin tendons. He said my hip joints were fine. My body had been used for many years to prolonged, continual and arduous exercise. Now I had stopped all that, my muscles went into spasm the moment I tried to start it again. The pains were a muscle and nerve thing and not due to worn-out bone joints. I later had blood and urine tests with which he said he was 'delighted, as they were all very good.' He added that I was the fittest 72-year-old he had ever met. He made me feel a million dollars and glad to be back in the area.

With time to kill before actually moving into the flat, I drove over to Llandeilo and met Steve and his new wife, a very attractive, intelligent lady with a PhD in biology. His film company boss, Richard Reece, joined us and we discussed the possible film about my wildlife work and treks in Spain. They were going to a major Wildscreen conference the following week and hoped to get backing for the project. They might even do it in four half-hour programmes. Steve was grinning from ear to ear and I had no idea his boss had gone for it in such a big way. I felt it could be a wonderful project; Steve and I working together would make something magical. Richard, who was a hill man himself, wanted all my wildlife videos, insisted I get them from Caballo and wrote out a cheque for the lot there and then. Golly, he must be serious, I thought.

Steve then drove us to Llandovery where I bought lunch, then took me to the Gigrin Farm red kite feeding station. To say I was wafted back into a wildlife paradise is an understatement. It was a truly fabulous day with red kites. I got over fifteen excellent minutes on my Hi 8 camera, which suddenly began working perfectly, having been on the blink for months. At the start, a wrinkled, bent old man singled me out and began chatting in a soft voice. I thought at first that he was just a local yokel, but the more he talked, the more I admired him. He was Eithel Powell, the farmer who had started it all. He had a fine mind, espoused brilliant ideas and told me how it had all started four years before, when he saw eight red kites on his land. He felt that if he fed them, they might stay, so from that day on he bought offal and off-cut meats from a slaughterhouse, drove it back and distributed at least 60 lbs a day over a rough field, beside which he eventually built some large, wooden public hides. Soon the kites began to gather from all directions, and that day most of Wales' new kites must have been there because I counted 160!

It was truly wonderful to see them circling, weaving, diving down to snatch up meat and winging away again. A heroic raven stole meat from below a kite's beak on the ground. A buzzard kept grimly nipping at a chunk of meat, only ducking its head an inch or two when dive-bombed by a kite. In all I had some marvellous film, my best ever of red kites, including the footage I'd shot in Spain. Eithel said he would like me back and that I was welcome at any time. I felt complimented that he had chosen to talk to me out of forty folk in the hide, and later sent him my video At Home with Eagles.

The next day, I drove down to Sussex to complete a lot of important business and to spend a few days target shooting with my old pal Peter Spear, who had been gamely sending on my mail to wherever I was for the past year. Back in Hawick, because old Caballo had again been making odd metallic noises, I booked him into Thornwood Motors who had always done a good job on him. Two hours later, Derek, the mechanic, rang me to say it would cost between £1,500 and £2,000 to repair, rebuild, service and get Caballo through his MOT. I thought how much I loved him, of all we had been through together, my faithful old 'horse,' and didn't hesitate.

'Do it. Get him through!' I said. 'Are you sure?' asked Derek, incredulously. 'Yes, I am. Get him through!' I replied.

On 17 October, I moved into the new flat. After sixteen hefty carryings of my gear from the basement where I had been allowed to unload it, I sat down for a first dram. I stared at my scattered belongings and thought, 'Hey ho. I'm back in town. In seven years I have come full circle.'

25

INSPIRATION IN THE AIR

The fact that I was once again town-based did not stop me from filming eagles, and having heard that the Forestry Commission and the RSPB had started a project taking donation-paying bird lovers to a large wooden hide on the island of Mull overlooking a sea eagles' nest, I booked myself and Steve Phillipps in for a visit in early June. It rained heavily for two days before we caught the ferry from Kilchoan and although we reached the sea eagles' pick-up site early so that we would be at the head of the queue, we were in the end in front of only three other cars.

Ranger Joyce Henderson, who had done a lot of work on the project, led us four miles down the forestry track on the north side of Loch Frisa to the big wooden hide. There, head ranger David Pool unlocked its door to let us in, then took me aside to say that he had started reading my wildlife books, especially those on golden eagles, at the age of 16 and that they had had a powerfully inspirational effect on him. I felt enormously chuffed. Steve and I were then set up outside the hide so that we would be on firmer ground, a bit nearer the nest and away from the amateurs, who could be talkative.

Steve spotted the huge nest first, fairly low in a big spruce about 350 yards away, and we were almost level with it. I thought it a bit far but that we'd surely get good footage if the adults came in. The single chick was six weeks old and thus able to feed itself. By now the sun was shining and the skies mostly clear, except for a few scenic, high, fluffy white clouds.

Within an hour the first sea eagle appeared, sailing in from the northwest with something whiteish-grey in its talons, and landed on the nest. For the next five hours I felt I was in paradise. David had told me that the main prey items by that stage were fulmars from the Treshnish Isles. I filmed four landings on the nest and five take-offs from it, as well as many circlings, the sun gleaming metallically on their white tails as they sailed like galleons around the sky. I also got the male landing with a baby rabbit, leaping over the big chick and bouncing up from the far side of the nest to land on a tall spruce, lift one set of talons into his chest feathers and go to sleep. Steve missed this sequence as he had gone with David to climb a steep hill so that he could film a fulmar on the nest with the chick. I didn't want a fulmar in the nest, just the sea eagles, so I had stayed where I was. I hadn't wanted to climb the steep hill, either, I have to admit. David later told me that to judge from their leg rings, the female had fledged nine years before from a nest on Loch Ba, and the male two years later from a nest in Skye. He and Joyce produced some interesting facts. While the eagles may have been preying mainly on fulmars, the nest had also contained hare, rabbit, sheep carrion, a lapwing, golden plover, barn owl, shag, young raven and sparrowhawk, a puffin, lumpsucker fish and a toad. They did not fish the freshwater Loch Frisa, despite nesting by it. They had been seen to chase ospreys until they dropped their fish prey, then swoop down and pluck it from the ground. This pair had first bred four years before and raised one chick. The following year, the chick was blown out of the nest in a storm, skewering itself on a sharp twig on the way down, and was found dead at the foot of the nest tree. They raised two chicks in each of the next two years. That year just one egg had been laid but, as we had seen, the chick was doing well. It was a remarkable breeding record for just one pair.

I had long suggested in my books that landowners, farmers and crofters should encourage rare eagles on their lands, not be against them for the very rare taking of a live lamb. After all, the tourists who stay in their bed and breakfasts, holiday chalets and caravans want to see the great birds and are huge contributors to the Highland economy. I told David Pool I thought this was the best wildlife project I had ever known and he explained the modus operandi. When the sea eagles were re-introduced, some locals and farmers were unhappy, especially if the odd lamb was found in a nest, and the birds themselves needed protection from egg and chick thieves, not to mention amateur enthusiasts who get too close to breeding nests. All the conservation bodies therefore got together – Forest Enterprise, which owns the land where the nest is, the RSPB, Scottish Natural Heritage, and the Mull and Iona Community Trust – to work with the local community, not against it. It was decided to run a project where they took birdwatchers on strictly supervised visits, no more than twenty at a time, to a hide at a safe distance from any nest. Donations were asked for and the money collected was given to the local community trust at the end of the season. There was also a scheme to compensate farmers if they could prove that a live lamb was taken. In such ways, sea eagles could be seen as an asset. Now it was known that Mull was the best place to see sea eagles and the birds brought many tourists to spend money in the hotels, cafés, pubs, shops, garages and B and Bs , so helping the local economy.

As David said, you could say the sea eagles were worth their weight in gold. Even so, as I write, a large volunteer force has been mobilised on Mull, led by police, local rangers and wardens, to monitor closely every sea eagle nest in the period between laying and fledging. As we left, I told David that I thought the whole project fabulous and that I was amazed I'd never heard of it before. He said they had all been trying to get better publicity but had failed, so I said I would see what I could do.

Back home I immediately rang the features section of The Scotsman and persuaded them – over several calls, I might add – that the Mull sea eagle project was a marvellously uplifting story. The end result was that they sent their ace feature writer Robert McNeil to Mull, after he had interviewed me at great length, and he did a brilliant job. The whole story, 'Inspiration in the Air', came out three weeks later, splashed over two whole pages of the paper.

David Pool rang me with profuse thanks. 'You achieved on your own what the combined press officers of the RSPB, SNH, FC and Community Trust could not!' Hmm. I felt happy to have been of help. Maybe this old hack ain't finished after all, I reflected. I thought back to my most cherished memory of the sea eagles, the moment when the male leapt over his chick, bounced off the far side of the nest, landed on the neatly bent-over top of a spruce tree, lifted one foot into his chest feathers, and went to sleep. He was having a siesta.

And now it's time for mine. This has been a long book. I have been on a long journey, but will head back to the Highlands soon, running wild again of course. Adiós por ahora mis amigos.

HE LIVED CLOSER TO NATURE THAN PEOPLE HAD DARED FOR
PERHAPS A HUNDRED YEARS. HIS WRITINGS OPENED THE EYES
AND CHANGED THE LIVES OF MANY. *The Herald*

ALONE IN THE WILDERNESS

...a compelling story... Wonderfully written, it is as
entertaining as any novel. *Yorkshire Post*

...a fascinating story of self-sufficiency ... in the majestic
wilds of British Columbia. *Writers' News*

ISBN 978-1870325-14-1   £18.99

BETWEEN EARTH AND PARADISE

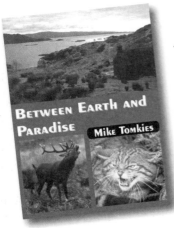

...is a treasure house of outdoor knowledge ... ...a golden
offering. It should be read slowly to fully appreciate its
value. *The Scots Magazine*

The awesome extent of his struggle to build an
uncomfortable but self-supporting writer's life alone
in an isolated crofter's cottage is vividly and lyrically
described. *Sunday Express*

ISBN 978-1904445-41-8   £18.99

WILDCAT HAVEN

'...a fascinating and inspiring new book' *Evergreen*

'a timely reminder of the need to conserve our only native
feline...' *Scottish Field*

ISBN 978-1904445-75-3   £19.99